DRAWING LIBERALISM

DRAWING LIBERALISM

Herblock's Political Cartoons in Postwar America

SIMON APPLEFORD

UNIVERSITY OF VIRGINIA PRESS
Charlottesville and London

University of Virginia Press

Printed in the United States of America on acid-free paper

First published 2023

9 8 7 6 5 4 3 2 1

Library of Congress Cataloging-in-Publication Data
Names: Appleford, Simon, author.
Title: Drawing liberalism : Herblock's political cartoons in postwar America / Simon Appleford.
Description: Charlottesville : University of Virginia Presss, 2022. | Includes bibliographical references and index.
Identifiers: LCCN 2022034830 (print) | LCCN 2022034831 (ebook) | ISBN 9780813948881 (hardcover) | ISBN 9780813948898 (ebook)
Subjects: LCSH: Block, Herbert, 1909–2001—Criticism and interpretation. | Editorial cartoonists—United States—Biography. | Cold War in comics | Liberalism—United States—History—20th century. | United States—Politics and government—1945–1989—Caricatures and cartoons.
Classification: LCC NC1429.B625 A66 2022 (print) | LCC NC1429.B625 (ebook) | DDC 741.5/6973—dc23/eng/20220915
LC record available at https://lccn.loc.gov/2022034830
LC ebook record available at https://lccn.loc.gov/2022034831

Cover art: Herblock in the 1960s. (Library of Congress, Prints and Photographs Division; C-DIG-ppmsca-22212)

For Liam and Skye

CONTENTS

ILLUSTRATIONS

ACKNOWLEDGMENTS

A project of this scope, which has been a daily part of my life for so long, inevitably incurs more debts than I can ever truly repay.

This book would not have been possible without the help and support of Vernon Burton, who from the moment I first emailed him as a prospective graduate student has taken me under his wing and become both a mentor and a friend. His support over the years has made me a better historian and, more importantly, a better person. I have also benefited from the generosity of several talented scholars who have read portions of this book in various stages of its development. Dianne Harris, Ray Fouché, Clarence Lang, Jim Barrett, Elizabeth Elliot-Meisel, Heather Fryer, and Adam Sundberg have all offered careful and insightful readings, and I owe them considerable thanks not just for pointing out myriad ways in which my arguments could be improved but also for their encouragement throughout this process. Jennifer Guiliano has been a sounding board, reader, editor, colleague, and conspirator during this whole journey. An incredibly talented historian and practitioner of the digital humanities, she is an even better friend.

I am grateful to the Herb Block Foundation for their permission to reprint over forty of Block's cartoons in this book. I must also express my thanks to the librarians and staff at the Library of Congress Manuscript Division, who were patient and supportive as I invaded their space with my digital camera and tripod. Librarians and archivists at the Truman, Nixon, and Clinton Presidential Libraries and at the Princeton and Yale University Archives have all been equally generous during the research of this project. Jeff Nichols generously sent me archival material related to Block's time working in Chicago that he encountered while working on other projects.

Support from Creighton University, and especially Bridget Keegan, dean of the College of Arts and Sciences, provided me with the time and resources necessary to turn this into a finished book. A George F. Haddix Pre-Tenure Sabbatical gave me the opportunity to dedicate a semester to the final drafting of the manuscript. A Summer Faculty Research Fellowship from Creighton's Center for Undergraduate Research and Scholarship supported the research that became the fourth chapter of this volume, while a *Magis! Investigatio* Research Award provided additional support as the manuscript moved through production. My colleagues at Creighton, especially those in the History Department, have been unstinting in their support and encouragement of my scholarship. I have also benefited from the insights of my many talented students over the last several years. Hailey Austin, Wade Peyou, Cole Crawford, Eric Howard, Kathleen Bever, Alisha Baginski, Kate Albrecht, and Katherine Consola have all assisted in various aspects of the project.

At the University of Virginia Press, Nadine Zimmerli has championed this project from the moment it landed on her desk. Her guidance and suggestions helped hone the book's argument and turned it into a much more focused work. Wren Morgan Myers ushered my manuscript through the production process while Margaret Hogan's careful copyediting has captured numerous errors that had escaped previous rounds of review and greatly improved the clarity and readability of my work. I am also grateful to the two anonymous readers whose comments and feedback helped make this a significantly better book.

My friends and family have all supported me throughout this process in more ways than I could have expected or hoped. The Obrecht clan, Catherine Callard, Susan Requa, Beatrice Smith, Troy and Robin Smith, Stephen Spackman, Jason Thatcher, Vetria Byrd, Megan Shockley, Christopher Woodall, Leslie Cornell, Audrey Shoemaker, Nick Jaworski, Stephanie Seawell, Sally Heinzel, Heidi Dodson, Jason Jordan, and Clara Wong have all in their own unique and individual ways provided me with much needed support at various stages of this project, and I am grateful for their continuing friendships.

Thank you to my grandparents, who through their unconditional love influenced not just this book but who I am as a person, in ways impossible to express in just a few words. My parents, Ann and Michael, have been my biggest supporters throughout my life and have always done everything in their power to give me every opportunity to succeed. I don't tell them often enough how much their love means to me. Thank you for always believing in me.

Finally, this project would never have been completed without the love and support of Rebecca Appleford. From encouraging me to write to forcing me to take a break, she has done more to make sure that this book is finished than anyone else. Her patience, generosity, and passion inspire me. You are my North Star, and I love you!

This book is dedicated to our children, Liam and Skye. They bring constant joy to our lives and are never afraid to remind us of what is truly important.

DRAWING LIBERALISM

INTRODUCTION

IN THE SPACE OF A single week in March 1951, the *Washington Post*'s editorial cartoonist Herbert Block, better known by his *nom de plume*, "Herblock," received plaudits from two of America's most prominent liberals. "I have long admired your work," declared the noted Harvard historian Arthur M. Schlesinger Jr., "both from an artistic point of view and as a cogent expression of political and social liberalism."[1] Later that same month, Chester Bowles, the former governor of Connecticut, also congratulated Block on the consistent and high quality nature of his work. "I honestly do not know anyone in the publication field or radio field," Bowles wrote, "who is presenting a liberal viewpoint more effectively and consistently than you."[2] That Block was lauded as a key proponent of liberal ideology by such public figures is not surprising. By 1951, he had been drawing political cartoons professionally for over twenty years. He was in his fifth year as the *Washington Post*'s resident editorial cartoonist where he had established himself as both one of the nation's most prominent political cartoonists and a leading voice for liberalism in the post–World War II era. Over a professional career that lasted seventy-two years and encompassed the presidencies of thirteen men, from Herbert Hoover to George W. Bush, Block drew liberalism for a much broader national audience than was reached by the writings of other liberal writers and intellectuals, helping shape how the American public understood and reacted to the events of the day.

This monograph is the first book-length, critical study of Block's work to date. It shows how Block drew cartoons to further the goals and priorities of liberalism in the three decades following the conclusion of World War II. By complementing close readings of these cartoons with the responses they generated from readers across the country, it argues that Block's cartoons interpreted, influenced, and reinforced postwar liberal opinion. Block was not an uncritical supporter of every tenet of postwar liberalism, but he was one of the most visible and productive members of this intellectual movement. In drawing liberalism he played a critical role in shaping public discourse and opinion across a wide range of political and social issues. Whether Americans agreed with or rejected postwar liberalism, there is no doubt that its policies changed the nation's society and politics. To understand postwar America one must also understand why liberalism took the form it did and why Americans either supported or rejected it as a political ideology. In the context of his daily editorial cartoons, which were regularly seen by Americans across the country, analyzing how and why Block chose to support, attack, and even ignore certain topics and events offers a distinctive lens through which to understand how liberalism and the events of the third quarter of the twentieth century were distilled, understood, and interpreted by the American public. His cartoons, far from simply reflecting liberal ideology, reveal the nature and limits of twentieth-century American liberalism.

Postwar liberalism articulated a belief in a benevolent but activist and expansive federal government that could shape society by keeping in check the worst excesses of capitalism. It could protect the civil rights and liberties of individuals and social groups while providing citizens with social welfare programs to afford them protections at all stages of their lives. Block's cartoons made him as important as more recognizable contemporary intellectuals and politicians such as literary critic Lionel Trilling, historian Richard Hofstadter, and lawyer and politician Adlai Stevenson in defining liberalism. Block also engaged in regular correspondence and considered himself friends with many of liberalism's intellectual leaders.

As shown by the letters he received from Schlesinger and Bowles in March 1951, they thought of him as one of their number and an important proponent of, and advocate for, liberal ideology.

Overshadowing this mutual admiration and belief in postwar liberalism was the Cold War and anticommunism. Rhetoric of both national prestige and national security supported the massive programs of government spending that postwar liberals advocated under the auspices of the Cold War (1947–1991). The looming threat of the Soviet Union encouraged Americans to follow a series of conservative values that placed clear limits on what attitudes, behaviors, and beliefs were acceptable to hold within American society. These normative assumptions included commitments to the principles of hard work and personal responsibility, the preservation of traditional gender roles, and an unwavering belief that the American system of government was superior to all others. Even liberals—eager to purge their consciences of their prewar ties and sympathies to Marxism—acquiesced to anticommunist sentiment at home.[3] So prevalent were these attitudes in postwar American society that in 1949, Arthur Schlesinger could describe how "the vital center," by which he meant liberal ideology, was critical in the defense of the ideals of American democracy from extremists on both the left and right of the political spectrum.[4] The following year, Lionel Trilling declared without any hint of embarrassment or irony that "in the United States at this time, liberalism is not only the dominant but even the sole intellectual tradition. . . . There are no conservative or reactionary ideas in general circulation."[5]

In 1952, however, Republican Dwight Eisenhower swept to victory against Adlai Stevenson—the darling of the liberal establishment, who was the losing Democratic presidential candidate in both 1952 and 1956—by winning over 55 percent of the popular vote and beating Stevenson 442 to 89 in the electoral college.[6] Combined with the culture of fear that Wisconsin senator Joseph McCarthy's anticommunist crusade engendered across America, it appeared to many observers as though the liberals' moment was over. Yet historians have come to recognize that many of the achievements of the Eisenhower administration—including massive federal funding on public works projects, support for civil rights, and welfare program reform—were also liberal priorities. As such, the core beliefs of each political party overlapped significantly.[7]

This overlap has led scholars such as journalist and historian Godfrey Hodgson to describe the postwar era in the United States as "an age of consensus." Hodgson argued that "whether you look at the writings of intellectuals or at the positions taken by practicing politicians or at the data on public opinion, it is impossible not to be struck by the degree to which the majority of Americans in those years accepted the same system of assumptions."[8] This so-called liberal consensus—at least for white, heterosexual, and middle-class men—manifested itself politically in a strong bipartisan commitment built around six central and connected tenets: (1) capitalism, especially as found in the American free-enterprise context, was the best economic system in the world; (2) American democracy was the best political system in the world; (3) class distinctions were in the process of being eliminated, and American society was naturally growing more equal; (4) any existing social problems could be solved by the benevolent application of social science and appropriate resources; (5) communists, both at home and abroad, represented the major threat to the advances that the liberal consensus promised; and (6) it was the duty and responsibility of America to contain and eliminate this Soviet threat so that the rest of the world could benefit from America's social, economic, and political advances.[9] Richard Hofstadter was thinking of America's past when he famously wrote in his 1948 book *The American Political Tradition* that "the fierceness of the political struggles has often been misleading; for the range of vision embraced by the primary contestants in the major parties has always been bounded by the horizons of property and enterprise." But this statement of political consensus applied just as well to the postwar nation.[10]

Postwar conformity was very much a white, male, and middle-class ideological construct. Behind its facade lay significant differences in how Americans understood and experienced their position in society.[11] On the political left, alleged communists and communist sympathizers were subjected to aggressive investigations and congressional hearings to answer for their alleged subversive activities, bringing to national prominence the likes of McCarthy and then-Senator Richard Nixon and threatening the nation's constitutional commitment to the principles of free speech, freedom of assembly, and a free press. Starting in the 1940s and growing increasingly vocal in the 1950s and 1960s, those Americans that were excluded from the full benefits of postwar society—most notably African Americans but also women, Mexican Americans, Indigenous peoples, and lesbians and gay men—pushed back against the restrictions imposed on them by the normative pressures of postwar liberalism to try and ensure access to the legal and constitutional rights other Americans already enjoyed. In tandem, America's youth rose up in violent protest as they struggled to assert their voices against a political establishment that did not represent their interests.

The political and social dominance of liberalism was opposed just as strongly from the political right. For a growing number of conservatives, the events and developments that characterized and altered America from the late 1950s onward seemed to threaten the values that they believed ensured the prosperity and security of both themselves and the nation. These insecurities included fears by white conservatives over the effects of the end of segregation and an increasingly militant African American freedom struggle. Similarly, the Christian Right became fearful that secularization was creeping through American education and popular culture. Many American men came to believe that feminism, gay rights, and changes in the economy were undermining the traditional patriarchal family. And, perhaps most significant was the simple fear among many Americans that society and culture were changing in ways and at a speed they could not comprehend. These tensions, coming from both the left and the right, crystallized during the 1960s into national movements that sought to overturn the existing political establishment, leading to the final collapse of postwar liberalism during the presidency of Richard Nixon and the ascendancy of a new conservative politics that became closely associated with Ronald Reagan.[12]

From the moment he joined the staff of the *Washington Post* in January 1946, Block used his cartoons to draw postwar liberalism and counter conservative viewpoints by familiarizing his readers with the central tenets of liberal ideology—the importance of a federal government committed to social reform and protecting the civil rights and liberties of individuals and social groups while also combating the threat of communism. In doing so, he positioned himself as one of liberalism's most forthright advocates. Block was described as "simply the greatest cartoonist of his era" and a "genius" by those who shared his political leanings, while his critics labeled him a "master of sick invective" and "an enthusiastic water boy for the powers that be on the left."[13] Examples of his cartoons can be found in politicians' personal collections across the country—ranging from Democratic president Harry Truman to segregationist Strom Thurmond. Block himself received countless requests from people and organizations—of all political persuasions and whether they were presented in a positive or negative light—for copies of the cartoons in which they were depicted.

Block was one of several prominent cartoonists working in the postwar years. Among his most notable contemporaries were the *St. Louis Post-Dispatch*'s Bill Mauldin, the *Miami Daily News*'s Anne Mergen, the *Los Angeles Times*'s Paul Conrad, and the *Denver Post*'s Pat Oliphant. Block's status as cartoonist for Washington's only morning newspaper afforded him a privileged position that allowed his cartoons to appear in the newspaper most likely to be read by the nation's powerbrokers and to influence their responses to the day's events. As a result, his cartoons were inevitably the subject of public comment, admiration, and condemnation. Harry Truman, for example, famously responded to a question about whether the House Un-American Activities Committee's actions posed a threat to educational freedoms by encouraging reporters to look at that morning's Herblock cartoon as it "pretty well answered" that question.[14] Meanwhile, Lyndon Johnson's 1968 comment to British Labour Party leader Harold Wilson that, although Block was "our best," he would "come over and eat your cookies, but then . . . go back and draw a cartoon giving you hell the next day," is typical of the dichotomy his cartoons provoked among the targets of his satire.[15]

Rhetoricians Michael A. DeSousa and Martin J. Medhurst have theorized that cartoonists generally draw on one of four themes or "major inventional resources: political commonplaces, literary/cultural allusions, personal character traits, and transient situational themes" when building their scenes. Taking each of these in turn, *political commonplaces* are those scenarios and topics in which a reader might naturally expect to see the subjects of political cartoons act, which allows the cartoonist to draw a cartoon without having to provide their readers with additional context. In other words, when one sees a character standing outside the White House, the cartoonist is likely commenting on presidential politics. When that same character is instead standing next to a stock ticker or atop planet Earth, the theme is more likely to be economics or something of global import. By the same token, placing a recognizable politician in a swamp or on the beach also primes the viewer as to the cartoon's intent. Setting a cartoon in a doctor's office, a grocery store, or a married couple's living room are all everyday settings that instill the cartoon with specific expectations and assumptions.

Cartoonists also frequently make use of *literary and cultural allusions,* drawing on anything from Greek myths to the latest Hollywood blockbuster to draw a connection between the subject of their cartoon and some more broadly understood context. Depending on the specific context and how a group of characters are portrayed, depicting them as Marvel's Avengers can instill them with heroic qualities, but it can also mock them, suggesting characteristics that the subjects may imagine they possess but the cartoonist feels they in fact lack. This intertextuality can deepen the layers of meaning within a cartoon but can also be a barrier to understanding if the viewer is unfamiliar with the analogy being made.

Personal character traits are those defining physical, emotional, and personal characteristics that caricaturists tend to highlight and exaggerate. In the hands of a skilled political cartoonist, though, these characteristics are used not simply to mock the subject of their pen but instead to reveal some inherent truth about that subject's personality. In rare occasions, those exaggerations can come to define who that political figure truly is for millions of readers.

Finally, *timely and transient situations* are the result of specific events or short-term controversies that often provide cartoons with their immediacy and timeliness on the day they are published. Timeliness, though, can make them indecipherable when separated by a period of months or years from the events that inspired them. As such, political cartoons are inherently ephemeral in nature. To fully understand their meaning and the cartoonist's original intent, a reader must not only recognize all the portrayed characters but also the historical and political context of the day and any cultural or literary allusions that are being employed.[16]

Block saw his work as an integral part of the *Washington Post*'s editorial content. While delivering the second annual Joseph Pulitzer Memorial Lecture at the Columbia School of Journalism in February 1957, for example, Block discussed the "power and responsibility" of a free press to "use its freedom to protect the freedom of everyone." He began by describing the symbiotic relationship that existed between his own work as a cartoonist and the editorial page of a newspaper. "The cartoon and the editorial," he declared, "are much the same thing—the means for speaking up and expressing opinions." Yet, it is the editorial cartoon that is the more "natural medium for vigorous comment" because it is "a type of work which is not calculated to induce in the practitioner an undue reverence for public officials."[17] In contrast to written editorials, which provide readers with the newspaper's official stance on a newsworthy event, political cartoons therefore offer a more personal and visceral reaction that shows why readers should care about a specific issue. To do so, they make use of a variety of visual, thematic, cultural, and rhetorical devices that allow the artist to embed within them a multiplicity of meanings. They contain both visual and textual messages on political and social events that are presented to their audiences through cultural symbols which have been interpreted and filtered by the cartoonist. Cartoons are assumed to be funny. But just as often they provoke anger, sadness, or joy, while their social impact derives from their simultaneous appeal to the eye, intellect, conscience, and emotion. They frequently rely on a visual shorthand, including caricatures, stereotypes, recurring symbols, and the juxtaposition of text and image, to give the cartoonist the latitude to draw what editorial writers arguably cannot write.[18]

Political cartoons are many things. But one of the things political cartoons are not is an accurate representation of the truth. Instead, they reveal *a* truth, a representation that the cartoonist wants to make apparent to their readers. Cartoons may or may not depict events and show politicians and public figures engaged in activities that actually occurred. But the best cartoons go beyond a single moment to reveal the true significance and hidden motivations of their subjects.[19] As the political scientist Charles Press wrote in 1981, "Cartoons present a picture as the essence of truth, a message as to what ought to be done on behalf of the deserving, and a mood created through artistic technique and allegorical imagery of how the viewer ought to feel over what is happening."[20] The intersection of all these factors offers a unique lens through which historians can understand a society's interests, prejudices, and values, allowing an insight into how the behavior of international, national, and local figures was interpreted by their contemporary audience.

Politicians who have been the subject of a particularly scathing cartoon were painfully aware of the impact cartoons might have on their political ambitions. Perhaps most famously, the nineteenth-century cartoonist Thomas Nast undertook a sustained attack on the corruption he saw in New York City's Tammany Hall boss William Tweed, which "in its passion and effectiveness . . . stands alone in the history of American graphic art."[21] As a result of these cartoons, Nast was reputedly offered a $500,000 bribe to stop his attacks and leave the country, leading Fiona Deans Halloran, a recent biographer of Nast, to describe him as "a man whose work could change minds, topple leaders, and influence leaders." Halloran argues that his cartoons were more than mere editorials that supplied evidence in support of his personal opinion. Instead, Nast used visual imagery to grab the public's attention and provoke a response.[22] Tweed's demand upon viewing an especially powerful Nast cartoon was that his lieutenants "stop them damned pictures" because "I don't care so much what the papers write about me. My constituents can't read. But, damn it, they can see pictures." This remains a ubiquitous anecdote used by scholars to highlight the impact of, and politicians' reactions to, political cartoons.[23] Boss Tweed was not the only political figure to directly link his public image or political fortune to the work of Nast. During the Civil War, Abraham Lincoln described Nast's drawings as the North's "best recruiting sergeant," while Ulysses S. Grant credited his victory in the 1868 presidential election on "the sword of Sheridan and the pencil of Thomas Nast."[24] Indeed, Nast's influence on American culture extends far beyond his unabashed support for the Republican Party or his attacks on Tweed's corruption, as he is credited with introducing both the donkey and elephant as symbols for the Democratic and Republican Parties and even for creating the modern image of Santa Claus, visual devices Block himself regularly used.[25]

Because of their ability to express complicated ideas in an easily understandable visual form, political cartoons have often found themselves treading a fine line at the limits of acceptable free speech, and cartoonists have frequently become the targets of governmental action when it seems they crossed that line. In 1917, for example, the Woodrow Wilson administration unsuccessfully used the Espionage Act to prosecute the cartoonists Henry Glintenkamp and Art Young for two cartoons critical of America's role in World War I that were printed in the periodical the *Masses*. Although the charges were ultimately dropped after two trials that both ended in hung juries, prosecutors alleged that the cartoonists, together with several of the *Masses*'s editorial writers, were guilty of "conspiring to cause mutiny and refusal of duty in the military and attempting to obstruct recruiting and enlistment"—treasonable offenses.[26] Dictators and the instruments of their power, inevitably obsessed with their public image, have been particularly forthright in their attempts to control how they were depicted in political cartoons. During the Second World War, several Polish cartoonists were executed for drawing anti-Nazi cartoons, while Joseph Goebbels applied considerable pressure on the British foreign secretary in an unsuccessful attempt to stop publication of David Low's highly critical cartoons of the Nazi regime in late 1937.[27] Block himself received a firsthand lesson in how his cartoons were received by a less than friendly regime when, in 1969, he was refused a visa to visit Soviet Russia, reputedly on the personal instructions of Leonid Brezhnev, who did not like how he was depicted in Block's cartoons.[28]

In shaping and influencing public opinion, Block created cartoons for what Benedict Anderson has described as an "imagined political community"—a public that shared a common set of assumptions and desires which were connected to each other not through personal interactions but through their readership of his cartoons. In Anderson's conception, print culture plays an instrumental role in establishing ideas of citizenship and nationalism as it makes "it possible for rapidly growing numbers of people to think about themselves and relate themselves to others in profoundly new ways." Thus, readers of newspapers participate in an "extraordinary mass ceremony" that is "replicated simultaneously by thousands (or millions) of others of whose existence he is confident, yet of whose identity he has not the slightest notion." This knowledge allows the consumer to be "continually reassured that the imagined world is visibly rooted in everyday life," thereby creating a "remarkable confidence of community in anonymity that is the hallmark of modern nations." Visual objects contribute to this process as they draw on recognized symbols of nationhood and patriotism to project specific representations of the nation to their audience.[29]

Because of their ability to appropriate multiple cultural and emotional symbols in their efforts to visualize collective attitudes around events, nations, and individuals, political cartoons are especially important tools in the establishment of these imagined communities. Recent scholarship—in contexts as varied as nineteenth-century Anglo-American relations, the shaping of anti-Irish sentiment, the development of a Japanese nationalist movement at the start of the twentieth century, and efforts to control the political participation of women in the Ottoman Empire—has begun to reveal the important role that political cartoons have played in shaping and influencing public opinion.[30] Block similarly worked to create an imagined community of readers in postwar America that was largely made up of the white, northern, white-collar, and male readership whom he believed to be the primary consumers of the news and editorial pages of newspapers such as the *Washington Post* and the *New York Times*. It was on this readership that Block's cartoons worked to create, disseminate, and strengthen a set of assumptions and ideals about the world, both physical and mental, which they inhabited.

Political cartoons are therefore rhetorical devices that express and propagandize a position in much the same way written newspaper editorials function. In fact, Block participated in a process referred to by scholars as media framing. As summarized by Todd Gitlin, media frames are used by journalists as a mechanism by which they organize the world, both for themselves as they report on it and for the readers who consume the news. As such, although journalists and the news media are perhaps not able to tell readers what to think, they are able to influence what readers think about. Media frames are thus "persistent patterns of cognition, interpretation, and presentation, of selection, emphasis, and exclusion," designed to help newspapers, and by extension staff members such as Block, filter the news they report and comment on to reflect, reinforce, and shape the attitudes of their readers.[31] Despite this, however, the influence of a cartoonist on his audience is not easily measured, especially when the public is constantly confronted by different media interpretations of world affairs. Block's cartoons form just one element of the newspaper's editorial page, appearing alongside both editorials and readers' letters. The spatial arrangement of text, headlines, images, and even white space on a page all provide the reader with visual clues as to how that page should be read and what elements of the page should be given precedence over others before they even begin to read. As Johanna Drucker has argued, "We *see* before we read . . . [which] predisposes us to reading according to specific graphic codes before we engage with the language of the text."[32]

Although Drucker was referring specifically to the graphic presentation of the poetic form, her insight is equally valid for visual materials such as a newspaper editorial page. Figure 1 shows a generic representation of the layout of the *Washington Post*'s editorial page throughout the time that Block worked at the paper. The focus of the page is intended to be on the two left-hand columns of editorials that extend vertically down the length of the page. The placement of the daily Herblock cartoon in the center-top of this page, however, inevitably draws the reader's eye to this graphic element, granting it precedence over the textual elements of the page. This placement also makes it easier to be seen by a reader who is simply flipping through the newspaper and who might otherwise avoid reading the editorial page altogether. As a result, Block's cartoon had the opportunity to influence the reader's understanding of the day's events before other editorial content in the newspaper were read and contemplated.

In the world of Washington politics, with its frequent upheavals, the daily Herblock cartoon became the city's most constant feature for over half a century. Block's unprecedented tenure at the *Post*, and the accompanying high profile that his work enjoyed through the syndication of his cartoons both nationally and internationally, transformed him into a ubiquitous presence in American politics. His awards and honors included Pulitzer Prizes in 1942, 1954, and 1979, while also being cited along with three other *Washington Post* staff members in the 1973 Pulitzer awarded to the paper for its Watergate reporting; multiple awards from the American Civil Liberties Union; multiple awards from civil rights organizations; several honorary degrees; and in 1994 the Presidential Medal of Freedom.[33] This platform allowed Block to articulate the values of liberalism to a much broader national audience than was reached by

FIGURE 1. Typical layout of the *Washington Post*'s editorial page, based on the paper's August 21, 1953, edition

the writings of other liberal writers and intellectuals. His deliberately unpresumptuous style had the effect of making his message easily accessible to all viewers. His cartoons were often tongue in cheek, for the most part taking a light-hearted approach to their themes and offering something for his readers to laugh at. Because of this, Block was able to pitch his cartoons at a broad audience that extended beyond readers of the *Post*'s editorial page. But Block's cartoons were more sophisticated than they initially appear, and it takes effort and thought on the part of the reader to grasp fully their deeper meaning. As a result, he played a critical role in shaping mainstream American public opinion. His work for the *Post* covered almost every major issue of the second half of the twentieth century. In addition to presidential administrations and wars, he regularly drew about issues including the U.S. economy, civil rights, environmentalism, the influence of special interests on congressional activities, and gun control.

It is for his cartoons depicting two of this period's most infamous politicians that Block is best remembered and that made his most enduring contributions to the public memory of the third quarter of the twentieth century. An early and fierce opponent of the activities of the House Committee on Un-American Activities, Block has been widely credited with introducing the term "McCarthyism" into the American political lexicon, after he used it as a label on a March 1950 cartoon that depicted the GOP elephant being dragged toward an unsteady tower made of tar cans by Republican senators. Block's portrayal of Richard Nixon haunted the former president from his earliest days in Congress. Block's Nixon was a sewer-dwelling thug whose features were defined by dark jowls and an ever-present five-o'clock shadow, and who was shown to be constantly working against the civil liberties of ordinary Americans. It was an image that Nixon actively strove to distance himself from, even as it came to define him in the minds of millions of Americans. Nixon made this explicit during the 1960 presidential election when an aide accused him of having thus far run a "kid-glove" campaign. He was urged to start attacking John F. Kennedy's policies. The Republican candidate agreed but cautioned, "I have to erase the Herblock image first."[34]

Despite his importance as an advocate of postwar liberalism, and in contrast to other liberal intellectuals from the era, Block has received relatively little scholarly attention. Outside of general histories of political cartooning where he can warrant anything from a couple of paragraphs to several pages of discussion, Block's work is rarely discussed except in passing. Steven Kercher's 2006 study *Revel with a Cause,* which includes an extended discussion of Block's anti-McCarthy cartoons, is a rare example of a scholar engaging with Block's cartoons as a significant historical source.[35] Block is even largely absent from histories of the *Washington Post.* The autobiography of Ben Bradlee, the *Post*'s longtime executive editor, mentions Block on just three occasions and only once as more than a passing comment. Leonard Downie Jr., Bradlee's successor, does not mention Block at all in his memoir, despite joining the *Post* in 1964 and heading the paper's editorial department at the time of Block's death in 2001.[36]

This book makes no effort to offer a complete analysis of every politician, event, or controversy that Block commented on over the course of his career. Such an endeavor would result in a work many times longer than the current volume. Among the issues that are not discussed here are Block's longstanding commitment to statehood for the District of Columbia, his staunch environmentalism, his condemnation of the American Medical Association's obstruction of efforts to reform the nation's health-care system, and his personal opposition to the tobacco industry. Also largely absent from these pages is a discussion of how Block depicted America's foreign policy. This is not to say that foreign policy is ignored, but the focus of this monograph is on how Block's cartoon's reflected and shaped liberalism in the domestic sphere. As a result, after an introductory biographical chapter that charts Block's career up until his arrival at the *Washington Post* in 1946, subsequent chapters are each structured around a case study that together demonstrate how Block's depiction and reaction to a specific controversy of the postwar era illustrates the fractures of postwar liberalism in theory and practice.

Chapter 2 explores how Block's commitment to anticommunism mirrored a division within the Democratic Party that came to define liberalism throughout the postwar period. It argues that Block's cartoons defined the efforts of anticommunists to root out alleged subversive activities in the federal government as something that itself threatened the foundations of American democracy. If the second chapter explored who was allowed to be an American in the postwar era, chapter 3 asks an equally profound question: who is allowed to be a citizen? Like many liberals, Block identified the fight for African American rights as one of the most important social and political movements of the mid-twentieth century. This chapter argues that Block's cartoons reveal the limits that were placed on efforts for racial justice by a white political establishment interested only in incremental change. The question of what values should define American society increasingly dominated Block's work during the 1960s as politically conservative and religiously conservative Americans pushed back against the social changes that dominated the decade. Chapter 4 demonstrates how Block's cartoons served as proxies in the early stages of a national debate over the so-called culture wars that has characterized much of American political discourse for the past fifty years.

Chapter 5 focuses on Block's response to the emergence of the so-called New Left as a major force in politics in the 1960s. It argues that Block, despite his own sympathies for the New Left's demands for an end to the war in Vietnam and far-reaching racial and political reform, failed to give any legitimacy to protest movements that threatened the stability of the postwar liberal order. Of all the subjects that Block drew throughout his career, there is perhaps no one who he is more closely associated with than Richard Nixon. Chapter 6 explores how Block's cartoons played a critical role in transforming a young congressman from California, who was admired by his supporters for both his good looks and his principled stance against communism, into an archetype of corruption, a chameleon whose position on the issues of the day changed based solely on political expediency, and whose features became synonymous with the abuse of power.

In drawing liberalism for an audience that might not otherwise have been interested in the topics and events he illustrated, Block's cartoons offer a unique lens through which to interpret and understand the shifts and contours of twentieth-century American political culture. Political cartoons are generally designed to comment on contemporary events in a humorous and satirical fashion and, as a result, they can easily cause offense to those whose actions are depicted or whose beliefs are challenged by the cartoonist's pen. But they can also be used by the cartoonist for the specific purpose of manipulating public sentiment in favor of their beliefs. Block's cartoons did both. They were, and continue to be, offensive to the people and organizations whose political beliefs and stances he challenged on a daily basis. Still, Block also used his cartoons as a tool with which to further the postwar liberal agenda and to defend its goals and priorities against those individuals and groups ideologically opposed to liberalism. For men like Block, after all, liberalism defined the core values that represented what it meant to be an American.

1

"AN UNINHIBITED VOICE OF LIBERALISM"

Becoming Herblock

POLITICAL CARTOONS, WROTE HERBERT BLOCK in 1977, are a "signed expression of personal opinion" whose most important characteristic is that they have a "view to express" and that they do so unapologetically. He argued that, although cartooning can be described as "an irreverent form of expression, and one particularly suited to scoffing at the high and mighty," it is equally important to remember that "if the prime role of a free press is to serve as critic of government, cartooning is often the cutting edge of that criticism." Indeed, the best political cartoons are not content to simply accompany and illustrate the news nor to merely poke fun at a politician for the sake of an easy laugh. Instead, it is the responsibility of a cartoonist to provide both an analysis and a judgment on specific events and situations.[1] Because of this intensely personal relationship between cartoonist and cartoon, Block fought hard to ensure that the views expressed in his cartoons were his alone and not those of his employers. Put another way, and to use an analogy that Block himself often employed when describing the function of his work, the cartoonist is akin to "the kid in the Hans Christian Anderson [*sic*] story who says the emperor has no clothes on. . . . [They are] someone who hollers, 'Stop, thief!'—who criticizes and prods the government."[2]

This first chapter illuminates the influences and experiences that transformed Block into one of the nation's foremost cartoonists and advocates of postwar liberalism. It provides an overview of the early trajectory of Block's career and highlights how his background shaped his subsequent career. It explores how his political ideology developed and matured because of his experiences growing up in Chicago and as a young cartoonist in the years leading up to the Second World War. In particular, the chapter investigates how Block's early cartoons reflected prevailing contemporary attitudes on such issues as equal rights for women and African Americans, and how his responses to the national crises of the Great Depression and World War II transformed him into, in the words of *Newsweek* magazine, the nation's "uninhibited voice of liberalism."[3]

Born in Chicago on October 13, 1909, Herbert Lawrence Block was the youngest of David Julian and Theresa Lupe Block's three sons. His parents profoundly impacted his early life, and it is clear from his autobiography—a book dedicated to "Dave and Tessie"—that he idolized them both. David Block had been born in Fort Wayne, Indiana, in August 1874, to Maurice and Julia (née Wolff) Block, immigrants from Bavaria and Alsace-Lorraine, respectively. By the early 1890s, David had moved to Chicago, where he studied at the Armour Institute of Technology, a school founded in 1890 with an explicit mandate to prepare students of all backgrounds for meaningful careers in the changing industrial society of the late nineteenth century. After graduating, he embarked on a career as a journalist for the *Chicago Record* while also contributing cartoons and poems to publications such as *Life, Puck,* and *Judge.*[4] His passion, however, was as an inventor and chemical engineer, and by 1900 he had already received attention from the local media for several inventions, including a process for "taking photographs through opaque substances" and a device that automatically measured the intensity of sunlight.[5] In 1902, he married Theresa Bacigalupe, the daughter of Italian immigrants who was born in Chicago in 1879, and together they soon started a family. During the First World War, David aided the war effort by developing synthetic rubber dyes that had previously been imported from Germany and also supervised the construction of the first American plant to manufacture aspirin.[6]

Although this work did not make the Blocks rich, it did allow David to ensure his family was able to engage in social mobility. At the time of Herbert's birth, the family was renting a home on Pearl Street in Chicago's 20th Ward, a working-class neighborhood just a handful of blocks west of the city's so-called Little Italy district on the Near West Side. Ten years later, the Blocks' economic situation had allowed them to move to the more prosperous Far North Side and a rented property on Rosemont Avenue in Chicago's 25th Ward; by 1930, the family owned a $40,000 property on Fuller Lane in Winnetka, an affluent village north of Chicago.[7]

Block's own memories of his childhood reveal an idealization of life in the early decades of the twentieth century. In his memoirs, he reflects on the innocence of the age, describing a generally simpler time before the advances of modern life had complicated and corrupted American society. It was a "time when more explicit and pungent words were not part of the general vocabulary," he wrote. "There was no cellophane, plastic or widespread pollution—but also no penicillin, no 'pill,' no by-pass surgery, none of the hundreds of innovations generally described as the greatest thing since sliced bread—and no sliced bread either."[8] Yet this description stands in stark contrast to the reality of life in the Chicago of Block's youth.

Chicago experienced considerable growth during the first decades of the twentieth century, adding over a million residents between 1900 and 1920 to become America's second largest city. Located on the Great Lakes and home to one of the world's largest railroad hubs, Chicago proved an ideal center for trade between America's eastern states and those in the Midwest and West. With the city's manufacturing and retail sectors booming and jobs plentiful in a wide range of industries, including steel, clothing, railroads, and timber, Chicago was also a natural place for immigrant and native-born workers alike to come seeking employment and stability in their lives. Most of these new arrivals were unskilled Jewish and Catholic immigrants from eastern and southern European countries such as Germany, Russia, Poland, Italy, and Greece, who established their own ethnic communities within the city.[9] When the First World War put a halt to immigration from Europe and created a significant labor shortage, as many as fifty thousand African Americans arrived in Chicago from southern states to help fill those jobs, doubling the city's Black population in just four years. Tensions among all these groups, exacerbated by competition for jobs after the war, contributed to an eruption of violence that occurred in July 1919 and resulted in the deaths of thirty-eight people.[10]

Through all of this, Block's parents allowed him a great deal of latitude to enjoy his childhood. Yet they still retained a strong influence on him, instilling in him a sense of "what was right and wrong, the confidence to express his views openly and the courage to stand up for what is right."[11] One area in which his parents failed to influence the young Block, however, was religion. Born and raised a devout Catholic, his mother tried throughout Block's childhood to instill the same sense of religious duty in her son that she herself felt, just as she had with his two elder brothers. But despite her best efforts, the young Block showed little interest in Catholicism and managed to avoid becoming at all religious, maintaining what he described as a healthy skepticism of organized religion throughout his life.[12]

What Block wanted to do was draw. The first caricature that he recalled drawing was of Germany's Kaiser Wilhelm II, an illustration in chalk on the sidewalk, both so that people could admire the young artist's handiwork and so he could glean a grim sense of satisfaction from its inevitable destruction as people trod on his subject's face. This interest in drawing was encouraged by his parents, especially his father, who not only provided him with drawing materials and art books but also taught him basic techniques. When Block was eleven, his parents sent him to Saturday afternoon classes at the Art Institute of Chicago where he soon received both a full scholarship to continue his studies and the first of his many awards.[13] Block was further inspired when he read as a teenager a biography of the great nineteenth century cartoonist Thomas Nast, with the influence that Nast had on the politics of his day something that Block later highlighted as a characteristic he actively strove to emulate.[14] By the time he was a junior at Nicholas Senn High School, located on the North Side of Chicago, Block was already convinced his future career would be as a political cartoonist.[15]

Block sought opportunities to hone his abilities and contributed regular cartoons to the school paper that commented on the experiences he witnessed daily as a student. These cartoons reflect his school spirit and support for the school's sporting teams, while also extolling his fellow students to work hard and achieve the highest grades of which they were capable. But the drawings also reveal a nascent interest in the issues to which he would later dedicate his career. On September 24, 1925, for example, he drew a cartoon asking his classmates to vote for candidates to the student council based on their qualifications rather than their personalities and popularity, while on October 1 he demonstrated his willingness to speak for those without a voice by encouraging his fellow students to look out for and support the incoming freshman class of students.[16] While Senn High provided the young cartoonist with an opportunity to develop his skills and voice, perhaps his most important lesson came from Helen Harris, his English and Journalism teacher and faculty advisor for the school's newspaper. It was from Harris that Block learned not just "how to read a newspaper" but also to be skeptical of what he read. As he later recalled, she instilled in him the insight "that everything that appears in print ain't necessarily so," and that it was critical, "not only as journalists, but as readers and citizens," to discover the truth behind a story.[17]

Block's career as a published satirist began while he was still at high school when he began submitting content to the *Chicago Daily Tribune*'s long-running daily "A Line o' Type or Two" feature, which collected humorous reader-submitted poems and paragraphs into a single column on the paper's editorial page. There was, however, a problem: contributors to this column generally submitted their content using fake names to hide their true identities. His father therefore suggested combining his first and last name, both solving the problem of what Block should call himself and creating a moniker that would become more recognized and celebrated than they could possibly have anticipated at the time.[18] On August 30, 1926, the first of these paragraphs to appear under the "Herblock" byline was published in the form of a fake telegram mocking the inability of the authorities to enforce prohibition.[19] Block's submissions won him enough of a following with the column's readers that he quickly established himself as a regular contributor to the column, which he continued to provide material for until 1929.

After his graduation from Senn High in 1927, Block decided to follow in the footsteps of both his father and his older brother Bill, a reporter at the *Chicago Tribune* and later the *Chicago Sun*, by finding work as a police reporter for the Chicago City News Bureau. This did not last, however, as the reporting position was only temporary. It was not long until Block enrolled at Lake Forest College in Illinois, where he studied English and political science. While attending Lake Forest and still only eighteen years old, Block began to contribute regular cartoons to the *Evanston News-Index,* a daily newspaper for one of Chicago's most affluent suburbs. Stylistically, these cartoons are very different from those that Block became most closely associated with decades later at the *Washington Post.* Instead, they are highly reminiscent of the style of cartoon popularized in the mid-nineteenth century by publications such as *Harper's Weekly* and *Punch.* In particular, the lines and shading are strongly emphasized, a consequence of Block's medium of choice at this time, ink, which resulted in cartoons that are starkly black and white with indistinct outlines and edges. More significantly, although the cartoons from this era clearly have something to say, they lack the biting satire and humor for which Block became renowned later in life and are instead more observational in nature. These cartoons did, however, focus on many of the themes and topics that Block would regularly confront throughout his career. His belief in the power of scientific progress to benefit society, for example, is shown in his August 13, 1928, cartoon "Evanston Streets, Now—and When?" which depicted the positive good that would result from the installation of streetlights in residential areas on both security and community spirit. "Exaggerated? Not Very Much," published five days later, revealed his strong concern for the impact of human activity on the environment. And October 6, 1928's "Get Ready for the Cleanup" is an early illustration of Block's lifelong battle to inspire the public's engagement in the political process as the best defense against corruption, in this instance by encouraging voter registration ahead of the upcoming national and local elections (fig. 2).[20]

Toward the end of his second year at Lake Forest, Block applied for a summer job as a cartoonist at the *Chicago Daily News.* His timing proved fortuitous for only a handful of days later a staff cartoonist at the paper announced his intent to leave, and Block, whose initial inquiry for summer work at the paper had been politely turned down, was offered the now vacant permanent position.[21] His first cartoon for the *Chicago Daily News,* which condemned the destruction of America's forests, appeared on April 24, 1929, marking the start of Block's career as a full-time professional cartoonist when he was still only nineteen years old.[22] Whereas the

FIGURE 2. *Evanston (IL) News-Index,* October 6, 1928

cartoons Block had drawn at the *Evanston News-Index* tended to focus on local concerns, his work at the *Daily News* displayed a growing awareness of both national and international events. Over the course of his first month at the *Daily News,* these cartoons ranged in theme from national concerns—such as the effectiveness of prohibition enforcement and

President Herbert Hoover's battles with Congress—to international affairs, including commentary on the disarmament process in Europe and the threat Benito Mussolini represented to world stability.

Block's time at the *Daily News* would prove to be formative in the development of his visual style. While working there, he became friends with fellow cartoonist and Chicago native Vaughn Shoemaker, under whose influence Block increasingly began to follow the style of what historian Lucy Caswell has described as the "Midwestern School of Editorial Cartooning." Caswell points to the large number of early twentieth-century cartoonists who were born and raised in the Midwest and argues that they shared many stylistic characteristics, including the liberal use of "symbols and labels" to represent specific concepts and a strong, but not uncritical, belief in the importance of the ordinary man.[23] Shoemaker's creation "John Q. Public"—a generic character designed to represent visually the interests of the "common man"—later became one of Block's most used and familiar characters. Block's cartoons underwent a more practical change in the early 1930s as he began to draw using pencil and black crayon. This allowed him to create a more nuanced style of illustration that used shading to soften the overall tone of his drawings and make them more accessible to a general audience. As the only cartoonist on the *Daily News* staff using this medium, this change also allowed Block to develop his own distinctive voice on the paper. And because his cartoons were not specific to local events in Chicago, they were syndicated by his newspaper to a national audience, exposing Block for the first time to a much larger readership.[24]

These cartoons also reveal a strong affinity to the Republican Party and its policies. Although the *Daily News* was politically independent, some of Block's earliest published cartoons had appeared in the *Chicago Republican,* which as the name implies was the local mouthpiece for the Republican Party. This led Block to comment wryly in his autobiography that this arrangement "involved no sacrifice of principle" because the Republican Party had been "the party of Thomas Nast" and had received "a lot of support from contemporary cartoonist 'Ding' Darling," whose work Block admired and sought to emulate.[25] During the interwar period, Republicans believed in a laissez-faire ideology of free-market capitalism that was best summed up by President Calvin Coolidge's famous declaration that "the chief business of the American people is business." With Republicans controlling the White House, Senate, and House of Representatives throughout the decade, they were able to pass a wave of pro-business policies that substantially reduced federal income tax rates, cut spending at every level of the government, and deregulated the economy and private industry. The result was an unprecedented economic boom that saw the stock market reach new heights while white Americans had access to higher levels of disposable incomes, allowing them to purchase, often on credit, more and more consumer goods. Republicans also supported an isolationist foreign policy and protectionist tariffs on foreign imports while also enacting strict immigration limits designed to prevent alleged radicals and communists from southern and eastern Europe from entering the country.

Block's cartoons clearly demonstrate his broad support for the pro-business agendas of Calvin Coolidge and Herbert Hoover. During the 1928 election cycle, for example, Block drew cartoons strongly supportive of Hoover's candidacy while directly linking his Democratic opponent, New York governor Al Smith, to the corruption of Tammany Hall.[26] This allegiance continued throughout the Hoover administration and can be seen in cartoons such as January 6, 1930's "A Suggestion for Mr. Hoover," which shows the president lighting a bonfire made up of a mountain of mail critical of his policies. Similarly, November 25, 1931's "Housing Plans" contrasts Hoover's plan to provide $2 billion in housing projects that would benefit the public with the partisan goals of the Democratic Party toward both the House of Representatives and the White House in the 1932 election cycle.[27] Block similarly drew cartoons that were supportive of the effort to pass a new protectionist tariff bill, advocated cutting government spending at the federal, state, and local levels to finance tax cuts, and approved of the effort to curtail the number of immigrants arriving from eastern Europe. His two-panel July 16, 1929, cartoon "The Pleasure Is All Ours," for example, shows Uncle Sam packing a giant picnic hamper that is to be sent back to Europe with bearded and dangerous-looking "Undesirable Aliens" (fig. 3).[28]

But Block was not unquestioning in his allegiance to Republican orthodoxy, a nuance in his politics that was evident in his regular depictions of Mussolini, Russia, and China as potential threats to world peace the

FIGURE 3. *Chicago Daily News,* July 16, 1929

global community could not afford to ignore, and perhaps most clearly in his concern about the unregulated nature of the stock market. This was shown in his October 14, 1929, cartoon "Stock Market Fever Chart." Mindful of the volatile nature of investing in the stock market, and likely aware that the London Stock Exchange had crashed the previous month causing some market instability, Block's cartoon shows an average investor becoming increasingly exultant over the rapid increase in value his stocks are achieving, only to experience a dramatic fall back to reality as the value of those stocks plummet to nothing. The cartoon proved prophetic as between October 24 (just ten days after it was published) and October 29, the Dow Jones Industrial Average suffered a loss in value of almost 25 percent that swept away billions of dollars of savings from ordinary Americans.[29]

The stock market crash precipitated a global economic crisis popularly known as the Great Depression. As brokerage firms began to call in their debts, many Americans rushed to withdraw money from their banks. But unable to cope with the sudden demand for cash, thousands of these banks failed, causing many Americans to lose their life savings and become even less able to weather the financial storms that engulfed the nation. Purchases of the types of consumer goods that had helped create the prosperity of the 1920s slowed to almost nothing. With the collapse in demand for their products, businesses, which had anticipated continued economic growth, found themselves unable to sell the large inventories they had stockpiled and started firing employees to cut costs. As a result, between October 1929 and December 1932, millions of Americans lost their jobs, resulting in a national unemployment rate that hit 23.6 percent in 1932 and peaked at 25 percent the following year. In Europe, the collapse of manufacturing in Germany led to that country's inability to pay the reparations demanded by the Treaty of Versailles, in turn pushing Great Britain and France to default on their World War I–era debts to American banks, further exacerbating the domestic crisis.

Chicago was not spared the ravages of the Great Depression, with the industrial and manufacturing sectors, so crucial to Chicago's growth earlier in the century, especially hard hit. By 1931, the city's unemployment rate stood at 30 percent, notably higher than the national rate.[30] Yet Block's cartoons only occasionally reflected the challenges faced by so many of his fellow citizens, with most of his work from the period commenting on such topics as Chicago politics, the inaction of Congress, local and casual sporting events, and events abroad. But when the Depression did feature, Block was careful to highlight the challenges faced by so many Americans. Hobos and tramps asking for assistance from the better off made regular appearances during these years, with the cartoon's punchline often showing that the person being asked for help was himself struggling financially. Cartoons such as September 25, 1930's "Profit and Loss," meanwhile, suggested the economic strain American families were under by showing a husband and father overwhelmed by the stack of bills coming due. Most frequently, though, Block looked to highlight optimistic signs of a potential recovery. August 19, 1931's "Smoke Clouds and Silver Linings," for example, is a two-panel cartoon that in its top frame depicts a couple complaining "a few years ago" at the sight of pollution pouring out of the chimneys of a large factory. Below is a second scene, set "today," that shows the same couple excitedly reacting to a few whiffs of smoke emerging from a factory labeled "Industrial Revival."[31]

Block's work for the *Chicago Daily News* garnered him enough of a professional reputation that in late 1932 he was asked by the Newspaper Enterprise Association (NEA) syndicate to join their organization as their sole editorial cartoonist. His move to the NEA's base in Cleveland in January 1933 had a massive impact on his career. Not only were his cartoons now syndicated to a much larger number of papers across the country, broadening his readership significantly, but they also increasingly focused on responding to events drawn from national politics.[32] His move to the NEA also coincided with a significant shift in Block's political ideology, which, like that of many of his generation, was forever changed by his growing admiration for the liberal policies of the new Democratic president and his experiences of Franklin D. Roosevelt's New Deal.

The ideology that underscored the New Deal had its origins in the various reform movements which emerged during the progressive era at the beginning of the twentieth century. These reformers had sought to address societal problems by pushing for the government to provide a basic level of support to its citizens and thereby solve social and economic problems caused by laissez-faire economics, industrialization, urbanization, and political corruption.[33] This reform spirit became less vibrant during the 1920s as the economic prosperity of the decade, which was seemingly driven by Republican policies that fully embraced laissez-faire economics, made it harder for progressive reformers to build the political coalitions necessary to enact change. All of this changed with the Great Depression. President Hoover's unwillingness to use the apparatus of the federal government to ease people's suffering drove people from the Republican Party. A new electoral coalition of northern urban voters, labor unions, African Americans, and southern whites swept Roosevelt to victory in November 1932 for the first of an unprecedented four presidential terms.

Roosevelt's New Deal took inspiration from the earlier reform movements to redefine the social contract that existed between the federal government and society. At its heart, however, was a belief that the resources of the federal government should be leveraged to ensure the economic well-being of the state. Thus, in Roosevelt's words, New Deal liberalism was committed to "a changed concept of the duty and responsibility of government toward economic life."[34] In pursuit of this goal, the federal government embarked on a massive program of expansion. It created work relief programs and authorized massive public works initiatives to stimulate job creation and employment. It also enacted social welfare reform by passing a Social Security Act in 1935 that guaranteed benefits to the unemployed and retirees and paid out a lump-sum amount at death. The New Deal's achievements, however, have been criticized from the left because of its perceived failure to challenge the engrained interests of capitalism and to not do enough to improve the prospects of women and minorities, and from the right for being socialistic and going too far in its labor and taxation reforms. Nevertheless, the New Deal gave the American public confidence in the country's ability to recover from the economic impact of the Great Depression and illustrated to millions of Americans the potential benefits of allowing the federal government to assume an unprecedented level of influence in their social and economic lives. Block could have been speaking for a generation of liberals when, years later, he recalled how the New Deal "brought home . . . what government was capable of doing to service its people."[35]

Block's move to Cleveland came just two months before Roosevelt's inauguration as the nation's thirty-second president, and his cartoons quickly reflected his belief in the new president's message of hope to the American people. On March 14, 1933, just ten days after the inauguration, for example, he drew "Dealing with Both Hands," a cartoon that depicts Roosevelt sitting at his desk with one hand resting on his relief legislation and his other knocking out a figure representing pessimism with a right hook that would have made any boxer proud (fig. 4).[36] Block was fortunate to have a steady income with which to support himself throughout both the Depression and the New Deal, but he saw the suffering around him and increasingly used his work as a vehicle for progressive reform, drawing cartoons that supported Roosevelt's New Deal policies. This newfound

FIGURE 4. Syndicated cartoon, March 14, 1933

political affiliation is seen through cartoons such as January 5, 1935's "The Difference," which depicts a man at two different moments of his life. In the left-hand frame, he is shown huddled over in front of a relief roll, counting the only loose change he has to his name. The image highlights the desperation the average man felt at the height of the Depression. In the right-hand frame, however, the same man is shown to be proudly heading to work, holding a lunch pail in one hand, with renewed purpose and vigor. This time, he is in front of a sign marked "Pay Roll: Citizens Earning a Living through Work on Useful Projects."[37] The intent of this cartoon, and the many similar ones that Block drew after Roosevelt took up residency in the White House, was to illustrate the positive impact the New Deal had made to the everyday lives of American workers.

Not that everyone agreed with this assessment. Although the New Deal undoubtedly helped ease people's suffering, progress was slow, and in the meantime many Americans continued to be unemployed and struggled to feed themselves and their families. It was therefore perhaps inevitable that charismatic figures would emerge, promising not just relief from people's economic suffering but fundamental change to American society. Two such men were Father Charles Coughlin and Louisiana senator Huey Long, both of whom Block denounced in his cartoons for what he viewed as their dangerously violent rhetoric.

Block's appraisal that Coughlin preached a "kind of home-grown fascism laced with antisemitism [and] was virulent in his attacks on the Roosevelt administration" was shared by many Americans.[38] Based in Detroit, Michigan, Coughlin came to national prominence thanks to a weekly radio broadcast that he used first to rally support for Roosevelt's campaign in 1932, telling his listeners that "the New Deal is Christ's Deal." After the election, Coughlin increasingly claimed to speak on Roosevelt's behalf. But when the policies he championed on his radio show failed to be enacted, Coughlin turned against the president, railing against Roosevelt and invoking antisemitic language to hint darkly that a small group of private interests were profiting off ordinary Americans' suffering. During the 1936 presidential election, Coughlin began openly praising the fascist policies of Adolf Hitler and Benito Mussolini, and in an infamous speech in Cincinnati, denounced the president as "anti-God and a radical" and urged his audience to prepare for armed resistance if Roosevelt won.[39] In response, Block drew Coughlin at a microphone-laden pulpit, his clenched fists, angry features, and incendiary words contrasted against the biblical teachings to "love thy neighbor as thyself" and to "not bear false witness against thy neighbor."[40]

It was Huey Long, who promised a radical plan to redistribute the nation's wealth by capping individual wealth at $4 million and guaranteeing all Americans an annual income of between $2,000 and $3,000, that Block focused much of his efforts on discrediting. Long's proposals attracted a substantial and dedicated following of over 7.5 million Americans, but he was also accused of bypassing the democratic process to push through his policies in Louisiana. All of this fed into Block's belief that Long was a dangerous demagogue, as can be seen in cartoons from 1934 such as August 4's "Louisiana—There She Stands," which directly compares the senator to France's Louis XIV, the "First Ruler of Louisiana," and November 16's "Feeding the Hungry," which depicts Long ramming legislation down the throat of Louisiana's legislature. Block also sought to highlight Long's corruption, drawing, for example, "The Long, Long Trail" on August 5, 1934, a cartoon that foreshadowed his later work highlighting the corruption of the Nixon administration by depicting an investigator and bloodhound following a litany of corrupt actions attributed to Long. Perhaps the most powerful of these cartoons, however, was April 18, 1935's "The Crown Jewels," which shows Long giving his infamous "Every Man a King" speech while standing next to a cowed and chained figure representing Louisiana.[41]

As another European war became increasingly likely, American politicians and officials were concerned about foreign operatives infiltrating and destabilizing federal and state governments. In response, the House Committee on Un-American Activities—popularly known in the late 1930s as the Dies Committee after its first chairman, Democratic representative Martin Dies of Texas—was constituted in 1938 to investigate alleged disloyalty and subversive activities perpetrated by both fascists and communists. But the committee instead focused most of its investigative powers on the latter group, hauling suspected socialists and communists to answer charges that they supported the destruction of the American government on the flimsiest of evidence. Block's earliest cartoons on the committee's work satirized the overly zealous efforts of its members to root out "un-American" activities across the country. In August 29, 1938's "Attention, Committee on Un-American Activities," for example, Block urged the House committee to investigate such threats to national security as "American restaurant proprietors who bestow foreign titles on hamburgers and turnips," "people who think that a cultivated English accent is preferable to clear enunciation," and "the unnecessary use of Roman numerals." Block was even more biting in that December's "Wait Till the Dies Committee Hears about This!" Drawn after a member of the committee accused the Elizabethan playwright Christopher Marlowe of being a communist, Block suggested that Father Christmas—with "headquarters close to the Soviet Union," "files on millions of Americans," "responsible for the fomenting of plots and secret actions in countless American homes," and "planning to enter the U.S. illegally and under cover of darkness"—should be considered a potential subject of investigation (fig. 5).[42] Although tongue in cheek, both cartoons clearly anticipated the minimal evidence with which the committee

FIGURE 5. Syndicated cartoon, December 3, 1938

pursued charges against accused Americans and helped establish Block as a prominent and vocal critic of its work.

But there are other aspects of Block's cartoons from this era that require further discussion. Block's depiction of women in the 1920s and 1930s was highly problematic. In some of these cartoons, women are featured in what is clearly intended to be a positive role—teachers, nurses, and mothers—but their most consistent function is that of the errant housewife who neglects her duties at home or spends her husband's hard-earned money and the socially mobile woman who threatens traditional male roles both socially and politically. These themes were seen from the very start of his tenure at the *Daily News*. Block's second published cartoon there, titled "Some Day There'll Be an Uprising," drawn on April 25, 1929, depicts a mob of angry men marching under the banner "The Bridge Players' Husbands" and holding signs declaring, "Give Us Back Our Homes" and "We're Tired of Eating Canned Salmon."[43] More explicitly, "Cheer Up! The Worst Is Still to Come," published just two days later on April 27, shows in one panel a man chastising his wife for having spent $57.50 on an antique chair only to reveal in the cartoon's second panel that she has later spent over $400 on an impractical, stylistically modern chair, much to her husband's horror.[44] Likewise, October 4, 1930's "Fairy Tale" can be seen as a relatively straightforward critique of the cult of celebrity, but a closer reading reveals that it is in fact a staunch defense of traditional gender roles: Block was clearly implying that the actress he depicted in his fantasy would have been able to live "happily ever after" if only she had eschewed the trappings of fame and instead settled down with a good husband.[45]

If Block was critical of modern women in his cartoons for what he perceived as their neglect of their traditional roles as wives and mothers in pursuit of fame or materialistic comforts, he was even more dismissive of their increasing role in the political arena. "Then and Now," dated August 29, 1930, is a typical example. Split into two frames, the top image depicts three young women in 1900 as demure members of the "Young Ladies' Sewing Society," while the lower image shows three similarly young but modern women who are now members of the "98th Ward Political Club" planning a political campaign.[46] If a reader was unfamiliar with the broader context of Block's cartoons from this period, one might interpret this cartoon as a celebration of the progress women had made, and in particular of their ability to engage in political activities that would have been impossible at the start of the century. Yet the already long list of cartoons Block had drawn by 1930 that critiqued organized politics precludes this from being a realistic interpretation of the cartoon. Indeed, Block drew a second cartoon dated August 29, 1930, which clearly illustrates his disdain for organized political activities by suggesting that the law was incapable of policing the illegal contributions and resulting corruption that was rampant across the political process.[47]

In this context, it is telling that, when reminiscing about his parents in his 1993 autobiography, Block remembered his father in terms of his achievements as a chemist and his enthusiasm for helping his sons with their homework and taking them to "movies, vaudeville shows and baseball games." In contrast, his mother's defining accomplishment was her prowess as a cook, something she did "marvelously well and was about as inventive in the kitchen as Papa was in the laboratory."[48] Block's attitude toward women, as represented by these cartoons, was consistent with what scholars have identified as a crisis in middle-class men's sense of their own masculinity as they struggled to adapt to the changes in American society precipitated by modernism. Men felt especially threatened by the rise of the "New Woman" and their perceived encroachment into traditionally male activities such as being the primary provider and decision-maker in the domestic arena and, especially, politics.[49] This is explicitly seen in his cartoon "'Tis a Sad Story, Men!" originally published in the *Chicago Daily News* on May 6, 1929 (fig. 6). As with many of Block's cartoons from this period, it is split into two frames. The top vignette, set in 1909, depicts two men laughing at a group of suffragettes passing on the opposite side of the road while holding a sign demanding equal rights. The bottom panel is set in 1929 and shows three fashionable young women snickering at a disheveled man whose angry cry "We Want Equal Rights!" articulates the anxiety and loss of control over their own lives that many white, middle-class men felt during this period.[50] It might be argued that Block intended his cartoon to be read satirically, that he was mocking the closed-minded attitudes of men and their histrionic reaction to modern women. But his full body of work from this period makes that conclusion unlikely. Block's cartoons typically presented their subjects

FIGURE 6. *Chicago Daily News,* May 6, 1929

in a very sober and matter-of-fact fashion that ultimately precludes this interpretation, giving an overall impression of a man who felt threatened by the relatively modest achievements of suffrage and believed that his readers felt exactly as he did about the subject.

Block's depiction of nonwhites during this period was also problematic. His cartoons were drawn primarily for a white, male, middle-class audience, and people who did not fit that description—especially those who were not white—rarely made an appearance in his cartoons as active subjects. The late 1920s and 1930s was a time when African American culture enjoyed a renaissance through popular literature and jazz. These developments were not reflected in Block's cartoons, which demonstrated no awareness of either the daily indignities that African Americans endured in the Jim Crow South or the Urban North, the specific economic and political challenges that defined their everyday lives, or the political activities of the National Association for the Advancement of Colored People as it strove to acquire equal rights. Nevertheless, Block was clearly aware of the resurgence of white racism that occurred across the country during the 1920s and 1930s. In particular, he responded to the horrific lynching of African Americans by white mobs that was still all too common across the South by using his cartoons as a platform from which he could condemn this form of institutionalized racial violence.

Works such as May 28, 1936's "It Can't Happen Here," which conjures a nightmarish world of shadows where a lynch mob emerges from the darkness wearing masks to obscure their faces and dark clothing adorned with white skull-and-crossbones insignia, stand as strong statements against this violence.[51] At a time when his work was becoming increasingly reliant on visual humor to carry its message, this cartoon stands apart as a serious reflection on the reality of life for African Americans across many parts of the country. Inspired by Sinclair Lewis's 1935 satirical novel of the same name, which imagined an America ruled by a totalitarian dictatorship, it is not hard to see the statement that Block was trying to make: so long as this horrific extralegal violence was tolerated across large segments of the country, America was little different from the terror-based regime of Nazi Germany.

On a different theme, "Nobody Knows de Trouble I've Seen," dated November 12, 1935, is a startlingly insightful commentary on the exploitation of Africa by European and American powers from slavery to fascist Italy's imperialistic ambitions in Abyssinia.[52] Yet this cartoon also demonstrates how Block's attitudes toward nonwhites were shaped by prevailing norms of white popular culture. The cartoon depicts an African tribesman wearing nothing more than a loincloth, staring glumly at the large footprints left by Western colonial powers over the centuries. On the horizon are yet more ships approaching the African shore, ready to strip the continent of more of its natural resources. Despite this sophisticated understanding of the nature of colonial oppression, it is the tribesman that catches the eye of a modern reader. Although somewhat indistinct, his facial features are drawn with a wide nose; thick-lipped mouth; and large, wide-open eyes. This stereotypical depiction of Africans and African Americans, which had long been employed by American political cartoonists and was still extremely popular with the white working classes because of the minstrel performances of white men such as Al Jolson, is reproduced in every cartoon drawn by Block between 1929 and 1943 featuring depictions of Black people.[53] One of the most egregious examples is July 29, 1932's "The Spirit of Democracy," in which Block drew an upper-class man, wearing morning dress and adorned with a monocle and drooping mustache, asking a stable hand for tips on which horses to bet on at the races.[54] The intent of the cartoon, indicated by its title, is seemingly to celebrate the breaking down of social conventions enabled by democratic ideals. But this message was undermined by the way the cartoon depicts its subject. Block chose to draw the stable hand not only with blackface-style features but half the size of the white gambler beside him, highlighting the social gap that existed between the pair and accentuating paternalistic assumptions about the nature of African American identity and character. The intended joke was therefore not just that the white gambler would stoop to talk to his implied social inferior for betting advice but that the stable hand was assumed to be his intellectual inferior as well.

It was not just Africans and African Americans that Block treated in this stereotypical way. His disregard for cultural awareness is evident in cartoons such as one he drew on September 17, 1930, nine months after the Indian National Congress declared independence from Britain and in the wake of Mohandas Gandhi's protest over the taxation of salt, which had increased international attention on his efforts against British colonial power. Titled "One Reason for Gandhi's Costume," the cartoon depicts a hypothetical discussion between two Indians, dressed in the traditional Indian style of *dhoti* and *pagri,* over a potential meeting between Gandhi and the British authorities. "Listen," Block imagined one of the Indians saying to his compatriot, "If Gandhi gets into a conference with those British diplomats, he'll lose his shirt!"[55] Even as a clear statement of how little Block thought of Gandhi's attempts to end British colonial control over India, it is hard to imagine a more dismissive representation of Indian culture and of what Gandhi's choice of clothing—specifically his affiliation with India's poorest citizens—was meant to symbolize. Similarly, November 20, 1930's "The Land of Opportunity" imagines that the most natural calling for a muezzin—the person charged by a mosque to lead the call to prayer and worship—in America would be as a train station announcer, supposedly the sole profession where his undecipherable language, imagined by Block as "Oogully, oogully, galumph," would be acceptable.[56]

One could argue that with cartoons such as these, Block was attempting to tread the fine line between caricature and stereotype. The specific challenges of cartooning—where an artist has to effectively communicate a message to their readers while using techniques such as space, line, and form as efficiently as possible—necessitates the representation of people in their most basic characteristics as a form of visual shorthand to assist the viewer in identifying who is being depicted. But this enterprise is inevitably fraught with peril for the cartoonist as it is all too easy for what was intended to be a comedic caricature to become an offensive stereotype. Many nineteenth- and early twentieth-century cartoonists deliberately relied on racial identifiers to provide visual cues within their cartoons, for example depicting African Americans as lazy and comic figures; the Irish as perennially drunk, immoral, and wasteful; Jews as penny-pinching Shylock types; and Native Americans as barbaric, threatening figures to be feared by "civilized" society.[57] Although Block was to become a master of the art of caricature, cartoons from this period that depict nonwhites clearly demonstrated a propensity for relying on popular stereotypes that provided a comedic visual shorthand to entertain his imagined audience of middle-class, white men.

As the political situation in Europe became increasingly volatile, Block ardently believed that America needed to prepare itself for being caught up in the ensuing conflict—an eventuality that he saw as inevitable. Throughout the 1930s and into the early 1940s he drew numerous cartoons that challenged the prevailing spirit of isolationism which dominated American society during the period, attacking the fascist regime in Italy and lamenting the violence of the Spanish Civil War. Most important, though, were his cartoons laying bare the inherent evilness of Hitler and Nazi Germany, producing work that, in the words of scholar Harry L. Katz, "exposed Nazi activities, giving them graphic form and visual power." His work during this period was characterized by cartoons that depicted "metaphors for the resilience of the human spirit, the inhumanity of war and the duplicity of dictators, finding heroes among innocents and victims, and taking to task villainous politicians."[58] Block's earliest depiction of Hitler's rise to power came in October 1930 after the Nazi Party unexpectedly won over one hundred seats in the German Reichstag, making it the second largest party in parliament. Titled "Evolution in Germany," the cartoon imagines the changing fortunes of German workers and is split into three discrete spaces that begin with a depiction of a hard-working, white-collar employee who loses his job, turning him into a homeless "black-collar" tramp contemplating his situation on a park bench. The final image is of him angrily marching as a Mussolini-inspired "black shirt" while holding a flag proclaiming his new political allegiance: "fascisti." In January 1933, even before the Nazi leader was sworn in as Germany's chancellor at the end of that month, Block drew "Hail Hitler!" in which Hitler is saluted by the medieval torturers Coercion, Intolerance, Bigotry, and Ignorance. In March 1934, Block's cartoon "The World as It Looks Right Now" depicts the world leaders of the day sitting on top of a black 8-ball, awaiting the inevitability of its being struck.[59] His anti-isolationist sentiments were made most specific in August 1936 when he drew the cartoon "In World Affairs—," which contrasts America in the twentieth century with the Roman and British Empires. In Block's rendering of history, Rome was born great and is shown as teacher of the young world, Britain achieved greatness and pulls the rest of the world behind it, but an isolationist America is resisting the best efforts of the rest of the world to have "greatness thrust upon" it.[60]

After Germany's invasion of Poland, and Britain and France's subsequent declaration of war in September 1939, Block's cartoons became even more graphic and insistent as he celebrated Allied resolve and attempted to educate his readers as to what was actually at stake in Europe. A notable example from this time is the September 1940 cartoon "Hands across the Seas," which depicts a triumvirate of Japan, Germany, and Italy clasping their bloody and dripping hands over America, and was clearly intended to warn Americans that the conflict in Europe would ultimately engulf the United States.[61] His cartoons also increasingly represented idealized views of American masculinity, which were used to affirm the readiness and potential of America's human and industrial resources. In "Waiting," a cartoon dated August 24, 1940, for example, he drew a chisel-jawed and muscular representation of "U.S. Manpower" standing in front of the U.S. Capitol building ready to be mobilized in support of the war effort.[62] More explicitly, "American Labor," drawn a week later, imagines an American worker, again heavily muscled and with features set with deep resolve, towering over America's industrial resources, as well as a sign that reads, "Free Men at Work," to indicate both the anticipation of Americans' labor and the value of a democratic society. Block contrasted this figure of American manhood by depicting in the cartoon's foreground shadowy figures chained together as part of a slave gang with the clear implication that their efforts could never match America's economic output.[63]

Block's internationalist views brought him into direct conflict with the management of his syndicate, which, like many in the country prior to the attack on Pearl Harbor in December 1941, was opposed to American intervention in what they saw as a European problem. Despite regular pressure from newspaper editors across the country and equal pressure from his superiors, however, Block refused to stop producing cartoons with a strong anti-isolationist message. As his increasingly liberal views more frequently diverged from those of the NEA management, Block was required to send rough sketches to New York for personal approval from the company's general manager.[64] Block's views were ultimately vindicated in 1942 when he won the first of his Pulitzer Prizes for a cartoon originally published on March 7, 1941.[65] Drawn at the height of the Blitz and captioned "British Plane," the cartoon is set in occupied France and shows a German soldier clenching his fist while staring hopelessly at the skies as an (unseen) British bomber flies overhead to unload its own payload and do its part fighting back against the Nazis. Behind the German, however, are shown three French citizens, whose own hopes are revealed by their furtive smiles.[66] In his autobiography, Block wryly explained how this Pulitzer award not only served to solidify his growing reputation as one of the country's foremost political cartoonists but also likely saved his job, as news of the award arrived only minutes before he was scheduled to go into a meeting with his syndicate's president in which he fully expected to be fired.[67]

Block ultimately stayed with the NEA until early March 1943, when he was drafted into the U.S. Army. Unlike other contemporary cartoonists such as Bill Mauldin and Gregor Duncan, who saw action in Europe and drew cartoons based on their experiences for the armed forces' *Stars and Stripes* newspaper, Block was not deployed abroad and never saw combat.[68] Instead, he was posted to the Army Air Force Tactical Center in Orlando, Florida, where he spent his days drawing cartoons that were printed in the camp paper. Frustrated and bored in Florida, he requested a transfer to Europe to replace Gregor Duncan on hearing that his colleague had been killed.[69] This transfer never came through, however, and instead he was redeployed to New York where he drew cartoons and wrote editorials that were distributed as part of a clipsheet of materials sent out to army papers across the world for the army's Information and Education Division.[70] The majority of cartoons from this period reflected the reality of working as an enlisted soldier on the home front whose work was intended for an official army publication. They reveal little about the lived experience of soldiers on the front lines and instead are straightforward gag cartoons intended to build morale among the troops while humorously educating his fellow soldiers about such topics as the importance of saving some money from their paychecks, encouraging the purchase of war bonds, behaving appropriately around women, and even being careful about where and when they smoked.[71]

With Japan's surrender in August 1945, the army began the process of demobilization, and Block, now holding the rank of sergeant, found himself looking for a job once he was mustered out. On a trip to Washington, DC, he was introduced to Nelson Poynter, then editor of Florida's *St. Petersburg Times*, and together they discussed his future plans. Several days later, Poynter happened to meet an assistant to Eugene Meyer, publisher of the *Washington Post*. Meyer, it transpired, was on the lookout for an editorial cartoonist to fill a vacancy at his paper that had existed since January 1943 and was interested in meeting Block to discuss the position.[72] At the time, the *Post* was severely under-resourced and, with anemic advertising revenues and a daily circulation that ranked it third of Washington's four newspapers, barely profitable. But Block was intrigued at the opportunity of working in the capital as it would give him the opportunity to observe the nation's decision-makers—the subjects of his cartoons—up close and in person.[73]

With their mutual interest established, the two men soon arranged a meeting at the Yale Club in New York where they sounded each other out to determine if Block would be a good match for the Washington paper. Meyer requested samples of Block's prewar work so he could get a sense of the cartoonist's style and skill, but in a letter dated October 11, 1945, also sent to Block examples of the *Post*'s editorial content so that Block in turn could become better acquainted with the paper and make an informed decision about moving to Washington.[74] Block had been entertaining several employment options at this time. But after his struggles with NEA's management over the content of his cartoons, one of the major attractions of Meyer's offer of employment with the *Post* was the assurance he received that his new boss would have "no idea of suggesting cartoons." Meyer instead informed Block that he believed it was important to simply "get good people and let them do their work."[75] A second meeting between the two men on November 6 went well, with Meyer crucially agreeing to allow Block to have his cartoons nationally syndicated. On December 26, the paper was able to proudly announce on its front page that the Pulitzer Prize–winning cartoonist would be joining their staff, with his first cartoon to be published a week later, on January 3, 1946.[76]

When Block first began working at the *Post,* the paper had a reputation as a strong supporter of the Republican Party, thanks largely to its anti–New Deal stance and advocacy for fiscally conservative policy.[77] But the cartoonist took at face value Meyer's assurances that he would not be subjected to any form of editorial control and immediately launched into a series of cartoons that revealed his commitment to postwar liberalism. In just his first month at the *Post,* Block's cartoons tackled such subjects as the importance of government intervention to manage fiscal policy and fight the threat of inflation, congressional obstructionism that was preventing needed reform in such areas as civil rights and welfare reform, anxiety over the dangers presented by atomic energy, and a desire that the United States assert itself in international affairs as a deterrent against the threat of communism.[78] With cartoons such as these, Block established himself as a strong and unique voice on the paper's editorial page, and as early as January 9, the *Post* had already received and published the first of countless letters sent by appreciative readers of the daily Herblock cartoon.[79]

Block's cartoons not only depicted current events but also regularly supported those other causes—such as environmentalism, gun control, and especially civil liberties—that he viewed as critical to ensure and maintain the continued quality of life to which Americans in the postwar era aspired.[80] Standing against these goals, though, were corrupt politicians and selfish special interest groups who frequently worked together to undermine the benefits that postwar rhetoric promised to all Americans. The connection that Block drew between the two groups was seen as early as March 1946, when he imagined a conservative congressman prostrating himself at the altar of the "Inflation Lobby," with cuts to housing reform legislation and the Office of Price Administration scattered on the floor as sacrifices.[81] It was, Block believed, his primary responsibility to be the person who stood up against these ingrained interests in support of the "little guy." It is no surprise, then, that in speaking primarily to the interests of white, urban, and middle-class citizens who made up the *Post*'s core readership, Block depicted this group of Americans as both the hero and the voice of reason of his work. And for Block, the greatest threat facing both these people and American democracy in the early postwar era was that posed by forces, whether at home or abroad, which sought to infringe on personal liberties.

2

"THE FEAR-AND-SMEAR RACKETEERS"

Protecting Democracy

"FOR THE PAST FEW YEARS the air of fear around here has been pretty thick," Block wrote in *The Herblock Book,* his first anthology of political cartoons, which was published in late 1952. "There's not always something you can put your finger on," he continued, "but there are plenty of people anxious to put the finger on somebody."[1] Block was writing at the height of the second Red Scare, a moment in American history that stretched from the late 1940s into the early 1950s and beyond, when the fear that communist spies had infiltrated American politics and society reached almost hysterical levels. Federal employees were investigated by government-sanctioned "loyalty boards," which peered into Americans' private lives to root out any perceived left-leaning associations. In the entertainment industry, screenwriters, actors, directors, musicians, and many others were placed on so-called blacklists and denied employment because of their suspected political beliefs. The anticommunist crusade extended into almost every facet of American life, with not even teachers or librarians exempt from scrutiny.

Unlike many other liberal commentators, Block was openly critical of the excesses of these anticommunist investigations from an early date.

His primary concern, however, was not over the goals of these efforts but their methods. "Close to 100 per cent of us in this country are against Communism," he assured readers of *The Herblock Book*. But he denounced what he described as the "Fear-and-Smear racketeers"—those politicians who leveraged "the fear of what Communists might do to us" and turned it into an opportunity to advance their own self-interests—for having "hijacked a legitimate public concern about Communism and steered it down their own dark alleys." The result was that they "bellow that they're protecting us from subversion while at the same time actually subverting just about everything this country stands for. And they have tried to take over the word 'Americanism' in exactly the same way that their Communist counterparts have tried to take over 'Peace' and 'Democracy.'"[2]

This chapter examines the visual devices that Block used to persuade his audience of the truth behind these statements. At a time when any criticism of anticommunist activities was used by politicians and others as all the justification needed to become the subject of an investigation into alleged subversive behavior, Block's cartoons defined the efforts of anticommunists to root out alleged subversive activities from the federal government as something that itself threatened the foundations of American democracy. By subverting the rhetoric and behavior of anticommunist leaders, Block's cartoons demonstrated to his readers how, far from protecting American values, anticommunist hysteria instead posed a serious threat to the continued stability of American values and way of life. Furthermore, Block's opposition to these initiatives helped elevate his reputation as a public defender of civil liberties, positioning him as an influential spokesperson for liberal values. At the same time, however, his uncompromising attacks on the leaders of these investigations and other activities marked him as a target of conservative fury that would continue throughout the remainder of his career.

Block, like other postwar liberals, believed that the American system—specifically its economic and political structures—stood above all others. As he wrote in the introduction to his government-printed and internationally distributed pamphlet *Herblock Looks at Communism*, he was able to work as a cartoonist because "personal liberty is a part of American democracy." More than this, however,

> If such liberty existed in communist lands . . . we would all be living in a happier world. That the communist rulers do not allow their people to seek the truth or to speak their minds is tragic for those people. But when those rulers systematically poison those minds against the people of other countries the results can be tragic for all of us. . . . I do not think another world war is inevitable. I think it can be prevented if communism, like fascism, is opposed by all who want to live as free men.[3]

Block's cartoons unabashedly depicted this stance in graphic form. It was, for example, explicitly seen in his March 1947 cartoon "Put Me In, Coach! Put Me In!" which depicts a football game in which a group of propped up strawmen labeled "Fascists," "Monarchists," and "Imperialists" are lined up against a tough-looking communist. On the sidelines is an even larger player, a representative of Democracy, begging his disinterested coaches, Uncle Sam and John Bull (a commonly used symbol for Great Britain), to let him enter the game and face the threat represented by communism.[4]

This cartoon was published just days before Harry Truman gave a speech before a joint session of Congress that is now widely heralded as marking the beginning of the Cold War. The cartoon's original context was the postwar efforts of both the United States and the Soviet Union to assert their influence in the Mediterranean and Middle East. In March 1946, a civil war had erupted in Greece in which communists were seeking to wrest political control from the ruling monarchist and fascist-sympathizing government. With Britain no longer able to offer the anticommunist forces the financial support they had been providing, leading American strategists feared that a Soviet-supported victory for the Greek communists would allow them to apply pressure over Turkey for control of a vital maritime link between the Black Sea and the Mediterranean. In Iran, meanwhile, which was then jointly occupied by the United States, Great Britain, and the Soviet Union as it moved toward independence, the Truman administration feared losing control of the nation's vast oil reserves. It was in this geopolitical context that Truman declared, "It must be the policy of the United States to support free peoples who are resisting attempted subjugation by armed minorities or by outside pressures," and requested $400 million from Congress to provide economic and financial aid to support the Greek government's efforts to put down the communist threat in their nation. Although Truman's address was specific to the Greek and Turkish context, his intent was to establish a precedent by which the United States would work to contain communism in Europe and elsewhere to the existing spheres of Soviet influence, a policy that became known as the Truman Doctrine.[5] For Block, the relief that Truman was finally taking a strong stand against the communist threat was tempered by a belief that the proposed action did not reflect American values and democratic principles. Thus, his initial response to Truman's speech was a cartoon showing a strong and determined Uncle Sam standing astride a globe and confronting Stalin with the words "I'm Here to Stay, Too" in a clear statement of resolve. But this endorsement was followed the next day with a cartoon depicting a badly battered Greek citizen lying in a war-torn landscape, while in the background Truman is shown to be naively handing over a sack of U.S. aid to a representative of the Greek government and unconvincingly asserting that the money was intended to provide economic aid for the war's victims.[6]

Communism's threat to world stability was perceived to be twofold. As articulated by George F. Kennan, then an American diplomat based in the U.S. embassy in Moscow, in a dispatch sent to the State Department in February 1946, global communism was "like a malignant parasite which feeds only on diseased tissue." There could be no cooperation with the Soviet government, he continued; the threat to American interests and global democracy could only be contained.[7] But the competition for political and ideological superiority that this so-called Cold War fostered itself created a dangerous cycle as the United States and Soviet Union developed ever more powerful and destructive weaponry. The United States' development of atomic bombs, and Truman's decision to use them against the Japanese cities of Hiroshima and Nagasaki in August 1945, forever changed the global balance of power. American political and military leaders were determined to keep their tactical advantage for as long as possible as a deterrent against the communist threat abroad. The Soviet Union's successful testing of atomic weaponry in August 1949 only spurred Americans to develop the even more powerful hydrogen bomb, which they successfully tested for the first time in November 1952. When the Soviet

Union once again caught up with American technology by testing its own hydrogen bomb the following year, each country focused on developing more advanced warheads and delivery systems. This ever-escalating arms race led many Americans to fear the inevitably of a devastating nuclear war, an anxiety that was captured in popular culture with science-fiction films such as 1954's *Godzilla* and *Them!* basing their plots on the horrifying consequences of nuclear accidents and radioactive fallout.[8]

Block was concerned about the American military's control of atomic power early in the postwar era. The opening of his proposed but unpublished book "What's Going on Here?" which was drafted in late 1947, is an extended meditation on the devasting power of atomic weaponry. Comparing the impact of an atomic bomb detonated in a body of water with a gas attack, Block warned that "the area covered would be measured in miles instead of yards and the radioactive mist would be infinitely more powerful and more penetrating. There would be no defense against it." The buildings in an urban center unfortunate enough to be targeted in such an attack would "remain intact," he continued, but "the city would be uninhabitable for years or ages." Writing over a year before the Soviet Union had successfully tested its own atomic weaponry, Block went on to warn his potential readers that America's monopoly on this technology would not last. "People all across the country are worried that the secret of the bomb might be stolen," he wrote. "What worries the scientists is that so many people think there is a secret. All of them agree that The Bomb is no secret." The only way to protect both America and the rest of the world against the dangers of the bomb, he concluded, was greater international control of this new class of weaponry.[9]

Block's words were never published, but readers of his cartoons would have recognized the sentiments he expressed. As early as January 26, 1946, Block put forward his belief in the importance of international oversight over atomic power. Inspired by the first of Hercules's mythical labors, he drew atomic power as the Nemean lion while Hercules, taking the place of the United Nations, which was meeting in General Assembly for the very first time, cautiously approaches with chains to tame the vicious animal.[10] As important to Block as ensuring international cooperation, however, was the need to safeguard that this technology remained under the development of independent scientists and that it not become solely a tool of the military. Cartoons such as "A Choice of Genii," originally published on March 6, 1946, imagined Uncle Sam as Aladdin and "Atomic Energy" as the genie of the lamp in two different scenarios. In the first, Aladdin's lamp is labeled "Scientific Freedom," with the emergent genie benevolently offering wealth and bountiful fruit. In the alternative, where the genie is under "Military Control," the bellicose and militaristic spirit is shown threatening its erstwhile master.[11] As tensions with the Soviet Union increased, though, the threat of atomic power became more explicit, culminating in Block's creation of the anthropomorphic Mr. Atom.

A threatening presence in the classic rocket-shape of an atom bomb, which Block depicted ominously looming over the American public, world leaders, and the globe itself, Mr. Atom became the personification of Block's anxieties over the dangers of atomic weaponry. The character first appeared in an April 1946 cartoon, interrupting a meeting of U.S. policymakers discussing the future composition of American armed forces with the words "I Ain't Got Any Traditions." This version of Mr. Atom was substantially different from the menacing monster who would stalk Block's cartoons for much of the rest of career, taking on an *almost* comedic appearance. The character is depicted leaning nonchalantly against a doorframe, while the rocket's tail fins become a crown, with a boater hat perched on one tip. Even so, the message of the cartoon, with the implied threat that the bomb's simple presence forced decision-makers to readjust their assumptions about traditional forms of warfare, made clear Block's fears about the impact of atomic weaponry.[12] By the time of Mr. Atom's next appearance in August 1946, however, the character had become something quite different. It had been flipped so that the top of the rocket now formed its head, while the tailfins had been discarded to give it a much sleeker and more naturalistic appearance. The cartoon, which showed Mr. Atom dressed in a suit casually asking a passerby ("World Diplomacy") the time, was drawn in a style emulating film noir, with deep shadows used to highlight the sinister nature of this otherwise seemingly innocent moment.[13] Ultimately, Block refined this depiction further, discarding the character's clothing but adding a Spartan warrior's helmet and a deep five-o'clock shadow. This latter trope would become one of Block's calling cards when depicting those he felt threatened postwar society. By transforming the very deterrent that the American government developed to help contain the spread of global communism into a thug-like character, Block highlighted how the threat posed by atomic weaponry was completely indiscriminatory in nature. This was not a problem for a single nation-state but one that endangered the entire world.

In the context of this anxiety over the potentially devastating impact of atomic weaponry and the Cold War and America's international entanglements against communism, it was perhaps inevitable that the United States would be susceptible to a wave of hysteria as politicians and the public alike became convinced that Soviet agents had infiltrated the federal government at its highest levels. Most famously, the House Committee on Un-American Activities (popularly known as HUAC), which had been first established as a temporary body in 1938 to investigate pro-fascist groups, was made a permanent standing committee in 1945 and given a specific mandate to investigate potential links to communism and other forms of disloyalty involving private citizens and public officials alike. Revelations from Canada in early 1946 of the existence of a Soviet-operated spy ring, coupled with similar claims from communist defectors such as Elizabeth Bentley and Whittaker Chambers that the Soviet Union had infiltrated the highest levels of the federal government, created a general atmosphere of unease around the nation. This seemed to underscore the importance of ensuring that all communist influences were expelled from America's public life and preventing communist spies from stealing the nation's atomic secrets. At the same time, opportunistic Republicans such as Richard Nixon, who in 1946 was running for office in California's 12th congressional district, found it politically expedient to accuse Democrats of being "soft on communism," which in turn prompted many Democrats to strengthen their own anticommunist rhetoric.[14]

Postwar liberals were complicit in this effort to remove communist influence from American life. Communists were driven out of labor unions by the leaders of those organizations, who were concerned about losing their own influence and power over their membership. Similarly, it was liberal executives, not conservative activists or politicians, who adopted the Hollywood blacklists.[15] But nowhere was this more clearly seen than in President Truman's Executive Order 9835, signed on March 21, 1947, just days after the Truman Doctrine was announced in Congress, and which the president hoped would not only nullify conservative attacks on Democrats for their lack of commitment to the anticommunist cause but also rally public opinion in support of his Cold War policies. This so-called Loyalty Order disqualified anyone from working in the federal government who was, or ever had been, a member of the Communist Party and gave wide-ranging powers to the Federal Bureau of Investigation to conduct background checks on any current or potential federal employee. The Truman administration's endorsement of this type of anticommunist activity deepened an ongoing crisis within the American left that would have a lasting impact on both the Democratic Party and Block's own politics. Starting in the mid-1930s, New Deal liberals, social democrats, and communists had set aside their ideological differences to form the Popular Front and work together against the rising tide of fascism around the world. All three of these politically left-of-center groups had benefited from this alliance, but the postwar climate of growing hostility between the Soviet Union and the United States forced New Deal liberals, who viewed Harry Truman as an uninspiring leader unsuited for the demands of the presidency, to reassess the extent to which they were willing to work with American communists. The more progressive social democrats, meanwhile, found Truman's leadership lacking because they believed him to have unnecessarily provoked tensions with the Soviet Union but wanted to maintain the Popular Front's cooperation with the Communist Party.[16]

This debate over the future of liberalism would be resolved in the glare of the 1948 presidential election. The 1946 congressional midterm elections had seen the Republican Party win control of both the House and Senate for the first time since 1930, leading many Americans to speculate that Truman lacked the political skills to win a presidential election for himself. The progressive wing of the Democratic Party coalesced around former vice president Henry Wallace, the man who Harry Truman had replaced on the party's ticket in 1944 and who had resigned from Truman's cabinet in September 1946 after he seemed to imply in a speech that the United States should cede influence over Eastern Europe to the Soviet Union. Three months later, Wallace was instrumental in founding the Progressive Citizens of America (PCA), a left-leaning political activist group that welcomed members regardless of race and political affiliation, including members of the Communist Party. The following year,

Wallace, with the backing of the PCA, launched a third-party campaign for the presidency and positioned himself as the true standard bearer of the liberal agenda. Wallace ran on the promise of deescalating the Cold War by reconciling with the Soviet Union and proposed domestic policies such as the desegregation of public schools, a national health insurance program, and gender equality. Wallace's campaign attracted support from several prominent left-wing politicians and intellectuals, as well as some union members, but it was his decision to accept the endorsement of the American Communist Party that proved most controversial, with many liberals fearful that Wallace's candidacy would split the Democratic Party's vote and be a boon to the Republican Party's prospects in the upcoming election.[17]

In response to Wallace's growing national profile and fearful that the PCA's apparent embrace of communist support would threaten the continued enforcement of New Deal policies, more centrist New Deal liberals decided to establish their own political organization, Americans for Democratic Action (ADA). Founded by Hubert Humphrey, Eleanor Roosevelt, and Adlai Stevenson in January 1947, the organization counted among its members other liberal luminaries such as Harvard historian Arthur Schlesinger Jr., union leader Walter Reuther, theologian Reinhold Niebuhr, and even members of the Truman administration such as Chester Bowles, the chairman of the Economic Stabilization Board. In contrast to the PCA, the ADA embraced an interventionist and anticommunist foreign policy that was intended to create a new political consensus between New Deal Democrats and moderate Republicans. Although many individual members of the ADA opposed the Truman Doctrine because of its implied support of authoritarian regimes opposed to communism, the organization's leadership was more willing to support the Truman administration's foreign and domestic policy goals. This was most clearly seen in their enthusiastic endorsement of the Marshall Plan, which promised economic aid to assist in the recovery of war-torn Europe and was widely interpreted as an effort to further isolate the Soviet Union from the rest of the world. With Wallace and the PCA denouncing the plan as a misguided policy that both failed to address Europe's actual needs and threatened to further destabilize global politics, the ADA's leadership took the opportunity to highlight the anticommunism that differentiated the two organizations.[18] Despite positioning their organization as an advocate and supporter of the Truman administration, ADA leaders such as Humphrey and Bowles doubted the president's commitment to New Deal policies and worried that having Truman at the head of the Democratic ticket in 1948 would cost the party not only the White House but down-ticket races as well.

There is little doubt as to which faction Block identified with. Throughout 1947 and 1948, his cartoons reflected many of the concerns and priorities of the ADA, even echoing and reinforcing public statements of the group's leaders. Henry Wallace's candidacy for the presidency in 1948, for example, was portrayed at various points of the campaign as playing directly into the hands of both Republicans and communists. Just days after Wallace announced his intention to run, Block drew a cartoon that showed a member of the PCA excitedly telling Wallace to "Listen! Listen to the People Cheering!" while oblivious to the fact that the enthusiasm for Wallace's third-party candidacy came from a crowd of Republican operatives overflowing from the Republican Party's headquarters (fig. 7).[19] Block's cartoons also reflected the ADA's distrust of the sitting president. In depicting Truman early in the campaign carefreely sunbathing while storm clouds gather over the Democratic Party's election prospects and recklessly driving the party off a cliff edge, Block reinforced the ADA's concerns that Truman was not an electable candidate.[20] Similarly, after Franklin D. Roosevelt Jr., who was serving as vice chair of the ADA, openly called for the Democrats to draft General Dwight Eisenhower as its presidential nominee, Block's cartoons became a space that suggested the Democratic Party's best chance for electoral success in November would come if Eisenhower was indeed at the top of their ballot.[21] Later in the campaign, after Truman had secured the Democratic nomination, Block followed the ADA's lead in framing Wallace's refusal to drop out as a specific threat to liberal, ADA-endorsed candidates such as Hubert Humphrey, Chester Bowles, and Helen Douglas that would ultimately only support the destabilizing goals of the Soviet Union.[22]

Truman ultimately did win the election in what was arguably the most surprising electoral result of the twentieth century. Block, like most New Deal liberals, had resigned himself to a Republican victory, and his cartoons of early November did not hold back his delight at this unexpected

FIGURE 7. *Washington Post,* December 31, 1947

turn, depicting Truman's presidential train hauling the corpse of the Republican elephant as a trophy and being met in Washington, DC, by a cheering crowd of Americans that threatened to overwhelm the cartoon's frame.[23] Just as notable as Truman's victory was the Democratic Party's success in retaking both houses of Congress, with fully a third of those newly elected Democrats active members of the ADA. Among those arriving in Congress for the first time were Hubert Humphrey as senator for Minnesota and Eugene McCarthy, who was elected to the House from Minnesota's 4th district, while Franklin Delano Roosevelt Jr. won a special election to represent New York's 20th district in May 1949. And in other elections, Chester Bowles and Adlai Stevenson were elected governors of Connecticut and Illinois respectively. Numbering only 35,000 fee-paying members at the end of the decade, the ADA was nonetheless an organization whose political influence was vastly greater than its membership suggested, thanks largely to the participation of so many prominent liberals in its activities.[24] In the aftermath of the 1948 elections, several commentators highlighted the ADA's role in securing Truman's victory and suggested that the president turn to the ADA for support in enacting his political agenda.[25] One American who was clearly inspired by the ADA was Herbert Block. Not only did his cartoons continue to mirror the language of the organization's public statements but throughout the 1950s, he regularly spoke at events sponsored by and on behalf of the ADA, traveling to cities as far afield as New York, Cleveland, and Santa Barbara, California.[26]

One area where Block and the ADA did seem to differ, though, was in their various reactions to Truman's loyalty program. Formed as an explicitly anticommunist organization, many members of the ADA were sympathetic to its goals. The ADA issued a September 1947 statement broadly supporting the program, while Arthur Schlesinger, writing in the *New York Times*, rhetorically asked, "What Is Loyalty?" before declaring that "civil libertarians who honestly fear a witch-hunt must be reminded that in an imperfect world of spies and traitors a Government must be conceded the right of self-protection." Although he granted that the challenge was to "construct some means of ridding the security agencies of questionable characters, while at the same time retaining enough safeguards to insure against indiscriminate purges," the threat posed by communist activity in the United States was very real, and failure to act against suspected sympathizers "may well imperil national security."[27] Block, in contrast, dismissed the effectiveness of the loyalty program, pointedly asserting in 1952 that "since it is agreed that Communists have no compunctions about swearing falsely, these oaths can't very well separate the sheep from the goats."[28] His cartoons likewise made clear his antipathy toward the methods used to enforce this order, using symbols and situations that held everyday familiarity for Americans to ensure that they resonated with his audience.

On October 13, 1947, for example, he imagined a group of people enjoying a cocktail party in the heart of Washington, DC. One of the party's guests, however, is wearing a gag, leading a fellow reveler to state, "You're with the State Department, I Presume." Similarly, May 31, 1948's "Okay, Honey—Put It On," depicts a federal employee checking that no one was spying on his home before allowing his wife to add Russian dressing to his salad. And April 24, 1949's "You Read Books, Eh?" imagines a terrified teacher being questioned by state and local investigators rooting through her trash, preparing to cut out the Soviet Union from a map hanging on the wall, and even looking disapprovingly at a portrait of Thomas Jefferson (fig. 8).[29] The strength of these cartoons lay not just in their ability to present an everyday scenario Block's readers could readily identify with but in their seemingly effortless ability to subvert that same mundaneness to illustrate the sense of paranoia permeating American society against

FIGURE 8. *Washington Post,* April 24, 1949

the backdrop of these loyalty oaths, background investigations, and other anticommunist activities. It comes as no surprise then that, when the ultra-conservative and anticommunist magazine *Plain Talk* attacked the *Post* for being a "Trojan horse for totalitarianism" in March 1948, Block was specifically called out as a prominent member of the paper's alleged "'liberal' faction," with his cartoons coming under special criticism for leading the paper's "crusade against the loyalty program."[30]

It was his cartoons depicting the actions of the House Committee on Un-American Activities that most clearly demonstrated Block's anger over the abuses of power that anticommunist sentiment fostered. Between January 1, 1946, and December 31, 1949, Block drew a total of seventy-seven cartoons that specifically sought to expose the excesses of HUAC and underscore his concern that the civil liberties of Americans were being suspended unnecessarily. These cartoons, which depicted threats to Americans' civil liberties and reflected his unease that government and congressional activities threatened the ability of ordinary Americans to express their own thoughts and opinions without fear of reprisal, generally fell into one of three categories. The first was evidenced within fifty days of Block's starting work at the *Post*. In a cartoon satirically titled "American, All the Way Back," Block explicitly targeted the committee's activities by depicting its members, led by John E. Rankin, a Democrat from Mississippi, as a group of seventeenth-century witch-hunters, rushing with the tools of their puritanical trade to try a new victim.[31] Similarly, October 8, 1947's "Everybody Ready for Hallowe'en?" imagines members of the committee as a group of trick-or-treaters, armed with tar brushes and clubs as they prepare to hunt for their next victims.[32] This group of cartoons, with their depiction of members of HUAC working in isolation and with no visible target of their investigation evident, sought to focus readers' attention on the vacuous nature of the committee's activities and were effective at depicting the committee's methods as outdated and vindictive.

In other cartoons, Block did show members of the committee interacting with the subjects of their inquiry. In these situations, however, the subjects of investigations are invariably depicted as either innocent bystanders who have been randomly targeted or as members of America's scientific community engaged in important work for national security.

On April 10, 1946, for example, Block imagined an unthreatening scientist stripped naked and sitting underneath a bright light as a mob of congressmen question and harass him from the shadows; in a similarly themed piece drawn two years later, a short-statured J. Parnell Thomas, a Republican from New Jersey who assumed the chairmanship of HUAC in January 1947, is shown dumping a bottle of tar over the head of a hard-working nuclear physicist.[33] These cartoons were designed to illustrate the trumped up charges and character assassinations that those accused of communist sympathies faced when they appeared before the committee. But the reckless nature of these investigations was perhaps best illustrated in a cartoon drawn on October 30, 1947, that showed the indiscriminate nature of HUAC's accusations as members of the committee pursued their victims without regard to their likely guilt. "It's Okay—We're Hunting Communists" imagined Thomas and HUAC's chief investigator, Robert E. Stripling, recklessly driving a car down a crowded sidewalk, uncaringly knocking over innocent passersby.[34] Together, these cartoons portrayed members of HUAC as overzealous and malicious investigators, uncaring as to the damage they were doing to America and its citizens' lives. This was a theme that Block was to develop further in the third, and arguably most effective, category he employed when critiquing HUAC's activities.

In this final group of cartoons, Block depicted members of the committee engaged in activities that struck against the very symbols of American democracy. This was made explicit on April 8, 1946, when Block imagined John E. Rankin in the act of throwing a bucket of tar over a representation of American Democracy while a congressman jovially tells a concerned member of the public, "That's a Joke, Son—You Don't Seem to Get It." Similarly, on November 16, 1946, Block showed the committee's leadership as termites gnawing their way through a pillar that represented both the U.S. Constitution in general and the Bill of Rights specifically. Likewise, on March 27, 1947, he depicted a congressman accusing Uncle Sam of belonging to what was characterized as an international organization but in truth was the fledgling United Nations. And on June 1, 1947, Block drew a battered and bruised Statue of Liberty, her torch extinguished, lying underneath Thomas, who is holding a can of paint with which he has smeared his innocent victims, triumphantly declaring that there is no longer any danger of fascism.[35] The most powerful of Block's HUAC-focused cartoons from the late 1940s, however, was June 17, 1949's "Fire!" With its depiction of an overwrought man, labeled "Hysteria," holding a bucket of water and frantically scrambling up a ladder so that he can extinguish the Statue of Liberty's torch, the cartoon perfectly encapsulated the environment of paranoia and wanton fear that permeated American society and in Block's mind threatened the very values on which it had been founded and which supporters of HUAC purported to uphold (fig. 9).[36]

Yet it is important to emphasize again that what Block was critiquing in these cartoons was not the anticommunist rhetoric of either Truman's loyalty program or HUAC but rather their willingness to use their power for their own political edification. One of the most telling Herblock cartoons from this period was published on January 31, 1950, in which Block

FIGURE 9. *Washington Post,* June 17, 1949

drew a communist and a conservative reactionary working together to throw tar-smeared rocks at an innocent bystander labeled "Liberals." Clutched in the reactionary's hand is a sign declaring that "Liberalism and Communism are all the same thing," while the cartoon's caption, presumably spoken by the same figure claims, "That's the Line We Want to Get Across, Pal."[37] Block's point that smearing postwar liberalism with unfounded allegations of communist sympathies only served the interests of communists and conservatives alike could not be clearer. Indeed, in many ways this cartoon was echoing Schlesinger's argument in *The Vital Center* that "the [American Communist Party] has been a great ally of the American conservatives because of its success, for a season, at least, in dividing and neutralizing the left."[38] In drawing these cartoons, Block believed that he was speaking for and defending a liberal majority that opposed the smear tactics of HUAC, and the unadulterated climate of accusations, fear, and hysteria it bred, but nonetheless stood opposed to the spread of communism across the country. Although this stance put him in opposition to the public statements of many Democrats, Block's was not the only liberal voice speaking out against HUAC's excesses during the late 1940s.

As early as February 1945, the liberal magazine the *Nation* had accused the newly permanent HUAC of having "become more authoritarian in its methods than its notorious predecessor," and argued that "the only way to save the country from the indignity of these repeated witch-hunts is to abolish the committee."[39] Similarly, the *Washington Post* took a visible stance in support of civil liberties as HUAC began to pursue aggressively its anticommunist agenda, a campaign that drew considerable public criticism and accusations that the paper was a "defender of the Reds" staffed by "communist sympathizers."[40] In an unusually lengthy editorial published on December 14, 1947, in response to these accusations, the paper defended its ongoing disapproval of the committee by arguing that the *Post*'s criticisms had been "directed consistently at its methods rather than at its aims." Furthermore, it argued, because HUAC "has equated loyalty with conformity, has concerned itself with opinions rather than activities, has disregarded the most elementary rules of fair play in dealing with witnesses and persons accused by witnesses, its conduct has seemed to us to be more dangerously un-American than that of any of the groups or individuals it has investigated."[41] Block's cartoons were an especially visible aspect of this campaign, visualizing HUAC's abuses in ways that written editorials could not and helping strengthen the paper's reputation for being an active opponent of the activities of the committee, while at the same time pushing the *Post* even further in that direction. But Block's stringent opposition to the House Committee on Un-American Activities during the 1940s was just a prelude to the impact his work would have in the first half of the 1950s when Senator Joseph McCarthy of Wisconsin leapt to national prominence.

During an otherwise unremarkable speech delivered on February 9, 1950, in Wheeling, West Virginia, McCarthy dramatically produced a sheet of paper and was reported to declare, "I have here in my hand a list of 205 [names] that were known to the Secretary of State as being members of the Communist party, and who nevertheless are still working and shaping the policy in the State Department."[42] The speech initially generated only modest interest from newspapers across the country. But as McCarthy toured the West in the days following, doubling down on his central allegation but changing the number of communists he purported were employed by the State Department as he traveled, media interest steadily increased. By the time he had returned to Washington, DC, where he took to the Senate floor to enter the speech into the *Congressional Record,* the scope of his allegations had fallen from 205 active communists in the State Department to only 57 employees who were "loyal to the Communist Party."[43] Despite the speciousness of his charges, media attention continued to grow over the course of the month, and on February 22, the Senate unanimously voted to authorize "a full and complete study and investigation as to whether persons who are disloyal to the United States are or have been employed by the Department of State."[44] Over the next two years, McCarthy used his newfound platform to embarrass and discredit the Truman administration, accusing officials of doing nothing to weed out communists from government agencies and generally smearing liberals with unfounded accusations that they had communist sympathies.

The *Washington Post*'s own coverage of McCarthy began on February 12 with an Associated Press story, followed two days later by an editorial titled "Sewer Politics" that blasted the senator for the changes to his story and not being able to follow it up with concrete evidence, instead only citing "four [cases] out of the 57 or, if you prefer, out of the 205" about which he claimed knowledge.[45] McCarthy's first appearance in a Herblock cartoon, however, did not occur until February 22, two days after the senator's appearance in Washington, when Block drew a ghostly version of the Republican, labeled "McCarthy's Vague Charges against the State Dept," angrily shouting on the Senate floor and prompting a bemused-looking senator to ask his colleague, "Seem to You There's Something a Little Odd Here?"[46] The point of the cartoon, which echoed the *Post*'s editorial stance, was to express both the lack of substance Block saw in McCarthy's specific charges and the contempt with which the cartoonist held the attention the accusations were receiving. Over the next several weeks, McCarthy made increasingly regular appearances in the daily Herblock cartoon, with Block critiquing both the impunity of the senator's accusations against innocent individuals and the unwillingness he displayed to stand behind his own words.[47] It was on March 29, 1950, however, that the *Washington Post* published what was to become one of Block's most important and influential cartoons. "You Mean I'm Supposed to Stand on That?" depicts a reluctant-looking Republican elephant being dragged and pushed by Republican National Chair Guy Gabrielson and Republican senators Kenneth S. Wherry, Robert A. Taft, and Styles Bridges toward an election platform made up of buckets of tar and topped by a barrel labeled with a word that would soon enter the American political lexicon: "McCarthyism" (fig. 10).[48]

Historians, journalists, and other political observers have uniformly credited Block with coining the word.[49] Block himself was sanguine about the origin of the word, writing that he simply needed a way "to summarize the issue," and that there was "nothing particularly ingenious about the term, which is simply used to represent a national affliction that can hardly be described in any other way. If anyone has a prior claim on it," he continued, "he's welcome to the word and to the junior senator from Wisconsin along with it."[50] In fact, the term "McCarthyism" had made its first appearance in the public sphere at least a day earlier than the publication of "You Mean I'm Supposed to Stand on That?"

On March 27, the *New York Times* published a letter written by Henry L. Stimson, who had served the administrations of Herbert Hoover

"You Mean I'm Supposed To Stand On That?"

FIGURE 10. *Washington Post*, March 29, 1950

and Franklin Roosevelt as secretary of state and secretary of war respectively, that attacked McCarthy's tactics and declared "the man who seeks to gain political advantage from personal attack on a Secretary of State is a man who seeks political advantage from damage to his country."[51] Reacting to this letter in an editorial published the following day, the *Christian Science Monitor* declared that "Republicans have run into a crisis which should soon separate the men from the boys." Arguing that the results of the 1948 election had "persuaded some Republican leaders that they have little hope of finding a popular domestic issue," the editorial accused them of having instead "turned to foreign affairs . . . [and] the McCarthy witch-hunt." The editorial continued,

> Straightforward criticism of policies is one thing, irresponsible smearing of individuals is something else. Senator McCarthy's reckless mud-slinging fully deserves Mr. Stimson's resounding rebuke.
>
> But what have Republican leaders done about this wretched business? Senator Taft is reported to have told Mr. McCarthy to keep on plugging; if he didn't pin a red label on one State Department employee, he should try another. National Chairman Gabrielson and Senator Wherry gave the sniping their implied blessing. Now Senator Bridges announces a "parade" of Republican speakers to "go after" Secretary Acheson. . . .
>
> Possibly many rank-and-file Republicans have not realized how much harm was being done. But any lingering doubts about the damage from *McCarthyism* should surely now be removed by Mr. Stimson's letter.[52]

Whether or not Block was aware of this editorial when he began sketching his cartoon will likely never be ascertained. But the similarities between the *Christian Science Monitor*'s March 28 editorial and the following day's Herblock cartoon are striking and certainly suggest that Block found inspiration from this source. That the editorial calls out the same four men depicted by Block for their role in pushing the Republican Party toward a greater support of the "McCarthy witch-hunt," in spite of the harm it might do to their party's reputation, *and* uses the term "McCarthyism" in the same piece stretches the limits of coincidence. Regardless of its provenance, however, Block's usage of the word in his cartoon, coupled with its subsequent syndication in newspapers across the country, undoubtedly exposed the term to a much wider audience than would otherwise have occurred, and as the *Post* noted in May 1950, helped it "very quickly come into use as a convenient word to describe the politics of character assassination and smear."[53] The impact that it had on the public consciousness as a short-hand for describing McCarthy's tactics of smearing victims with unfounded rumor and innuendo can perhaps best be seen in the senator's own efforts to control usage of the word when he took it as the title of his 1952 book, *McCarthyism: The Fight for America*.[54]

After its first appearance, Block was only to use the word "McCarthyism" in three more cartoons over the course of 1950, despite drawing a total of forty-nine cartoons that year that touched on the Red Scare in some capacity. But it was clear that McCarthy—who was physically depicted in fifteen of these cartoons, making the Wisconsin senator the third most frequently depicted nonsymbolic character that year, behind only Joseph Stalin and Harry Truman—and his public posturing were at the forefront of Block's mind.[55] His initial cartoons focused on ridiculing McCarthy's propensity for backing away from his statements and accusations when pressed for more specificity. April 22, 1950's "Stop Ganging up on Me!" for example, featured a tar brush–wielding McCarthy being harassed by a mob of doppelgangers, each of whom is holding a banner on which is written an earlier public statement of is the senator's now harming his credibility. May 3, 1950's "How about If We Just Set the Bar on the Ground?" meanwhile, cast McCarthy as a pole vaulter who falls flat on his face after failing to reach even the lowest bar that has been set by Uncle Sam to prove his claims.[56]

Block's earliest efforts to expose McCarthy's excesses were welcomed by his audience. One *Post* reader who signed his letter "Nauseated Voter" and identified himself as an opponent of the Truman administration applauded Block's "You Mean I'm Supposed to Stand on That?" cartoon for causing him to consider "a phase of this business which I have not yet seen touched on in the press," namely the willingness of the Republican leadership to engage in "a smear campaign which for cynical and knowing dishonesty, or abysmal ignorance, or both, makes any other 'political' move of recent years seem clean by contrast." As a result, he was now reconsidering which party he would support in the 1952 presidential election since "our votes will be little more effective in getting us good government than the votes recently cast by the Russians in their own election." Another anonymous letter writer asserted that Block's "inimitable and devastating cartoons [attacking McCarthy] . . . have upheld decency, fair play and democratic processes."[57]

The tone of Block's depiction of McCarthy soon began to change. His initial characterization of McCarthy as a coward, unwilling to face either those he was accusing or his critics in a public setting, was soon replaced with something much more nefarious. This McCarthy, depicted as a permanent resident of the sewer, was given a heavy five-o'clock shadow and tar-stained hands to suggest the political thuggery that Block felt the senator represented. On August 8, 1951, for example, McCarthy was shown crouching in the corner of the Senate, surrounded by rotting trash and overturned buckets of tar, and on January 23, 1952, Block imagined Republican presidential candidates Dwight Eisenhower and Earl Warren taking the proverbial high road while fellow candidate Robert Taft, who had recently endorsed McCarthy and his methods, is shown wading through knee-deep mud with one arm wrapped around his fellow senator (fig. 11).[58] This thug-like, almost neanderthal depiction would become a recurring theme of Block's work, deployed to paint some of the most

FIGURE 11. *Washington Post,* January 23, 1952

prominent subjects of his cartoons—including politicians such as Richard Nixon and Barry Goldwater and representative characters of such groups as white supremacists, who Block considered to be a threat to the postwar liberal order—as figures who stood outside the mainstream of American respectability.

To emphasize the point, Block often juxtaposed McCarthy and other symbols of his tactics against the most nationalistic symbol of all: Uncle Sam. On August 13, 1951, for example, Block drew a tar brush–wielding McCarthy and his followers stalking the streets of Washington, DC, causing panicked federal workers to flee from their approach. In the foreground, Uncle Sam is sardonically asked by John Q. Public, in reference to one of Franklin Roosevelt's Four Freedoms, "Say, What Ever Happened to 'Freedom-from-Fear'?"[59] Cartoons such as this succinctly demonstrated the outrage that Block felt toward a man he later described as possessing "animal cunning and [an] instinct for publicity unfettered by any sense of morality or honesty, who personified the intellectual terrorism of the time."[60] The cartoons also hit the mark. Although Block was never accused of communist sympathies by McCarthy, the senator did keep a file on the cartoonist, noting in which countries his cartoons were reproduced. And Jean Kerr, who married McCarthy in September 1953, reputedly cried on seeing especially vicious Herblock depictions of her future husband.[61] But they were only a prelude for what would occur after the 1952 presidential and congressional elections.

Deeply unpopular because of the Korean War and the effect of ongoing Republican accusations of corruption and communist influence within his administration, Truman decided not to seek reelection. The Democratic Party nominated Illinois governor and prominent member of the ADA Adlai Stevenson, who ran on a platform that defended New Deal pluralism, condemned McCarthyism, and promised to take a strong stance against Soviet aggression while continuing the policy of containment. The Republican Party, meanwhile, selected Dwight Eisenhower as its candidate but only after a bitter primary campaign that pitted the retired general against the staunchly conservative Senator Robert Taft, who supported both a strongly isolationist foreign policy and the dismantling of the New Deal state. Eisenhower, in contrast, presented himself as a much more moderate candidate who would root out corruption within the federal government and "liberate" those who lived under communist "tyranny."[62] American voters, perhaps eager for political change after twenty years of Democratic presidents, renounced liberalism that November. Stevenson lost the popular vote by almost 7 million and won only 89 votes in the electoral college. With their gains in the Senate and the House, Republicans now held, for the first time since 1928, all three branches of government.

Under the new Republican leadership, McCarthy was appointed chairman of the Senate Committee on Government Operations from which position he launched investigations into communist influences in such State Department programs as Voice of America and the U.S. Information Agency (USIA), initiatives that sought to propagandize American values across the world. Block commented on each of these investigations in turn, critiquing McCarthy for damaging America's ability to fight the Cold War against the international communist threat. On March 2, 1953, for example, Block drew Joseph Stalin standing with one of his generals in front of a series of Soviet radio masts engaged in efforts to jam Voice of America broadcasts in their territory. The Soviet general is reading a newspaper report of McCarthy's latest hearings into communist threats, causing him to gleefully tell Stalin that it "Looks as if Congress May Save Us Money, Anyhow."[63] And on June 18, 1953, Block condemned the Eisenhower administration's acquiescence to McCarthy-led demands for thousands of books authored by supposedly procommunist authors to be removed from USIA libraries around the world, with some libraries going so far as to burn the offending books. The cartoon shows Uncle Sam staring accusingly at a nameless member of the administration as Father Time adds the United States to a list of notorious book-burning regimes that include both Nazi Germany and Communist Russia.[64] By connecting McCarthy's investigations directly to the ability of the United States to pursue its Cold War foreign policy in this way, Block reminded his readers that more was at stake in his portrayal of the hearings than a simple disagreement over the tactics employed to root out imagined communists.

This became even more urgent when McCarthy turned his focus in October 1953 to the U.S. Army, investigating first an alleged communist spy ring that operated out of the Army Signal Corps laboratory at

Fort Monmouth, New Jersey. When these accusations came to nothing, McCarthy launched an investigation of Irving Peress, a dentist who was drafted into the army in 1952 and promoted to major in November 1953. Before joining the army, however, Peress had been a member of the American Labor Party, an association that led him to invoke the Fifth Amendment on a loyalty-review form. When he learned of the case, McCarthy wrote to Robert Stevens, Eisenhower's secretary of the army, demanding that Peress and those officers who had promoted him each be court-martialed for fostering communist activities, but by this point Peress had requested, and been granted, an honorable discharge. McCarthy's ire was further raised in February 1954 when Peress's commanding officer, the highly decorated General Ralph W. Zwicker, refused to identify who had ordered the discharge, leading McCarthy to accuse him of being "not fit to wear [his] uniform."[65] Stevens initially sought to protect his officers, declining to release documents related to Peress's promotion and discharge, but shortly thereafter acceded to McCarthy's demands and promised to make available for questioning by McCarthy's committee any officer involved in the case.[66]

Although Block remained silent on these specific developments, his portrayal of McCarthy during the first months of 1954 underwent a significant change. The tar brush Block originally had given to McCarthy to indicate the work he did staining people's reputation was gradually replaced by increasingly more dangerous implements, and McCarthy himself was transformed from a peddler of lies and innuendo into someone that threatened not just the current administration but the very foundation of American democracy. Starting on February 5, 1954, McCarthy was shown holding a wrench with which he had beaten a person representing the Voice of America broadcasts. Then, on the same day that news broke of General Stevens's capitulation to McCarthy's demands, Block imagined the secretary of the army presenting the senator with a ceremonial sword, prompting McCarthy to thank Stevens with the words, "Okay, Bud. When I Want You Again I'll Send for You"—a clear indication that Block considered the army's credibility compromised. Three days later, McCarthy was depicted driving a massive wedge into the world that threatens to split it apart as Eisenhower impotently looks on. And in one of Block's most celebrated cartoons, McCarthy is shown holding a bloody meat cleaver while President Eisenhower seeks to protect himself with nothing more than a feather he has unsheathed as though it were a sword. McCarthy's transformation was completed three days later in "Relax—He Hasn't Got to You Yet," which depicts McCarthy physically stabbing representatives of the State Department and the U.S. Army in the back, with President Eisenhower next in line (fig. 12).[67] As Block imagined McCarthy engaged in ever more violent activities, so too did the senator's physical characteristics change to represent something far more dangerous than the self-promotional smear artist of his earlier cartoons. McCarthy's hairline seemed to recede further, while the five-o'clock shadow on his face, already prominent, became even darker. And in the absence of a brush or can of tar to blacken his hands, McCarthy was given a swath of

"Relax — He Hasn't Got To You Yet"

FIGURE 12. *Washington Post,* March 7, 1954

dark hair that extended to his knuckles. Together with the introduction of a noticeable slouch, under Block's pen McCarthy seemed to devolve into something almost primeval in nature.

These cartoons sought to peel away McCarthy's fabrications and expose the hypocrisy of his crusade, challenging his readers to question the senator's motives and reexamine their own Cold War fears. The images also reflected the emerging liberal view of the senator and his actions, which, in the words of one McCarthy biographer, came to portray the Wisconsin senator as a "ruthless, reckless, heartless, mindless fiend who had yet to utter his first honest sentence."[68] Several readers wrote to the *Washington Post*'s editorial page to express their appreciation for Herblock's February 26 cartoon "And I'd Still Like to See You Become President," which saw Eisenhower sitting at his desk in the Oval Office with a Republican voter from 1952 expressing his desire to see the president show some leadership in the matter of Stevens's capitulation to McCarthy's demands that the army cooperate with his investigations.[69] Another reader, however, took exception to the "viciousness" of March 7's "Relax—He Hasn't Got to You Yet," complaining that "once marked by light, clever sarcasm, Herblock cartoons have become of late bitter and irrational cynicism about the McCarthy issue. . . . The purpose of this cartoon," the letter writer continued, "amounts to illustrated character assassination, a sin which Mr. Herblock imputes to another, no doubt."[70]

In fact, this last series of cartoons anticipated what was to become, at least for the media, a defining moment in McCarthy's ultimate downfall. On March 9—two days after Block's "Relax—He Hasn't Got to You Yet" cartoon was published—CBS's *See It Now* documentary series broadcast an exposé of McCarthy's methods hosted by the journalist Edward R. Murrow. While the program used excerpts from McCarthy's own speeches to reveal the contradictions and hyperbolic hysteria he peddled, it also used carefully compiled and edited clips to give as negative a portrayal of McCarthy as possible. In the words of a sympathetic biographer, under Murrow's treatment the senator at times "seemed to sway in front of the camera, obviously under the influence of alcohol," and was variously shown "belching, picking his nose, ignoring or berating witnesses . . . and giggling" at his own jokes.[71] Although the specific characteristics that Murrow and his producers highlighted were different, they followed a template that Block himself had pioneered in his own efforts to discredit McCarthy and his methods.

Less than two months after CBS broadcast this edition of *See It Now,* McCarthy and Roy Cohn, his chief counsel, appeared before a Senate committee to answer allegations that they had sought preferential treatment for former McCarthy aide G. David Schine, who had been drafted into the army as a private the previous fall. The story had been developing since the end of January when the media first reported that the army was probing allegations that Schine had been "coddled through basic training."[72] Although initial reports did not directly accuse McCarthy of wrongdoing, by mid-March an army report into the allegations found evidence that Cohn and McCarthy had used their influence on Schine's behalf. With McCarthy strenuously denying the charges, claiming that they were being made in retaliation to his public statements against General Ralph Zwicker, the Senate Permanent Subcommittee on Investigations, which was usually chaired by McCarthy himself, was tasked with holding an inquiry into the allegations.[73]

In an unprecedented decision, the resulting hearings were aired nationally on the NBC and ABC television networks. This live coverage unflinchingly showed McCarthy trying to bully and stonewall witnesses and investigators alike. Meanwhile, newspapers across the country ran critical headlines and features at every opportunity; together this negative media coverage crucially turned the tide of public opinion against McCarthy once and for all.[74] Despite all of this, it was Block's cartoons—not the watching television cameras—that McCarthy was reportedly most concerned about: the pro-McCarthy radio commentator Walter Winchell reported having overheard the senator complaining during a break from the hearings that he had to shave twice a day "because of that guy [Herblock] and his cartoons."[75] Assuming the veracity of this anecdote, which has been oft repeated, McCarthy had good reason to be concerned with how he was being depicted by Block.

Throughout the hearings, Block continued to demonize the senator in the pages of the *Washington Post.* On April 22, for example, Block retold the story of St. George and the Dragon as an analogy for the just-beginning hearings. McCarthy is cast as the eponymous beast but is depicted as a pathetic, skunk-like creature crouching maliciously in the shadows of a cave, while a representative of the U.S. Army takes on the role of the brave knight, donning a gas mask to protect himself from the stench of McCarthy's allegations as he prepares to enter the dragon's den. Five days later, McCarthy was shown as a burglar, replete with a large bag of swag and a still-smoking gun, directing a bumbling Karl Mundt, who was chairing the Senate investigation, away from the footsteps that led directly to McCarthy.[76] These two cartoons earned Block a "vehement protest" for his "gross abuse of his editorial license" from a reader in Washington. "Whatever your editorial views may be as to the junior Senator from Wisconsin," he continued, "I fail to see how you can justify picturing him as either a dirty beast or a vicious criminal."[77]

Demonstrating how charged the story had become, and how powerful Block's cartoons were in telling that story, other readers quickly jumped to the cartoonist's defense. "Ridiculous!" declared Guy Sauterne in a lengthy rebuke to the earlier letter writer's protest over Block's use of symbolic imagery to condemn McCarthy:

> The symbol is the conventional means of presenting an editorial picture worth 10,000 words. So if Herblock believes, as the great majority of the American people have come to believe, that McCarthyism stinks, he will use a garbage can or dead fish or skunk to illustrate it. . . . Instead of finding fault with the skunks and cops-and-robbers symbols—both of which are conventional almost to uselessness—the vehement letter-writer should have delighted in Herblock's brilliant twist—that of making St. George confounded by something petty and obnoxious instead of dragon-like.[78]

Another letter writer found it only poetic that McCarthy was depicted in Block's cartoons as such an unsavory character because "Senator Joe has a way of labeling those who disagree with his power-crazed thinking with such titles as Communist-fronter, Red, commie-coddler, and so on."[79]

Arguably most powerful of all, however, was Block's cartoon of May 7, 1954. Early in the Senate hearings, a photograph was introduced into evidence that appeared to show Secretary of the Army Stevens and Private Schine engaged in a private conversation. The photograph had purportedly been taken after a specific request from Stevens, a claim he himself strenuously denied. It soon emerged, however, that the photograph had been cropped to make it look as though the two men were alone, leading to salacious headlines and commentary that accused the McCarthy camp of being deliberately dishonest and disingenuous in its defense.[80] This was compounded several days later when McCarthy produced a copy of a letter written on FBI stationary in 1951 to Lieutenant General Alexander R. Bolling, head of Army Intelligence, that was signed by FBI director J. Edgar Hoover and named thirty-five men employed at Fort Monmouth who were suspected of subversive activities. McCarthy went on to claim that the warning had been willfully ignored by Stevens and was evidence of the army's "gross negligence in eliminating 'dangerous' security risks" from the base. The FBI, however, denied that the letter was original, leading to allegations that McCarthy—who refused to reveal who had provided him with the copy—had once again used faked evidence.[81]

Block responded to these developments by depicting McCarthy standing at his desk holding two burning documents: in one hand is a "Doctored Photo" and in the other a "Faked Letter." But it is McCarthy's own demeanor that is most damning. The familiar tropes of the Herblock McCarthy are present—the dark five-o'clock shadow, and fingers, as ever, darkened with tar—but now sweat is seen to be dripping from his face as he makes ever more frantic efforts to evade his questioners. Compounding the impact of the image is the cartoon's caption, which takes the words that had first propelled McCarthy to national attention and turned them into a sharp indictment of everything the senator from Wisconsin had stood for over the previous four years: "I Have Here in My Hand—" (fig. 13).[82] As Block's imagined documents burned, so too did McCarthy's credibility in the eyes of the American people.

The hearings dragged on for another month with McCarthy visibly angry and frustrated as the army's lawyers, led by Joseph N. Welch, steadily dismantled his arguments and discredited his witnesses. The defining moment came when McCarthy accused one of the army's junior lawyers of being connected with the Communist Party. Stunned by McCarthy's audacity, Welch declared, "Until this moment, Senator, I think I never really gauged your cruelty or your recklessness," before asking him, "Have you no sense of decency, sir. At long last, have you left no sense of decency?"[83] Block's cartoon the next morning, which depicts a

"I Have Here In My Hand —"

FIGURE 13. *Washington Post,* May 7, 1954

housewife calmly asking her husband, "Well, Why Doesn't He See a Psychiatrist?" while they watched the hearings on their television, succinctly captured the impact this moment had for many Americans.[84] The hearings came to a close a week later, and although McCarthy ultimately was acquitted of wrongdoing by the Senate committee, the full Senate voted later that year by a margin of sixty-seven to twenty-two to censure him for contempt of Congress, a vote that effectively ended his political career.[85]

Throughout the McCarthy era, Block's portrayal of the Senator complemented the overall tone of the *Washington Post*'s reporting and editorials. Unlike many other American newspapers, the *Post* offered strong and early rebukes of McCarthy's rhetoric and actions from the earliest days of its coverage of the senator.[86] As Katharine Graham wrote in her autobiography, "The *Post*'s comments against McCarthy represented a very clear—and brave—position, and the paper took a lot of heat for its coverage. In fact, the war between McCarthy and the *Post* was vicious and frightening." But, she continued, most "effective of all probably was Herblock's series of cartoons depicting McCarthy and his various outrageous activities."[87] Certainly, Block's cartoons had the potential to reach a far wider audience than the *Post*'s other anti-McCarthy content. In 1950, when McCarthy first rose to prominence, the *Post*'s circulation was only 184,000, making it the third most read of Washington's four daily newspapers, but by July 1954, four months after the *Post*'s purchase of its local rival the *Washington Times-Herald,* circulation had more than doubled to over 380,000, which put the paper in roughly seven out of every ten households in the city of Washington.[88] Even so, Block's reach extended far beyond the DC metro limits. As the publisher's blurb for his 1955 book *Herblock's Here and Now* pointed out, by mid-decade his cartoons were syndicated to over 150 newspapers, both in the United States and abroad.[89] This wide reach gave Block's cartoons a platform from which they could influence a far broader group of readers than would otherwise have been possible and led Martin Agronsky, a radio and television commentator who was one of the first public broadcasters to criticize McCarthy, to assert that Block "had as much to do as anybody in our business with making people understand what Joe was; he really damaged him."[90]

If Block's attacks on the anticommunist activities of HUAC and McCarthy garnered him praise from his fellow journalists and other liberals, they also made him a target for criticism from the right, not just for the content of his cartoons but for his actions as a private citizen. Block's decision to donate the five hundred dollars he received from the Heywood Broun Prize in February 1950 to the Democratic opponent of Ohio senator Robert Taft—who was, according to one newspaper reporting the story, the "moral and intellectual leader of the Republicans in congress"—was broadly criticized among conservatives, leading Block to make a public defense of his donation on the letters page of the *Washington Post.*[91] A similar controversy occurred in May 1950 after Block agreed to connect an exhibit of his cartoons in New York City with a fundraiser for the National Art Division of the ADA. Block's syndicate objected to him associating his work with such an explicitly partisan organization on the basis that his work could be dropped from some newspapers in reaction. Informing him that "we must protect Herbert Block at all costs [because] the continuation of Herblock cartoons being reproduced throughout the country is the most effective way of promoting the liberal point-of-view," the ADA reluctantly agreed to minimize the connection between Block's exhibit and their own fundraiser.[92] The following year, the USIA's international distribution of *Herblock Looks at Communism* resulted in McCarthy openly wondering why the State Department would "subsidize this man who is actively committed to oppose attempts to drive communists out of government." Because of the pamphlet's distribution, Senator Pat McCarron, another frequent target of Block's cartoons, attempted to strip $10 million from a State Department appropriation.[93] And in 1955 an announced weekly satirical television show, which would have been called *Herblock's Week* and seen Block offering his views on current events, was abruptly canceled after the Fund for the Republic, a New York–based non-profit organization charged with promoting freedom and justice within the United States that had planned to underwrite the production, was attacked by prominent conservatives such as the popular radio host Fulton Lewis for providing a platform for Block and his longstanding agenda of "ridiculing congressional investigations, subversive activities, the federal security program . . . [and] portraying everyone involved in subversive investigations or security investigations as a thug or an idiot or both."[94]

Ultimately, Block's cartoons used a combination of highly personal attacks intended to discredit the leaders of these investigations and appeals to patriotic sentiment to persuade his readers of the importance of standing against the excesses of domestic anticommunism. Although his cartoons were not able to end the activities of HUAC and McCarthyism on their own, they nevertheless played an important role in demonstrating that opposition to their actions was possible and laid the groundwork for future media coverage of anticommunist activities. These cartoons also reveal one of the limits of postwar liberalism. The thesis of Arthur Schlesinger's *Vital Center*, which underscored much of postwar liberalism's ideology, was that the core values of American society lay at a political center in which like-minded men could solve the nation's problems by working together and providing greater access to society's benefits. In this construct, the communists and social democrats of the far left and conservatives on the political right stood outside of the political mainstream and as such represented a threat to American democracy that should be challenged. McCarthy and his supporters could thus be dismissed, in the words of the liberal historian Richard Hofstadter, as "pseudo-conservatives" who stood outside the traditions of American democracy.[95] But McCarthy did enjoy broad support for his activities for much of the first half of the 1950s. He easily won reelection to the Senate in 1952, gaining 54.2 percent of the vote and with many Wisconsinites specifically citing his willingness to stand against communism as a reason for their support, and in January 1954 he enjoyed a favorability rating in the Gallup Poll of 50 percent, with only 29 percent disapproving of his activities.[96] McCarthy may have represented the very worst impulses of anticommunism, but a more moderate version of those views were widely shared by many Americans, including liberals such as Arthur Schlesinger and Herbert Block.

Block may have spoken out earlier and with more passion than other liberals against the excesses of HUAC, Truman's loyalty program, and McCarthy, but he ultimately shared their commitment to anticommunism as a necessary protection for democracy. Because he was able to leverage the platform that he had constructed at the *Washington Post* into the national consciousness, Block's anti-HUAC and anti-McCarthy cartoons established him as a preeminent spokesperson for liberal ideology whose work demanded to be recognized as such from liberals and conservatives alike. As a result, the attacks aimed at him from conservative politicians, commentators, and voters became increasingly frequent, especially as his cartoons began to focus on the activities of the man who Block identified as the natural successor to McCarthy and his attempts to smear innocent Americans for his own political agenda: Vice President Richard Nixon.

But even as the majority of Americans found themselves repulsed by the tactics used by McCarthy, members of the Republican Party's right wing continued to find much to admire. The performative nature of McCarthy's exaggerated and angry rhetoric, coupled with his ability to dominate news cycles, was warranted in their eyes because his goal of eliminating communist influences from the government ultimately justified any and all of his excesses. What was more, supporters of McCarthy argued that opposition to his methods was simply evidence that the true danger to America's security lay not just in the alleged presence of communists within the nation's borders but also in the failure of the liberal establishment to treat this threat with the seriousness that it deserved.[97] Conservative Republicans' belief that liberals were seeking to undermine the foundations of America's democracy was further affirmed by the legal and political victories being won in African Americans' long quest for equal rights, an issue that was to become increasingly visible in Block's cartoons.

3

"THE MAJOR MORAL ISSUE OF OUR TIME"

Standing for Civil Rights

FOR MUCH OF SEPTEMBER 1957, the *Washington Post,* like most of the nation's media, breathlessly reported on events in Little Rock, Arkansas, where Governor Orval Faubus had ordered the state's National Guard to bar nine African American students from desegregating Central High School. In justifying his actions, Faubus unabashedly declared that he had called out the guard not in defense of segregation but to "preserve the peace."[1] Not that the northern press was fooled by these claims. In a scathing editorial entitled "Law and Order" printed on September 4, the *Post* made clear its stance on Faubus's actions. "Those who oppose desegregation in Arkansas and who threaten violence to protect it are guilty of lawlessness," it read. "Unhappily, it was on the side of those who threatened to defy the law that Governor Faubus intervened; and it is their conception of order, rather than the law's conception, that he has used National Guardsmen to maintain."[2]

Although he had no way of knowing it at the time, Little Rock came to represent a watershed moment in Block's engagement with civil rights issues, if not in terms of the actual content of his cartoons then in his sustained interest in a single incident. In his first cartoon commenting on events in Arkansas, Block unambiguously reinforced the *Post*'s editorial stance that Faubus's actions amounted to an extralegal reaction to integration. Published on September 5, 1957, and captioned "The Gov. Faubus 'Peace' Plan," in reference to Faubus's quoted statements on the role he claimed for the National Guard, the cartoon echoed in graphic form the sentiments expressed on the previous day's editorial page. It also encapsulated what Block would later identify to be the defining issue that lay at the heart of the Little Rock crisis: the efforts of "segregationists to launch a campaign of 'massive resistance'" and "forcibly [defy] the law by using troops to keep the Negro children out of school" (fig. 14).[3]

The first evidence of Block's intent with this cartoon is found in its title and the placement of quotation marks around the word "Peace." Whereas

FIGURE 14. *Washington Post,* September 5, 1957

Faubus claimed his actions were intended to "protect [Little Rock's] citizens," Block's use of punctuation served to expose both exactly who Faubus was referring to and his actual commitment to ensuring a peaceful resolution to the crisis.[4] This message was further reinforced by several visual clues that Block embedded in the cartoon to highlight his contention that the governor's actions were an illicit usurpation of the law intended to benefit one side of the crisis over the other. In this context, the pointedly diminished stature of Faubus serves to visually delegitimize his actions and moral authority while also suggesting he is in thrall to the demands of the thuggish-looking representative of "Anti-Integration Groups" with whom he is shaking hands. Meanwhile, the juxtaposition of the national guardsman idly grasping his rifle while sitting on top of a conspicuously white and immobilized child with schoolbooks and a sheet of paper labeled "U.S. Court Ruling" scattered on the ground creates a visual discordance that further unsettles the viewer while simultaneously strengthening the overall sense of illegitimacy that pervades the scene.

Over the course of the next thirty days, Block drew another twelve cartoons that commented directly on the ongoing drama in Little Rock. Faubus appears in all but three of these cartoons and is constantly characterized as a short-statured, insincere politician only interested in self-promotion and ensuring that he stayed in the limelight for as long as possible. It was not hard for Block to find examples of Faubus's words and actions to illustrate this narrative. On September 9, for example, Faubus held his first major news conference since the start of the crisis and once again attempted to portray himself as having acted in the best interests of the people of Arkansas and as an ardent defender of states' rights. Raising the specter of further violence, Faubus declared, "If the Federal Government moves into Arkansas by force, or in any other manner . . . and takes from the people of the state the right to elect a Governor, and depend on him to exercise certain discretionary functions of government, then we will have lost our last right of self government. If blood is then shed, my conscience will be clear, but I will weep for my people."[5] This quote became the inspiration for the following day's Herblock cartoon, "Tears," which showed Faubus releasing a crying crocodile labeled "Race Violence" onto school property, while holding a sign referencing Faubus's statement from the previous day: "If blood is shed then I will weep for my people."[6] The change was subtle but significant. By abbreviating and altering the word order of Faubus's actual statement, Block changed the context of those words, highlighting what he believed to be their true meaning. No longer was Faubus's self-proclaimed grief expressed as a warning against the possible consequences of a federal intervention into Little Rock and the violence that might ensue from that action. Instead, the words became a statement of Faubus's hypocrisy and his intent to provoke the situation without care for any potential repercussions, a sentiment strengthened by the popular understanding of "crocodile tears" being shed only when one is being insincere.

As events in Little Rock continued to escalate, Block sought to further undermine Faubus's position and reveal what he later described as the governor's true agenda during the crisis: an opportunity to "advance his own political interests."[7] One visual device Block employed to emphasize this throughout his run of Little Rock cartoons was to depict Faubus as an immature juvenile. In September 13's "Oh Boy—Lots of Headlines," for example, an oblivious Faubus is shown to be eagerly reading his own headlines, while leaders of Asia, Africa, and India are somberly reflecting on the same coverage. A clear companion to an editorial published in the previous day's *Post* that lamented that "racial incidents in Little Rock, Nashville, Birmingham, and elsewhere are doing the United States enormous harm abroad," Faubus is once again shown to be comically short, even more so in comparison to the leaders of Africa, India, and Asia, who are in the cartoon's background looking at the same newspaper reports but who nevertheless tower over the Arkansas governor.[8] In September 25's "Back to School," meanwhile, Faubus and a "Faubus-Inspired Thug" are represented as errant schoolboys sitting timidly at a school desk while Uncle Sam lectures them on U.S. law and history. And October 3's "How Can You Doubt My Good Intentions?" shows Faubus with a child's slingshot juxtaposed against the vicious-looking club held by a "Faubus-Inspired Mobster."[9] The cumulative impact of this exaggeration of Faubus's height, employed in every cartoon depicting the governor, is to subvert in readers' minds the governor's moral authority during the crisis and to suggest that his actions were intended to garner favor and political support from the thugs and white supremacists who invariably accompanied him in Block's cartoons.

Absent from any of these cartoons, however, are depictions of the three groups arguably most involved in events on the ground at Little Rock: African Americans, women, and children. The closest that Block came to depicting any of these groups in a meaningful way was in his September 6, 1957, cartoon "This Is an Explosive Situation," in which two—again conspicuously white—schoolchildren are present with other citizens as third-party observers to Faubus's attempts to inflame tensions at Little Rock.[10] In fact, every Herblock cartoon commenting on the crisis showed the principal actors to be either white male southerners, President Eisenhower, or Faubus himself. By doing so, Block eschewed the type of imagery that both accompanied contemporary newspaper coverage and has become part of the nation's visual shorthand for the crisis. Some of the most iconic imagery from the Little Rock crisis is of the nine African American children who desegregated Central High either having abuse hurled at them by crowds of white protesters or being escorted to class by the National Guard.[11] By privileging the actions of white elites such as the president and governor at the expense of other participants—most notably of the African American community but also of women and children—Block gave his readers a significantly distorted picture of the situation in Arkansas. Yet, the absence of African American agency and the corresponding focus that Block placed on the actions of white southerners was not uncommon for his civil rights–related cartoons, especially during this period.

By the time of the Little Rock crisis, Block enjoyed a national reputation as a strong and powerful supporter of civil rights. Already the recipient of awards given in recognition of his commitment to these issues, Block understood supporting civil rights to be among the most important imperatives of his time, something that spoke to the very nature of being American.[12] In his 1993 autobiography, for example, Block wrote that the fight against segregation was, along with the effort against McCarthyism, one of the "major moral issues of our time."[13] Thirty years earlier, in December 1963, while giving the Elmer Davis Memorial Lecture at Columbia University's Graduate School of Journalism, Block made a similar statement when he described how "the special indignities and restrictions that have been inflicted upon Negroes in many areas of American life . . . including that of unequal public accommodations" were perpetrated largely by "extremists, who seem to fear the word 'democracy.'" As a result, Block argued, all Americans who believed in democratic values and self-government "should be pressing for prompt correction of these evils." Block went on to describe what he believed was both the short-term solution to ending discrimination and a long-term corrective that would ensure the continued protection of Americans' constitutional rights: the enactment of new laws guaranteeing the right to vote to millions of Americans who at the time were disfranchised by states that sought to "deprive citizens of the franchise through the use of poll taxes, literary tests and other devices, including naked intimidation."[14]

Despite his early awards and public statements, Block's record in his first decade at the *Post* suggests only a limited interest in depicting the racial situation in postwar America. In fact, Block's depiction of the Black freedom struggle went through several different phases. For the first decade that Block worked at the *Post,* civil rights barely registered as a topic of interest in his published work. The number of cartoons he drew on this topic steadily decreased from 1946, when fourteen of his cartoons in some way dealt with civil rights issues, to a nadir between 1953 and 1955, when Block drew just two cartoons connected to the freedom struggle. The year 1956 saw the start of a renewed representation of issues related to African Americans, leaping to twenty-two cartoons that year and thirty-four in 1957. Block's engagement in the topic reached a peak in 1963 when civil rights–related cartoons represented over a quarter of the total number of cartoons he drew that year. Following the passage of the Civil Rights and Voting Rights Acts of 1964 and 1965, however, civil rights and race again became a less common topic for his cartoons, until it became a topic revisited only occasionally during the 1970s. This all suggests a far more nuanced understanding of how Block confronted issues related to African Americans than the typical narrative of him as an unwavering advocate for civil rights generally allows. The remainder of this chapter explores Block's pre-1965 cartoons to understand how his interpretation and presentation of issues of race reflected liberalism's own limitations in its response to racial injustice.

Block's faith in the ability of legislative reform to end discrimination across the South and his equating civil rights to a moral imperative were not unusual stances within mainstream liberal circles at the time. As historian Carol A. Horton has written, postwar liberals such as Block took a "strong, principled stand against racial discrimination" because they "believed that anti-African discrimination represented the preeminent moral dilemma facing the nation, as it conflicted with the fundamental principles of American liberalism."[15] This argument was popularized by the Swedish sociologist Gunnar Myrdal in his 1944 book *An American Dilemma: The Negro Problem and Modern Democracy,* in which he posited that although all Americans believed in a "liberal creed" of individualism, civil liberties, and equality of opportunity, some Americans nonetheless also embraced the racist belief that African Americans were inherently inferior. In this framing, racism was a problem that distorted and threatened American values but was one that could nonetheless be resolved if the federal government were to remove the legal barriers that prevented African Americans from participating fully in American society and white Americans were educated about the fallacy of their preconceptions.[16]

Arthur Schlesinger was just one of the more prominent postwar liberals to echo Myrdal's views when he declared in *The Vital Center* that "the sin of racial pride still represents the most basic challenge to the American conscience," and that the nation's domestic policies should therefore "demonstrate a deep and effective concern with the racial inequities within the United States." At the same time, liberalism's postwar embrace of anticommunism and its split from the social democrats limited the possibilities of its racial agenda to the prohibiting of overt discrimination in areas of public life such as education, transportation, and the workplace, with more radical forms of reform treated with suspicion and racial injustices considered to be a uniquely southern problem. Thus, Schlesinger was able to suggest that opposition to civil rights reform was an aberration in American politics, writing that "the South on the whole accepts the objectives of the civil rights program as legitimate, even though it may have serious and intelligible reservations about timing and method." Left unstated there, but an implicit part of his argument, was that those who continued to oppose progress toward racial equality were themselves acting against America's founding values.[17] Block amplified these ideas through his cartoons, emphasizing the importance of legislative change and depicting racist southerners as enemies of American ideals. In doing so, he brought them to the attention of a much larger audience than might otherwise have been exposed to the ideas of liberal intellectuals like Myrdal and Schlesinger.

During the first decade of his time at the *Post*, Block saw the battle for civil rights as primarily a legislative issue with its most important battleground being the chambers of Congress. As a result, many of the cartoons he drew on civil rights between 1946 and 1956 primarily commented on congressional activity, or more specifically decried congressional obstructionism and inactivity. This is clearly seen in a sequence of cartoons that began in January 1946. At the time, Congress had before it a bill to make permanent the Fair Employment Practices Commission (FEPC), which had been established five years earlier to ensure that defense contractors did not discriminate on the basis of race or religion. Southern Democrats had targeted it for repeal ever since. Block's initial engagement with the fight over the FEPC's future did not suggest he placed much interest in its fate. January 16, 1946's "It's Terrible, People Refusin' to Work!" depicts two congressmen discussing a newspaper headline that comments on a wave of strikes sweeping the nation in the early weeks of 1946. In the cartoon's foreground is a pile of neglected legislation, including at its bottom a bill labeled "FEPC," quickly gathering dust.[18] Block's intent was clearly to juxtapose the congressmen's accusatory comment about the striking workers with the legislators' own unwillingness to do the work of government. The FEPC is depicted as just one of several pressing issues—including new labor legislation, universal military training, health insurance, and unemployment benefits—that was being unduly delayed by an obstructionist and hypocritical Congress.

As the proposed FEPC legislation faced filibusters and stalled in the Senate, however, so too did Block's frustration manifest itself more clearly in his cartoons. On January 24, he suggested that successful passage of the FEPC was a matter of American foreign policy, and that southern Democrats' ultimately successful filibuster against it in the Senate was hurting American interests in the postwar world. The cartoon depicts two (white) soldiers in Europe questioning which event was hurting American prestige abroad more: their recent demonstrations demanding a prompt demobilization and return home or the heated arguments going on in Congress in support of segregation and prejudice.[19] If this cartoon was designed to play on fears of how America was viewed abroad and to position the continued funding of the FEPC as a potential instrument of propaganda in the country's nascent fight for democratic values in the postwar era, January 29's "I Got No Control over Myself" sought to make the issue personal. The cartoon is a naturalistic portrait of a southern senator in the aftermath of a weekend-long drinking binge fueled by a bottle of whiskey labeled "Old Filibuster" (fig. 15).[20] Block's depiction of a balding and disheveled senator, seen slouched in a chair surrounded by debris from his drunken rage and left to defiantly exclaim, "I Got No Control over Myself," turned the popular view of southern masculinity on its head. Far from the idealized image of the southern gentleman as

FIGURE 15. *Washington Post,* January 29, 1946

"aristocratic, graceful, honorable, manly, and well-spoken," this was the South of journalist W. J. Cash, who ripped away the myth and romanticism of the Old South to reveal, in the words of historian James C. Cobb, a "savagely racist, intellectually stunted, emotionally deranged society unwilling to admit it was sick, much less heal itself."[21]

Block may have been prompted to draw the cartoon by his mounting frustration at the successful efforts of southerners to prevent legislative reform, but the source of his belief in the importance of enacting this legislation lay in the daily incidents of violence and white supremacist activity that African Americans living in the South continued to face. This became clear in his June 29 cartoon, "Torchlight Parade," which continued his outright rejection of southern manhood as an honorable ideal. Ostensibly commenting on the reelection campaign of Mississippi senator Theodore Bilbo, and specifically the senator's recent call to "every red-blooded white man to use any means necessary" to prevent African Americans from voting in the upcoming primary election, the cartoon can be understood as a prototypical example of what was to become Block's standard depiction of white southerners.[22] Although the image only depicts his subject's arms and hands, they are drawn to emphasize their more barbaric traits—the man's sleeves are rolled up, suggesting an uncouth temperament and revealing arms covered in dark hair. In one angrily clenched fist, he holds a club labeled "Bilbo Election Campaign," while the other grasps a sheaf of papers, marked the "laws of the United States" and set alight to become the burning torch implied by the cartoon's title.[23]

The cartoon ultimately operates on multiple levels, drawing on the violent imagery and iconography most commonly associated with the activities of the Ku Klux Klan to highlight the overtly racist nature of Bilbo's public rhetoric and reinforce his and the Klan's betrayal of American values. The cartoon also foreshadowed the *Washington Post*'s own stance on Bilbo's racist rhetoric, which had first been noted in a brief June 25 article but was strongly denounced on July 1 in an extensive editorial that decried Bilbo's "routine expression of his characteristic bigotry" and went on to declare that through his threats of racial violence, Bilbo had "disqualified himself for membership in the Senate."[24] Block would repeat this position five days later in his cartoon "The Bilbo Election Case"—which depicts Bilbo, covered in reeking mud, striding purposefully toward the Senate doors emblazoned on which is the cartoonist's rhetorical question, "Political Fraternity House or the People's Legislative Body?"—and returned to it again in a sequence of cartoons published between September 1946 and January 1947 that relentlessly supported an ultimately successful movement by liberal Democrats and Republicans to not seat Bilbo in the Senate because of his violent rhetoric against African Americans.[25]

While Bilbo was seeking reelection to the Senate in Mississippi, former Georgia governor Eugene Talmadge was mounting a campaign to win back his gubernatorial position on a platform that prioritized restoration of Georgia's all-white primary system. Under Georgia law, counties were divided into three categories based on population. The 8 most populous counties were classified "Urban," the next 30 as "Town," and the remaining 121 sparsely populated counties were described as "Rural," with each county receiving 6-, 4-, and 2-unit votes respectively. To win an election a candidate had to win a majority of these county unit votes, 206 of the available 410 votes. Because there were many more unit votes available from "Rural" areas, election campaigning tended to focus in these parts of the state rather than in areas with larger populations. In the July 1946 Democratic gubernatorial primary, Talmadge won 242 of the unit votes but lost the popular vote by some 16,000 votes.[26]

Anticipating the more focused coverage that the *Post* would give to the story as it enfolded, Block's initial cartoon on Georgia's gubernatorial race appeared on July 19, 1946, a day after Talmadge's victory.[27] Imagining a scene at the Old Governor's Mansion, Block depicted a well-dressed white schoolboy who represents Georgia being dragged back to Tobacco Road by an angry-looking Talmadge, who is barefoot and wearing tattered clothing. The boy, who carries all his worldly possessions under his one free arm, is shown looking forlornly back over his shoulder and crying, "Thanks, Mr. Arnall! Thanks for Everything!"—a reference to the term-limited, New Deal–era Governor Ellis Arnall, who had implemented a Supreme Court ruling that banned the all-white Democratic primary and led Talmadge and his supporters to brand Arnall a "race-traitor."[28]

In an unpublished commentary written for his proposed 1948 book "What's Going on Here?" Block explained that he was inspired to feature Talmadge in his cartoons because he "represented a virulent form of ‘white supremacy’ politics, and his demagoguery was as blatant as the red suspenders he affected as a trademark.” In a revealing section that was marked for deletion, Block went on to explain that Talmadge’s victory in the election occurred because “many of the ‘backwoods’ counties enjoyed a ‘unit’ voting strength as great as that of the heavily populated urban areas.”[29] Block’s explanation of Talmadge’s electoral victory was accurate, but his dismissal of Georgia’s rural areas as a “backwoods” corresponds with a belief that those living in the country were less educated, less civilized, and less representative of American ideals than their city-dwelling contemporaries, which stood in contrast to Schlesinger’s claim in *The Vital Center* that most southerners supported civil rights reform and which would soon begin to become apparent in his cartoons.

Ten days later, Block’s daily cartoon revisited Georgia in response to the deaths of four African Americans at the hands of a mob of white men. The details of the crime—two young married couples were tied to a tree and murdered by a mob of whites in a hail of over sixty bullets—horrified the nation, with the *Washington Post* being typical of the northern response when its editorial page decried “the power of evil that stalks [the Georgia] countryside.” Without excusing the perpetrators of this crime, the *Post* left no doubt as to who must bear ultimate responsibility for creating an atmosphere in the state that allowed these events to occur without fear of reprisal: “the incendiaries who strut their stuff under that banner with its strange and mocking device, ‘white supremacy,’” and especially “the inflammatory Eugene Talmadge [who] won his campaign on the pledge that he would ‘keep the Negro in his place.’”[30] Block’s cartoon of that day echoed this assertion. The cartoon imagines the immediate aftermath of the murder, going so far as to graphically depict the victims’ bodies lying in pools of blood in the background. The focus, though, is on the group of casually dressed white men who are calmly holding shotguns and walking back to their cars, one of them reassuringly telling another, “It’s Okay—Ol’ Gene [Talmadge] Will Be Back in Soon.”[31] In contrast to the depiction of southerners in Block’s earlier “Torchlight Parade” cartoon, this image focuses the viewer’s attention on the apparent normality of the scene: the perpetrators of the crime could have as easily been returning from a weekend hunt as leaving a murder scene. By once again opting for a naturalistic style of drawing, Block highlighted how the white mob was ordinary, almost banally so, and by extension suggested the routine nature of white-on-Black violence in the Jim Crow South (fig. 16).

If this cartoon suggested the normality of racial violence in the South, Block soon began to portray the instigators and perpetrators of that violence in such a way as to highlight their differences from other Americans. This change was seen through a series of cartoons drawn in January 1947 that once again drew attention to the political situation in Georgia. Eugene Talmadge, who had comfortably won reelection in November, died after a short illness on December 21, 1946, leaving open the question of who would become the state's governor. The outgoing incumbent, Ellis Arnall, announced that he would only relinquish his position in favor of the newly

FIGURE 16. *Washington Post,* July 29, 1946

elected lieutenant governor (a Democrat), while Talmadge's supporters rallied around the candidacy of his son, Herman. In the first of three cartoons drawn after the state legislature had declared Herman Talmadge to be the rightful governor, Block depicted the thirty-three-year-old Talmadge as an ineffective child, showing him being held aloft from a balcony by a supporter as though he is inheriting his father's crown. This imagery was further evoked by both the cartoon's caption of "Attention, Subjects!" and the label of "Herman, the Boy Pretender" that Block appended to Talmadge's trousers.[32] The impact of this cartoon was such that in the first draft of his proposed manuscript "What's Going on Here?" Block claimed that after the image was printed in the *Atlanta Journal,* crowds started demonstrating in front of the Georgia State Capitol building with signs—inspired by the cartoon's title—that declared, "We Are Citizens, Not Subjects!"[33]

In two subsequent cartoons, Block further reinforced this theme by explicitly showing the same two characters actively usurping the will of the voters, represented first by "The People of Georgia" and then by Uncle Sam himself, in their efforts to assure Talmadge's ascension to the governor's mansion. January 18, 1947's "We Don't Want None of Your Outside Interference" juxtaposes the South's standard refrain against federal efforts to protect African American access to the ballot by showing the state legislature angrily remonstrating with "The People of Georgia" while Talmadge stands next to a turned-over ballot box. Four days later, Block recreated the scene, replacing the people of Georgia with Uncle Sam himself and the spilled ballots with a discarded book of federal laws.[34] In both instances, Talmadge and the state legislature were depicted to accentuate their differences from the ideals signified by the people of Georgia and Uncle Sam. Thus, Block's representation of the state legislature portrayed an older, balding man with hollowed cheeks, a crooked nose, narrowed eyes, and just a hint of stubble. Combined with his pronounced slouch and small stature, the character contrasted sharply with the straight-laced ideal of white manhood Block employed to represent first Georgia and then Uncle Sam.

Block's depiction of white southern racists as different to other Americans reached its maturity in his May 23, 1947, cartoon "Not Guilty," which was drawn in reaction to a jury's verdict of not guilty in the trial of twenty-eight white men accused of torturing and killing twenty-four-year-old Willie Earle in Pickens County, South Carolina, three months earlier. Reinforcing the *Post*'s editorial stance that "a jury of neighbors [had] looked at these men and found themselves mirrored among them, heard the story of what they had done and decided there was nothing wrong in it," the cartoon imagines a southerner, labeled "Lynch-Law Mentality," holding a rifle and rope in his bloody hands while standing in front of a mirror and practicing his declaration of innocence (fig. 17).[35] Block's implication could not be clearer. In the rural South, a white man accused of murdering an African American could expect to be tried by a judge and jury whose support of white supremacist violence was no different than his own. What made the cartoon notable, however, was that Block

FIGURE 17. *Washington Post,* May 23, 1947

had completed his transformation of the white southerner into a caricature completely separate from Block's depiction of Americans from other regions of the country. The southerner is drawn to exaggerate his size and his assumed lack of education: he is notably overweight and stands hunched over, while his head is undersized in proportion to the rest of his body with no hint of a chin, and his eyes are mere pinpricks. This image may have been developed to allow northern liberals to visualize the violent intent and severity of white supremacist activity, but it also allowed them to disassociate and absolve themselves of their shared complicity in the maintenance of a legal system of violence that terrorized millions of African Americans living in the South on a daily basis.

The emphasis of Block's civil rights cartoons shifted in 1948 from predominantly depicting local and regional events to focusing on national politics. Harry Truman's Special Message to the Congress on Civil Rights, which was delivered in early February 1948 and urged the investigation of discrimination and extralegal violence against African Americans, precipitated Block's change. Addressing Congress, Truman declared that "there is a serious gap between our ideals and some of our practices. This gap must be closed." To do so, he urged Congress to consider several measures, including establishing a permanent Commission on Civil Rights and a Civil Rights Division within the Department of Justice, providing federal protection against lynching, protecting the right to vote, prohibiting discrimination in interstate transportation facilities, and passing the FEPC to prevent unfair discrimination in employment.[36] Although suspicious of the president's commitment to their ideology, liberals were enthusiastic in response. Block's own reaction to the statement depicted a determined Truman ringing the Liberty Bell, and in doing so captured both Truman's appeal to American values as a rationale for civil rights reform and the urgency with which many northern liberals now saw the issue.[37]

Determined to not let this opportunity pass, members of the liberal group Americans for Democratic Action (ADA), led by Minnesota's Hubert Humphrey, pushed to include a strong civil rights plank mirroring Truman's proposals in the Democratic Party's platform for the upcoming presidential election. When the resolution reached the convention's floor, however, their effort was met with stiff resistance from a combination of moderates concerned over an electorally damaging rift within the party, supported by Truman himself, and southern Democrats who bitterly opposed any type of civil rights reform as a violation of states' rights. The measure ultimately passed in a close vote but only after an acrimonious debate that culminated in delegates from Mississippi and Alabama walking out of the convention hall in protest. Soon after the convention's close, these disgruntled southerners formed the States' Rights Democratic Party, popularly known as the "Dixiecrats," and nominated South Carolina senator Strom Thurmond as their candidate for president.[38] Block's own depiction of the convention fight, which he had witnessed in person as a member of the press, left little doubt as to his own stance on the platform. Imagining it as a boxing match fought on a still under-construction ring, the ADA-backed proponents of a strong civil rights plank were depicted as a hard-working carpenter, protected only with a small hammer, getting ready to fight against a grim-looking southerner clutching an oversized axe.[39]

After 1948, Block's depiction of civil rights issues focused on the growing split within the Democratic Party between moderate Democrats and southerners who opposed the passage of any civil rights legislation, which the party's national convention had precipitated. It was not until 1954, and the Supreme Court's historic ruling in *Brown v. Board of Education,* that state laws creating separate public schools for students of different races were declared "inherently unequal" and therefore an unconstitutional "denial of the equal protection of the law," that Block commented on a civil rights–related topic that was not connected to congressional obstructionism. Block again used the Liberty Bell, transporting the symbol of American independence to the forecourt of the Supreme Court in Washington, DC, and foregrounding the words "Proclaim LIBERTY throughout the Land" to affirm his belief that civil rights were a core value of American identity.[40] This iconography may have reflected postwar liberalism's positioning of racial discrimination as antithetical to American ideals, but this cartoon stands thematically isolated from those around it. It broke a twenty-two-month period in which no cartoons even alluded to civil rights or issues of race and was not followed by a similarly themed cartoon for another eighteen months. This isolation furthermore reflected liberal uncertainty over how best to respond to the Supreme Court's ruling in *Brown.* Although many liberals publicly celebrated its significance, they were also wary of pushing too hard to see the ruling enforced. Adlai Stevenson, who had been defeated in the 1952 presidential election but was already considering a second run in 1956, for example, worried that taking too firm a stance in favor of integrating public schools would provoke violence across the South, further alienate southern Democrats, and all but assure a second electoral loss for the Democratic Party.[41]

Block's infrequent interest in confronting civil rights issues before 1956 resulted in his ignoring many notable—and newsworthy—events. The trial of Emmett Till's killers in Mississippi, for example, garnered not just national but international attention from news organizations during September 1955. The *Washington Post,* unlike other northern newspapers such as the *New York Times, Chicago Daily Tribune, St. Louis Post-Dispatch,* and *Detroit News,* may not have sent a dedicated reporter to Mississippi, but it still printed a handful of syndicated stories on the trial, including a front-page story on September 24 after the jury delivered its verdict of not guilty on all charges.[42] During that month of September, however, Block did not draw a single cartoon commenting on Till's murder, the ensuing trial, or even the hatred and prejudice prevalent across the South that created a climate in which the brutal murder of a young boy could go unpunished. Instead, Block spent the month drawing cartoons that covered a wide spectrum of events and issues: the Strategic Arms Limitation Talks with the Soviet Union, the escalating political crisis in Argentina that culminated in Juan Perón's overthrow, the Eisenhower administration's agricultural policies, government spending, education reform, and, especially, anticipation for the 1956 presidential election, culminating on September 25 with "You're Going to Run Again, Aren't We?" which depicted Vice President Richard Nixon hanging onto Eisenhower's shoulders.[43] These were all worthy and important subjects in their own right, but with the exception of the disarmament talks and events in Argentina, none was especially unexpected or time-sensitive, and it is telling that Block would overlook an event attracting such nationwide coverage and interest.

Block also made no effort in his cartoons to explore the everyday experiences of African Americans beyond their exposure to violence at the hands of whites. To an extent, this reflects some of the limitations of political cartoons as a form of commentary. Political cartoons are designed to respond to, interpret, and critique a single day's headline. As such, it was much easier for a cartoonist such as Block to lampoon and vilify the racist attitudes of segregationists and white supremacists than it was to engage in a concerted exploration of the daily injustices faced by African Americans. But at a time in which he *was* regularly depicting the lived experiences and expectations of "John Q. Public" and what he viewed as the average American family, it is notable that the previously discussed 1946 cartoon "It's Okay—Ol' Gene Will Be Back in Soon," with its inclusion of the bodies of four black murder victims, is the only time in Block's first decade at the *Post* that he depicted an African American character. Instead, the actors in these cartoons were uniformly white men—whether politicians or the instigators of violence.

This absence of diversity in the characters he depicted did solve a problem for Block: how to draw African American characters without relying on the stereotypes of the day. When Block depicted African Americans during the 1920s and 1930s, he did so by using the conventions of minstrelsy with its focus on prominent white lips and wide-open eyes. Although he drew no cartoons between 1946 and the end of 1955 that clearly depicted African Americans, Block's treatment of Africa and Africans during this period suggests that in the immediate postwar period his style of drawing had not changed. In cartoons such as January 12, 1947's "Naive, Isn't He" and December 11, 1949's "Hm—You Don't Say!" for example, he imagined the conservative forces that opposed the progressive reforms of the Truman administration as a cannibalistic society in Africa. As such, Block relied heavily on the visual stereotypes of blackface to suggest the backward and primitive nature that he associated with conservative opposition to Truman.[44]

The relative lack of cartoons dealing with African Americans or civil rights issues—and especially the invisibility of African Americans within those cartoons he did draw—through the first half of the 1950s also reflected the *Washington Post*'s own struggles in the postwar era to attract a diverse readership. According to a 1946 survey, the *Post* had the lowest percentage of African American readership of any of the four Washington daily papers, while by late 1975 consistent increases in the cost of a subscription to the paper had ensured that "inner-city Blacks and less affluent whites were not readers." In his official history of the

Post, Chalmers M. Roberts sought to explain the low number of Black readers in 1946 by claiming that the paper's management had "deliberately centered its circulation-building efforts in the white community because the city's principal advertisers in large part ignored potential Black customers."[45] Scholars have come to recognize this firm, albeit unproven, belief among the majority of postwar advertisers that "white readers read white magazines and newspapers, and Black readers read Black magazines and newspapers" directly led to the "visual content of mass-circulation magazines of the period [being] overwhelmingly characterized by the whiteness of everyone and everything depicted."[46] Thus, even though the *Post* took steps in the early 1950s to improve its record on printing stories about African Americans, visual representations of nonwhites remained severely limited throughout the period. And when it did print photographs of African Americans together with whites, primarily with engagement announcements and during the Korean War, the paper's management inevitably received a barrage of complaints from angry white readers.[47] There is no evidence to suggest that Block limited his depiction of race and civil rights during this time as a result of pressure from either advertisers or the paper's owners, but given the whiteness of his own imagined community of middle-class readers, the coincidence is striking and suggests that he at least subconsciously may have placed limits on his own portrayal of African Americans to avoid a similar backlash from readers.

In 1956, however, Block made a significant change in how he dealt with the fight against segregation in the South. On December 1, 1955, Rosa Parks, a forty-three-year-old African American living in Montgomery, Alabama, was arrested after she refused to give up her seat on a municipal bus to a white man. This event sparked what would become a year-long boycott by African Americans of the city's buses that resulted in severe economic losses for white business owners. Although news of the boycott was widely reported, especially in southern and African American newspapers, the *Washington Post,* like other major northern publications including the *New York Times* and *Newsweek,* initially relied solely on wire service stories and gave only limited coverage to events in Montgomery.[48] It took until the end of February for either Block or the *Post*'s editorial page to acknowledge this high-profile civil rights campaign. In a carefully worded editorial, seemingly designed to express support for the legality of the boycott without inflaming white sensibilities, published on February 24, 1956, the *Post* argued that the "sense of frustration" articulated by Montgomery's white community over the tactics of their city's African American community was "easy to understand" because the protest, aimed as it was at the economic interests of white civic leaders, was "impeccably lawful, orderly, dignified—and effective."[49]

Block's first cartoon responding to the boycott, published four days later, seemed to take this editorial to heart as it imagined a scene in Montgomery in which two clearly agitated white men stand at a bus stop as a young family of African Americans calmly walk past them on their way to church. The family—a father, mother, and young son—is labeled "Passive Resistance," while the cartoon's title is taken from the stark assertion of one of the white men to his compatriot that "Somebody from Outside Must Have Influenced Them," a sardonic reference to white southerners' claims that interlopers from the North were irresponsibly encouraging the protest for their own nefarious purposes (fig. 18). The two white men stand with hunched shoulders, their dark suits noticeably wrinkled and their faces creased with angry scowls. In contrast, the family that is the object of their scorn stand tall and proud, immaculately dressed in their Sunday best and the very essence of middle-class respectability.[50] Block repeated this scene, almost exactly, in a second cartoon drawn a month later, on March 25, 1956. Again, he imagined an African American, this time a solitary male dressed in a business suit and holding books in his right hand, calmly passing an irate white man who is jumping up and down in anger at a bus stop in Montgomery. The cartoon's caption, "Tote Dat Barge! Lift Dat Boycott! Ride Dat Bus!"—a play on Oscar Hammerstein's lyrics to "Ol' Man River"—serves to suggest Block's belief that the white civic leaders of Montgomery felt the city's African American community was obligated to participate in the city's white-dominated economy by ending their boycott.[51] What is most notable about both these cartoons, however, is that they together mark the first time since 1946's "It's Okay—Ol' Gene Will Be Back in Soon" that Block chose to include a physical depiction of an African American in his work. Yet in both cartoons, the African American actors have their backs turned away from the viewer, their features—and perhaps, more significantly, the color of their

FIGURE 18. *Washington Post,* February 28, 1956

skin—hidden from the audience's view so that their race is only apparent from an appreciation of the subject and broader contexts of the cartoon. The result in both cases is to focus the attention of the viewer onto the attitudes and actions of the white southerners at the expense of the agency of the African Americans who were the victims of their abuse.

It was almost three more years until Block depicted a clear, front-on view of an African American. In a cartoon published on December 10, 1958, that would become one of his most celebrated civil rights–related cartoons, Block imagined an African American being barred from exercising his right to vote by a group of white men sitting beside a padlocked ballot box. Block made clear the hypocrisy of white southerners using literacy tests as a qualification for voting by juxtaposing the would-be voter's high level of education—demonstrated by his business suit, glasses, the books he is holding in one hand, and the briefcase that is held in the other labeled "Tuskegee"—against the white men's own lack of education, indicated by their casual dress and demeanor and the cartoon's caption, "Nah, You Ain't Got Enough Edjiccashun to Vote" (fig. 19).[52] Glossing over the assumptions that Block was making about the educational attainment of the average southerner, the overriding message of the cartoon was that regardless of the advancements this representative African American had made, his potential advancement in southern society would always be limited by barriers put in place by whites.

Despite this newfound willingness to include depictions of African American actors, they still made only infrequent appearances in Block's

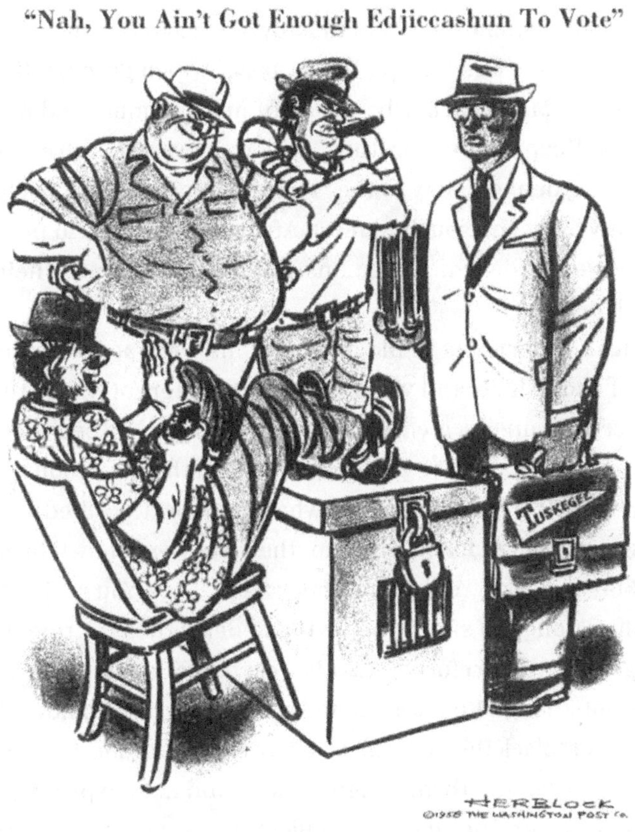

FIGURE 19. *Washington Post,* December 10, 1958

cartoons. Between January 1956 and December 1964, a period that saw Block produce 246 cartoons related in some way to civil rights, only 32 included a Black person in its frame. Furthermore, the common theme of these cartoons was their depiction of African Americans in positions of limited power, a framing Block consistently used for African American actors. In this regard, Block was no different than the other white editors and reporters that surrounded him in the *Post*'s newsroom. As historian Martin A. Berger has persuasively argued, photographic representations of the Jim Crow South and the civil rights movement that appeared in northern newspapers typically placed "Blacks in the timeworn positions of victim and supplicant . . . [and] allowed magnanimous and sympathetic whites to imagine themselves bestowing rights on Blacks."[53] Block's cartoons were no different in their participation in this enterprise as they tended to place African Americans in situations that portrayed them as passive objects without agency of their own. In cartoons such as April 28, 1959's "Poplarville, Mississippi, U.S.A., 1959," which graphically depicts the murder of Mack Parker by a mob of masked men, and August 14, 1960's "Pray Keep Moving, Brother," which shows a well-dressed father and son being denied entry to the "First Segregationist Church," Block consistently and consciously showed African Americans in positions of limited power while whites demonstrated and exercised their power over Black people.[54]

If African Americans in Block's cartoons were stoic and innocent victims of racist laws and violence, then his stereotype of the white southerner as an uneducated, violent thug, which he had been developing since the 1940s, became a regular component of these cartoons throughout the late 1950s and early 1960s. In what might be described as this caricature's most benign form, white southerners were shown in cartoons such as May 15, 1963's "You Don't Understand, Boy—You're Supposed to Just Shuffle Along" to simply be trying to delay the enactment of civil rights legislation and reform.[55] In other cartoons, including 1958's "Nah, You Ain't Got Enough Edjiccashun to Vote" and 1959's "Oh Boy—Wait Till They Discover 'Black Beauty,'" Block portrayed white southerners, in his own words, as "acting through ignorance—and not surprisingly, since they were raised in ignorance."[56] But Block's most common treatment of whites was as angry bigots, shown to be either contemplating or enacting violence to preserve their racially based way of life. In December 15, 1960's "You Know What I'd Like to Do? I'd Like to Push This Right Down over That Guy's Ears," for example, Block showed a group of white Christmas shoppers imagining the violence they would like to do to a man whose only crime was escorting a young girl to her newly desegregated school in New Orleans.[57] Meanwhile, cartoons such as February 28, 1964's "And, Over Here, the Enemy—People" and March 9, 1965's "I Got One of 'Em Just as She Almost Made It Back to the Church," which respectively show white police officers preparing to attack African American protestors and the satisfaction that Block imagined they gained from such actions, succinctly depicted not just the dangers that civil rights protestors faced in the South but also what Block understood to be the inherently violent nature of white southern society, including law enforcement, especially when it was faced with any form of resistance to its hegemony.[58]

Inevitably, Block's depiction of the white South angered many of his readers, especially those who lived in that part of the country. A common refrain among letter writers was that Block was one-sided in his treatment of white southerners, leading these correspondents to suggest he should draw cartoons showing the imagined barbarity and crimes of African Americans that, in their opinion, justified both the continued maintenance of the Jim Crow system and the legalized violence of that era. In response to Block's "Poplarville, Mississippi, U.S.A., 1959," and its depiction of the lynching of Mack Parker, who had been accused of abducting and raping a white woman, for example, a reader from Raleigh, North Carolina, wrote to request that Block provide a different side to the story by creating a drawing that shows "an innocent, pregnant mother crying and begging for mercy with an un-merciful, determined rapist in the 'prelude.'"[59] Similarly, an untitled cartoon, originally published on February 26, 1960, that depicts a cornered Senator James Eastland, labeled "Anti-Civil Rights" and holding a sign that reads "Be Nice to Minorities—In the Senate, That Is," led a reader from Atlanta to predict that, in time, Block might "become head man of the Washington chapter of the 'Let's rip the south association.' . . . [Or] may be presented an award from the N.A.A.C.P. for helping in the destruction of the country." Echoing the remarks of the earlier writer from Raleigh, this correspondent went on to ask, "Where is a cartoon of the rape beatings, and crime rate by negro citizens . . . [or]

a nice witty cartoon of the vast amount of tax (of any kind) paid by the good negro citizens."[60]

Block's portrait of white southerners served to emphasize not just their brutality but also their separateness from what he understood to be the accepted norms of mainstream American values and society. This was seen, for example, in a cartoon drawn during the Little Rock crisis that imagined a mob of white protestors holding a sign reading "Down with U.S. Interference in the U.S." Similarly, during the efforts to desegregate the city of Albany, Georgia, Block drew Laurie Pritchett, the city's chief of police, looking up at an approaching helicopter only to declare, "We Don't Want ANY Outside Interference."[61] Block's inspiration for the language in these cartoons may have come from the rhetoric of the white segregationists who led the protests and violence he was condemning, but his decision to make this assertion the principal motivating factor of the white actors in these cartoons underlines the extent to which he both depicted the actions of southerners as fundamentally un-American and, like most other liberals, understood the problems of desegregation and discrimination to be primarily southern issues.

This philosophy was most explicitly stated in a cartoon drawn during the summer of 1961 following an attack on a group of Freedom Riders in Montgomery, Alabama. The cartoon, dated May 23, 1961, has a straightforward composition, simply depicting three armed thugs, one a Ku Klux Klan member, leering threateningly at the viewer in front of a plain white background. The cartoon's caption, paraphrased from the words of the city's police commissioner, declares, "We Don't Want No Troublemakers from the United States," and makes explicit that, at least in Block's mind, the South did not share the rest of the country's values and system of justice (fig. 20).[62] This cartoon inevitably stirred up controversy, with one reader feeling compelled to write to FBI director J. Edgar Hoover, accusing Block of trying to inject a "type of poison . . . into the blood stream of America" and of using his "evil work" to stir up "racial and religious hatred" across the country. The writer went on to assure Hoover that he himself was "willing to go down fighting to the death, if necessary, for his love and belief in the South and [its] way of life," before concluding his letter with one last warning that Block was "transgressing the border line of the Southern States in his mad desire and intent of subversion of all

FIGURE 20. *Washington Post,* May 23, 1961

States."[63] White southerners may have taken exception to their portrayal in these cartoons, but for Block and other liberals this representation of white southern values served as a perfect proxy for the violent realities of life for African Americans in the Jim Crow South. Furthermore, by portraying white southerners essentially as residents of a foreign country, Block allowed his northern readers to imagine themselves as different—in terms of both their belief system and the nature of their liberal politics—to the violent racists they saw depicted not only in his work but in other visual imagery associated with the civil rights movement published by the same newspapers that syndicated and printed his cartoons.

With Block only rarely including African Americans in his cartoons, and even then depicting them primarily as nonthreatening victims of white racism and violence, the leaders of the civil rights movement were all but invisible in his cartoons. Whereas white southerners, such as South Carolina's Strom Thurmond, Arkansas's Orval Faubus, and Alabama's George Wallace, became infamous in the liberal media for their white supremacist rhetoric and activities and made multiple appearances in Block's work over extended periods of time, Martin Luther King Jr. appeared in just two Herblock cartoons drawn between 1946 and 1976: "Enemies of the Dream," published in April 1968 three days after his assassination, and 1975's "We Hadn't Planned to Include This in the Tour, Senator," which shows a portrait of King labeled "Hoover Enemy No. 1" hanging on the wall of a forgotten FBI office, surrounded by evidence of the agency's historic illegal activities.[64] Block did depict some of those students who helped desegregate the South's educational institutions—namely, Ruby Bridges, Charlayne Hunter, Hamilton Holmes, and James Meredith—in solitary cartoons, while Julian Bond, one of eleven African Americans elected to the Georgia legislature following the passage of the Voting Rights Act in 1965, appeared in a cartoon condemning that body's refusal to seat him after Bond refused to disavow the Student Nonviolent Coordinating Committee's opposition to the Vietnam War.[65] Over this thirty year period, only two African Americans other than King were depicted more than once in a Herblock cartoon: two cartoons featured Gerald Ford's secretary of transportation, William T. Coleman, while the controversial Adam Clayton Powell, who represented Harlem in the U.S. House of Representatives between 1945 and 1971 but was stripped of his chairmanship of the House Education and Labor Committee in 1967 because of budget mismanagement, appeared in six separate cartoons.[66] This is a striking divergence from the standard contemporary media representation of the civil rights movement, which tended to portray African American activism across the South as a monolithic movement led by a charismatic Martin Luther King who spoke as the nation's voice of conscience in the face of racial injustice.[67]

At the same time, the scenarios in which Block placed civil rights activists put them in opposition to white antagonists and denied them active agency. By almost completely ignoring the actions and rhetoric of the rank-and-file members of the movement, which stood in marked contrast to how he usurped the language of white southerners, Block gave greater significance to the civil rights–related actions of national institutions that were controlled by white elites—specifically, the presidency, the U.S. Congress, and the courts. In this framing, which is evident in Block's cartoons throughout the Eisenhower and Kennedy administrations, civil rights ultimately came about because benevolent white presidents listened to the emotional appeal of moderate African Americans. Thus, it is no coincidence that in his autobiography, Block introduced the subject of civil rights in the context of what he perceived to be Eisenhower's "absence of leadership" in the area, writing that his "cartoons showed [the President] more interested in deliberateness than 'all deliberate speed.'"[68] As a result, many of his cartoons from this period depicted the president's disinterest in using his authority to apply federal power to end segregationist activities, drawing a contrast between his inaction and the broader interests of the country, which were frequently represented by Uncle Sam. On April 3, 1956, for example, Block showed Eisenhower dressed as a fire chief observing homes burning down because of the "Civil Rights Crisis" and absent-mindedly telling a shocked Uncle Sam, "Tsk Tsk—Somebody Should Do Something about That." Similarly, August 28, 1958's "And All This Time I Was Hoping You'd Speak Up" imagined Eisenhower as the Egyptian Sphinx, holding a sign that reads "Let's Go Slower" while Uncle Sam, who is holding a piece of paper marked "Desegregation Question," reacts in disbelief.[69]

If Block chose to interpret the failure of civil rights reform in the late 1950s as, at least in part, a failure of moral leadership on the part of Dwight Eisenhower, Block celebrated Eisenhower's successor as a champion of those values. As early as the 1960 presidential campaign, John F. Kennedy was depicted as a prize fighter, bravely wrestling against the brutish "Administration–Byrd Democrats Coalition" in defense of the Democratic Party's support of civil rights reform within its platform.[70] With the Kennedy administration initially favoring a measured approach to civil rights, however, it would not be until June 13, 1963, two days after the president's famous address in which he declared civil rights a "moral issue . . . as old as the scriptures," that Block again directly incorporated Kennedy into a civil rights–related cartoon.[71] In "Washington, D.C., June, 1963," Block showed Kennedy standing on the White House's roof while raising an American flag and a banner quoting from his nationally televised address that reads, "The time has come for this nation to fulfill its promises." This connection between Kennedy and patriotic iconography continued for the remainder of the administration, with, for example, Block's November 6, 1963, cartoon "Cold War at Home" imagining Kennedy as a general being prevented from bringing his civil rights legislation to the Senate floor by a roadblock manned by the southern Democrats Richard B. Russell and Harry F. Byrd.[72] Just as the belief that Eisenhower was, at best, uninterested in the pursuit of racial justice became a standard narrative for both historians and the general public, Block's hypermasculine and patriotic depictions of Kennedy anticipated the mythologizing of Kennedy's commitment to civil rights reform that liberal commentators and historians engaged in following his death.

In the aftermath of Kennedy's assassination, Block was skeptical that the president's successor had either the will or the desire to continue the civil rights progress he imagined Kennedy to have fostered. As he later confessed in his autobiography, at the time that Lyndon Johnson became president, he "hardly seemed like a civil rights champion," and Block had not been "enthusiastic about him as a vice presidential candidate."[73] Block's suspicion of Johnson's civil rights record dated back to the Eisenhower administration and can be seen in cartoons such as one published in November 1956 that showed the then-Senate majority leader welcoming a liberal senator with proposals for new civil rights legislation into his office with the words, "Come in, Friend—I Welcome Suggestions." The cartoon indicated how insincere Block considered Johnson's support for these proposals to be by having him holding up a trash can and hiding a mallet behind his back. Six months later, Block reiterated this by imagining Johnson as a disinterested schoolboy living in a house of straw as a big bad wolf representing filibusters threatened to overwhelm the Senate's unsubstantial civil rights initiatives.[74] These cartoons demonstrated Block's displeasure with Johnson's efforts to build a bipartisan consensus among liberal northern and southern conservative Democrats that was shared by many other liberal commentators and senators, who believed Johnson was undermining their liberal ideology for political expediency and in benefit of the goals of the Eisenhower administration. But the cartoons also underestimated a genuine commitment to civil rights that had evolved during Johnson's congressional career and that saw him usher important civil rights legislation through the Senate in both 1957 and 1960.[75]

Johnson was ultimately to prove these liberal naysayers wrong, a fact that Block begrudgingly admitted in 1968's *The Herblock Gallery* when he credited Johnson with passing "three far-reaching civil-rights acts" during his presidency, despite sustained congressional opposition.[76] Regardless, Block never depicted Johnson as a champion of civil rights as he had done with Kennedy. Indeed, a physical depiction of the president is conspicuously absent from any of the sixty civil rights–related cartoons Block drew between Johnson's swearing-in on November 23, 1963, and the signing of the Voting Rights Act on August 6, 1965.[77] During this eighteen-month period, Block focused, just as he had in the late 1940s and early 1950s, primarily on the progress of civil rights legislation through Congress, most notably what became the Civil Rights Act of 1964 and the Voting Rights Act of 1965.[78] Instead of elucidating the specific gains that these pieces of legislation would afford to African Americans across the country, Block used these cartoons to criticize the opposition and obstructionist tactics of southern senators and congressmen such as South Carolina's Strom Thurmond, Mississippi's James Eastland, Virginia's Howard Smith, and Georgia's Richard Russell Jr.[79] In doing so, he framed the issue in the same moralistic tones that he had used in the late 1940s and early 1950s, portraying the conservative opposition to civil rights reform as a series of unsavory and violent characters—ranging from Confederate officers to violent lynchers and from a spider spinning a web of technicalities and delaying tactics to Charles Dickens's Ebenezer Scrooge taunting Uncle Sam as Block's John Q. Public character hangs over a lit fire in which a civil rights bill is burning—who were ultimately willing to do anything in their power to prevent passage of the relevant bills.

In many ways this emphasis was not surprising as a consistent theme of Block's depiction of civil rights was to give prominence to the actions and attitudes of white politicians and Americans over the activism of the African Americans who were fighting for equality. This is not to diminish the importance of these cartoons, which in many ways reflected the limitations of both editorial cartooning as a medium and postwar liberalism's attitude toward issues of race and civil rights. It was Block's job to distill complex ideas and emotions into a single easily understandable image that provoked a strong reaction from his readers, and as a cartoonist living in the nation's capital, it was somewhat inevitable he would choose to depict the legislative and political issues occurring around him. But postwar liberalism, committed as it was to a strong anticommunist agenda, was hostile to ideas and activism that originated from outside a narrow range of political bounds. As a result, the types of civil rights reform that were possible in the 1960s were limited to efforts to end overt discrimination in education, the workplace, and at the ballot. These were limitations that Block's cartoons, with their emphasis on the primacy of legislative action over community activism and depictions of white southerners as un-American thugs, reflected and shared with his national audience.

These cartoons also illustrated how Block had become increasingly concerned through the first half of the decade with critiquing a new threat to the stability of the postwar liberal establishment. The white southerners whose racist beliefs he so frequently condemned were also members of the Democratic Party whose obstructionism in Congress often prevented the passage of significant liberal legislation. As the civil rights movement gained broader national backing and won significant judicial and legislative victories, these Democrats increasingly found they had much in common with a new conservative movement that was gaining support throughout the nation but especially in America's sunbelt and western states. These conservatives believed that the liberal establishment was simultaneously not doing enough to fight communism and intervening too much in both the operation of business and the lives of American citizens. For them, liberal support of civil rights was merely one more example of a government that had gone too far in its effort to transform the country into a society that they no longer recognized. As this movement grew in popularity, Block increasingly sought to defend postwar liberalism against those who would see its achievements undone.

4

"NOTHING MORE THAN INFLAMMATORY PROPAGANDA"

Denouncing the New Right

BLOCK TREATED THE NEWS OF President John F. Kennedy's assassination with a combination of disbelief, shock, and horror. His November 23, 1963, cartoon depicted a strikingly diverse group of Americans standing in front of the stars and stripes at half-mast, their heads bowed in grief. The cartoon's caption was a line from Kennedy's inaugural address: "With a good conscience our only sure reward, with history the final judge of our deeds, let us go forth to lead the land we love."[1] The cartoons published over the next several days saw Block further process his grief, first imagining a family still trying to comprehend the assassination and then anticipating the long shadow that Kennedy's death would leave over the country's suddenly uncertain future. By November 26, his work seemed to reflect an acceptance of the reality of Kennedy's death by showing Father Time inscribing the Johnson administration as a new chapter of American history.[2] Block's interpretation of the assassination spoke to Americans' collective grief, but his November 27 cartoon revealed that his mourning had turned to anger as he sought to find an explanation for Kennedy's death. Imagining an advertisement for the type of rifle Lee Harvey Oswald had used in Dallas, the cartoon's headline screamed, "Sportsmen! Kids! Maniacs!" above marketing-style language that satirized the ease with which anyone could cheaply obtain these types of weapons (fig. 21).[3]

Block's attempt to highlight the potential role of lax gun control laws in a national tragedy was met with swift condemnation from conservative readers. Signing his letter "Constitutionally yours" and claiming to have seen the cartoon in "the local Prairie Pravda," one reader from Madison, Wisconsin, accused Block of an "usual inattention (or ignorance) of the facts," and stated that he was "guilty of false and misleading advertising" in suggesting that rifles of this sort could be purchased for as little as $12.78. The reader's indignant point was that to make the "outmoded" weapon usable, ammunition and a telescopic sight would have to be purchased separately,

FIGURE 21. *Washington Post,* November 27, 1963

thereby increasing the cost of ownership.[4] "It is nothing more than inflammatory propaganda," wrote another reader, this time from Warrington, Florida, "designed to agitate a people shocked and saddened by this national disaster and turn their feelings of frustration into those of rage against the weapon used!" After declaring that "it is *people,* not guns, that kill," and claiming otherwise "increase[s] the popularity of the minority groups trying to eliminate the heritage of a nation ready and willing to defend itself," the reader concluded by arguing that Block's "cartoon tries to channel unreasonable emotion into an issue that needs the most studied thought. For a man in your influential position, there is no excuse for this at a time that requires even more careful thought from such men."[5]

If these partisan reactions to Block's cartoon at a time of national mourning have a contemporary resonance, it is because they reflected the early stages of the so-called culture wars, which have characterized American political discourse since the 1960s. This decade was a period of significant unrest in the United States as new assumptions from both the right and the left about what values should define American society challenged the consensus politics of postwar America.[6] Coming to national prominence in the early years of the 1960s but present in American culture earlier, the resurgence of conservatism was initially driven by issues introduced in the previous two chapters. The failure of McCarthyism, coupled with a changing relationship with the Soviet Union, signified to conservatives that America was losing the fight against communism in the Cold War. Similarly, the end of segregation and changes in the racial status quo were transforming the power structures of American society. At the same time, religiously conservative Americans were convinced that secularization was creeping through American education and popular culture, undermining the traditional patriarchal family. And, perhaps strongest of all was the simple fear among many Americans that society and culture were changing in ways and at a speed they could not comprehend.

With most political commentators focused on the glamor of the Kennedy administration and the efforts of the conservative coalition of southern Democrats and Republicans to oppose the civil rights movement, the liberal establishment largely ignored or dismissed as extremism the rise of this so-called New Right. But postwar liberals underestimated the appeal of a new coalition made up of East Coast elitists such as

William F. Buckley Jr., midwestern activists like Phyllis Schlafly, politicians like Arizona's Barry Goldwater, and the grassroots members of conservative organizations such as California's John Birch Society that was opposed to the liberal agenda. Block framed the tension between the political ideologies of conservativism and liberalism as a battle between the forces of regression and progress, between an imagined past and a hopeful future. His depiction of these disparate figures and their grievances reveals how the liberal vision of American society was fundamentally different to that proposed by the emerging conservative movement, a conflict the consequences of which we still face today.

At the start of the decade, few prominent Americans would have given much credence to the idea that a conservative movement was a viable threat to postwar liberalism. Eisenhower may have held the presidency for Republicans for the previous eight years, but Democrats had made significant gains in the 1958 congressional elections and were looking forward to the next presidential election as an opportunity to regain the White House. Harvard historian Arthur M. Schlesinger articulated this optimism in January 1960 when he argued in *Esquire* magazine that there was a "New Mood in Politics." While the 1950s had been a decade of "passivity and acquiescence," that era was now "drawing to a natural end." Schlesinger identified cultural changes such as the emergence of the Beat Generation, a resurgence in religious activities, and the general popularity of books written by public intellectuals such as John Kenneth Galbraith to posit that Americans of all backgrounds were reacting against a "deepening concern with our character and objectives as a nation" and exploring myriad ways in which they could "seek a renewal of conviction [and] a new sense of national purpose." Suggesting that the "quiescence and respite" of the 1950s was the natural result of a "cyclic rhythm" in American politics that oscillated between passivity and activism, between conservatism and liberalism, Schlesinger looked forward eagerly to a new decade that would see Americans "fighting for individual dignity, identity, and fulfillment in an affluent mass society."[7] A year later, he could look back at his predictions and the outcome of the election with satisfaction. Although Kennedy had not been the first choice of many liberals—the leadership of ADA, for example, had favored their organization's cofounder Hubert Humphrey and were initially suspicious of Kennedy's commitment to many of their priorities—Kennedy's campaign rhetoric of a "new frontier" that would sweep away the staid policies of the previous administration and reinvigorate America's fight against communism, coupled with the confident declaration in his inaugural address that "the torch has been passed to a new generation of Americans," seemed to usher in a new period of American growth and optimism. That Kennedy openly embraced liberalism's intellectual leaders, bringing prominent ADA stalwarts such as Schlesinger, Galbraith, and Chester Bowles into his administration, only added to their belief that American liberalism was entering a new period of political dominance.

Again, Schlesinger offered one of the clearest articulations of liberal hopes for the new administration. Four years earlier, he had argued that the affluence of American society demonstrated it was time to move on from New Deal liberalism, which had succeeded in solving the Depression-era "problems of subsistence and survival." But for all the undeniable riches of the age, he lamented, "our schools become more crowded and dilapidated, our teachers more weary and underpaid, our playgrounds more crowded, our cities dirtier, our roads more teeming and filthy, our national parks more unkempt, our law enforcement more overworked and inadequate." Liberals, he declared, should embrace a new "qualitative liberalism" that would leverage the resources of the federal government to address these issues, and more, and in so doing improve "the quality of American life" for all Americans.[8] With Kennedy in the White House, Schlesinger now saw an opportunity for the government to invest its resources on "long-run factors—on the education and health of our people, on the guarantee of their equal opportunity, on the growth of our economy, on the development of our resources." Kennedy, he promised in an October 1960 campaign publication that contrasted the policies and characters of Kennedy and Richard Nixon, would provide strong presidential leadership to achieve these domestic policy goals, and in doing so would "revolutionize the moral tone of the country [and] inaugurate the new epoch of national progress." But the "national revival," Schlesinger continued, "is not just a matter of domestic interest." Instead, it was of the "most vital concern in our foreign affairs, since only a moral and intellectual revival within the United States can charge our foreign policy with the spirit of creative idealism necessary to restore the confidence of other peoples in our purposes." This explicit connection between domestic and foreign policy lay at the heart of liberal ideology. In order to defeat the communist threat abroad, Schlesinger declared, it was not enough to simply talk about "the great ideals of the American Revolution." Instead, "the key to peace lies in *doing* something about those ideals—in showing the world that the American Revolution is not dead in the land of its birth. It lies in leadership that will put American idealism to work."[9]

Block was not immune to this confidence in the new administration's commitment to liberal priorities and found himself thrust into the nexus of Washington's political leadership. Already friends with many administration officials, Block was a guest at numerous White House events, including at least one state dinner, and frequently attended dinner parties hosted at Robert Kennedy's Hickory Hill home. He later recalled how the Kennedys "brought an excitement, an intellectual stimulation and a desire to serve that hadn't been seen since the days of Roosevelt."[10] Many of Block's Kennedy-related cartoons reflected this enthusiasm, especially those from early in the administration. At its simplest level, Block's depictions of Kennedy emphasized his youth and rugged handsomeness. This visually reinforced the impression of a new president determined to bring a new energy and commitment to America's foreign and domestic policies. Whereas Block depicted Eisenhower as Soviet premier Nikita Khrushchev's stooge, he imagined Kennedy not just as Khrushchev's equal but as a paradigm of American masculinity.[11] For instance, Block's post-inaugural cartoon "Chief, I Just Don't Think He's Ready for the Idea" depicted a scowling Khrushchev (imagined as an undertaker replete with a wreath labeled "R.I.P. USA") looking on as Kennedy confidently strode onto the world stage followed by a gaggle of journalists struggling to keep up.[12] Similarly, the cartoon "Test" from 1961 showed Kennedy and Khrushchev engaged in an arm-wrestling contest as the two world leaders struggled for influence in Laos.[13]

Block similarly portrayed Kennedy as a dynamic force in domestic politics, ready to take on the challenges that faced the nation. An early inspiration came from the self-styled rhetoric of the campaign, with Block deploying a western theme that cast Kennedy as a courageous pioneer or clean-cut cowboy. The purpose of this iconography was twofold. It directly connected Kennedy to a mythological past, a simpler time when men worked hard and protected their families from the dangers posed by those who stood outside respectable society, generally bandits and Indians. But it also allowed Block to frame liberalism's postwar agenda in moralistic tones, presenting the administration as one side of a fight between good and evil. Block first employed the motif during the presidential campaign when he imagined Kennedy and Richard Nixon about to engage in a gun fight in the halls of the U.S. Capitol. The dark shading of Nixon—in contrast to the light tones used to depict Kennedy—left the reader with little doubt as to which man they should be supporting.[14] Block continued to rely on this imagery throughout Kennedy's abbreviated presidency.

Every western needs a strong villain, and after Nixon seemingly departed from the national stage following his electoral defeat, Block turned to an old threat to Kennedy's liberal priorities: the coalition of conservative Democrats and moderate Republicans who controlled the balance of power in the House of Representatives and Senate. This conservative coalition had stymied liberal priorities, especially those related to civil rights, since the Truman administration and represented an ongoing obstacle to the liberal agenda. Thus, Block cast this group of legislators alternatively as a wild bull needing to be tamed by the president-elect's brave and solitary cattle-handler, a stereotypical group of Native Americans threatening to attack Kennedy's train of pioneers, and as a gunslinger kidnapping the administration's legislative priorities.[15] Block's fears were well-founded. After the 1960 election, the Democrats maintained a majority in both chambers of Congress, but some of their gains from two years earlier were erased. The result was a notably conservative Congress whose balance of power was controlled by politicians unfriendly to liberal priorities.

Block portrayed conservatives as the natural opponents to the advances promised by Kennedy's New Frontier, but the cartoonist's framing of the opposition only partly captured the power of a new wave of conservatism that was emerging in American politics. In addition to the conservative coalition in Congress, a grassroots movement was steadily finding support in both America's western states and its suburbs. One sign that conservative ideas were gaining in popularity came in the January 1961 edition of *Esquire*. The magazine's profile of William F. Buckley, a right-wing provocateur and the founder and editor of *National*

Review, was in many ways a response to Schlesinger's year-old claim that there was a new mood in American politics. Like Schlesinger before him, Buckley found that many Americans were dissatisfied with the state of their nation. But whereas Schlesinger had identified liberalism as the panacea for America's ills, Buckley saw liberalism's commitment to federal social reforms as its cause. In a thinly veiled reference to the civil rights movement, for example, Buckley argued that "the idea that everyone is qualified to vote [is] one of the great self-delusions of democracy," and that "under certain circumstances, dictatorship is best." Likewise, the failure of conservatives in recent elections "does not mean that the fight was not worth fighting, or even that nothing was won by it; nor that the next thousand will not be worth fighting." Instead, "it means American conservatives should in their own self-interest abandon the nonsense about how 'all we need is a good conservative candidate.' All we need is a fresh set of voters. That, too, can be arranged." *National Review* and the broader right-wing movement, he concluded, were "in the business of trying to 'purify' conservatism."[16]

On this point, Buckley explicitly addressed an issue that had long been of concern to Block. He, like Buckley, was acutely aware both that the 1960 presidential election had been decided by fewer than 120,000 votes and that millions of Americans were either denied the vote or had their vote counted unfairly. Cartoons condemning the efforts of white southerners to prevent African Americans from voting had been a staple of his work since the mid-1950s, but Block was also regularly concerned about the disfranchisement of two other groups: residents of Washington, DC, like himself, and the estimated 3 million migrant workers employed to pick fruit and vegetables on America's farms.[17] Fair access to the ballot was requisite, but Block also believed that the system itself—in particular the electoral college—had inherent biases that disadvantaged liberals and consequently endangered their agenda. Across almost fifty cartoons drawn between 1946 and 1976, Block consistently depicted the electoral college as a senile old man, replete with white beard stretching to the ground and colonial-style clothes. Often shown carrying a musket, the character signified that the electoral college was a relic of an irrelevant past that actively resisted enfranchisement and the will of the people.[18]

As outlandish as Buckley's pronouncements likely sounded to *Esquire*'s liberal readership, they were an accurate reflection of the ideology he had set forth in *National Review.* In that magazine's first issue, published in November 1955, he argued that "literate America [had] rejected conservatism in favor of radical social experimentation." He promised that he and his contributors would stand up against the "socialist objectives" of labor unions to "tell the violated businessman's side of the story." He argued that the "largest cultural menace in America is the conformity of the intellectual cliques which . . . are out to impose upon the nation their modish fads and fallacies." In what he called the "profound crisis of our era," Buckley railed against those "Social Engineers" who sought to "adjust mankind to conform with scientific utopias," positioning himself in enlightened opposition, along with "the disciples of Truth, who defend the organic moral order." As a result, rapprochement with communism—the "century's most blatant force of satanic utopianism"—was "neither desirable nor possible, nor honorable," while internationalism and "the fashionable concepts of world government [and] the United Nations," which had "bewitched America's Liberal elite," was to be rejected because it amounted to the "surrender [of] U.S. sovereignty to a world organization." Buckley's ideology maintained that not only was it the sole responsibility of the federal government "to protect its citizens' lives, liberty and property," but that "all other activities of government tend to diminish freedom and hamper progress," and therefore "the growth of government (the dominant social feature of this century) must be fought relentlessly."[19]

In blaming the expansion of federal power on the "fatuous and unreasoned slogans . . . [of] 'progressivism' and 'bipartisanship,'" Buckley explicitly attacked one of the foundations of postwar liberalism's consensus politics. But during the second half of the 1950s, America enjoyed unprecedented prosperity, and the government policies Buckley decried were generally popular with ordinary Americans. For the liberal establishment, including Block, these arguments rang hollow. In their estimation, the only legitimate threat to the postwar establishment came from Congress—specifically the so-called conservative coalition of lawmakers that continued to trouble Block throughout the Kennedy administration. Any other groups that challenged the internationalism and social policies of the decade could easily be dismissed as the result of paranoia or extremism, as Richard Hofstadter did in an unpublished 1959 essay that described how "right-wingers . . . regard the involvement of the United States in affairs of the world [and] the rise of the welfare state . . . [as] the work of mischievous and malicious men of great power."[20]

One such group was the Daughters of the American Revolution (DAR), a nationalistic women's organization whose isolationist opposition to immigration and the United Nations were a theme of Block's cartoons from May 1947 to April 1961. Block drew members of DAR as overweight and elderly women, wearing flowery formal dresses and hats, pince-nez glasses, and adorned with the ubiquitous sashes of their organization. They were depicted as miserly busy-bodies who belonged to a different time. This image certainly matched the antiquated attitudes Block ascribed to them. Whether it was standing on the banks of Plymouth Rock furiously objecting to the arrival of refugees from Europe, obliviously insisting that American and UN troops engaged in combat against communist foes abroad be sure to properly display the American flag, or angrily informing an incredulous Uncle Sam that "some" members of the United Nations "aren't American at all," Block made clear to his readers that he considered their views a ridiculous form of faux patriotism.[21] Supporters of DAR inevitably found much to dislike about Block's portrayal of the group, and correspondents decried the cartoons as "outrageous caricature[s]" bereft of "even a touch of humor."[22] In response to a 1957 cartoon that depicted two indignant members of DAR standing outside a bookstore, flustered by the presence of a globe they view as anti-American propaganda, one letter writer contrasted how the daughters presented their views "calmly and courteously" while Block "demonstrated his superior grasp of the issues involved by lampooning their personal appearance and substituting a generalized sneer for an appeal to reason." Another simply found the cartoon lacking "honesty and justice."[23]

Block, meanwhile, remained largely nonplussed by these complaints and argued as early as 1952 that DAR exemplified what he described as "the practice of Mumbo-Jumbo." The term dismissively referred to the organization's "transference of devotion from a set of principles to the symbols and rituals that are built up around them," with the result that the original meaning of those principles are forgotten or even destroyed.

Block found it hypocritical that an organization which ostensibly honored the actions of their ancestors in overthrowing tyranny would object to the arrival of immigrants who might share those same ideals. Similarly, DAR's insistence that everyone in society should venerate the American flag and punish those who did not perform the requisite devotions was evidence that they had either forgotten, or never cared about, the freedoms and civil liberties that the flag was supposed to represent. In both examples, the symbol—America's founding fathers and the flag—had become rhetorically more important than the ideals for which they stood. Block's argument echoed one articulated at the time by historians who looked to such contexts as the antebellum South, the Jacksonian era, and the American West to argue that the way in which ordinary Americans remembered the past through symbols and myths was critical for understanding how they acted in the present. For all of Block's disdain toward DAR, he nonetheless acknowledged that many of its members, if "sometimes misguided in their zeal . . . also perform many good works which don't always bring forth editorial comment."[24] Such qualification was not extended to other conservative groups, most notably the John Birch Society, which in the minds of many liberals became synonymous with the resurgent conservative movement of the early 1960s.

The John Birch Society was founded in 1958 by former candy company executive Robert W. Welch Jr. At its height the society had as many as 100,000 members, the majority in America's western states, and held that the political consensus of postwar America had failed the nation. In itself, this stance was not dissimilar from other right-wing and conservative groups. The scale of the group's grievances was far grander, however. The increasing size of the federal government and its expanding intervention into Americans' lives, whether in the form of the welfare state, higher taxation, or increased labor protections, were described "as brakes on material progress and as destroyers of personal freedom." Likewise, the increasingly progressive decisions handed down by the Supreme Court under the leadership of Chief Justice Earl Warren, especially those supportive of civil rights, were decried for undercutting the principle of states' rights and increasing protections for the rights of communists and other leftists. The society condemned the civil rights movement itself as beholden to communist influence and working to undermine

American values. Developments in the Cold War that suggested a possible rapprochement between the United States and the Soviet Union were equally concerning. Nuclear disarmament talks, America's continued support of the United Nations, and Nikita Khrushchev's visit to the United States in 1959 all seemed to indicate that Congress and the Eisenhower administration were growing soft on communism. Welch even suggested that Congress might actually be working with communists as part of "a gigantic conspiracy to enslave mankind," that they were "willing to use any means to achieve its end," and that President Eisenhower was a "dedicated, conscious agent of the Communist conspiracy."[25]

Ideas such as these led journalists and liberal commentators to dismiss the resurgent conservative movement as a group of extremist fanatics. Alan Barth, an editorial writer at the *Post* who also regularly contributed short essays to the *New York Times,* ascribed their emergence to the success of the liberal agenda in reshaping American society and protecting the most vulnerable members of its society. This "tremendous transformation," he wrote, was "opposed by some . . . as contrary to traditions of free enterprise and individual initiative." Coupled with anxieties over the Cold War and the potential impact of nuclear war, Barth argued that "today's tensions have led to a proliferation of 'conservative extremists'" but nonetheless dismissed them as a group which offered "no novel solutions to the problems that plague them" and instead represented "not a wave of the future [but] a voice of frustration and despair, a wail from an irrevocable past."[26] Richard Hofstadter was blunter but no less representative of liberal thinking when he dismissed the ideology of the John Birch Society and other right-wing groups as "pseudo-conservatism" and linked their opposition to postwar liberalism to a "profound if largely unconscious hatred of our society and its ways."[27]

Block portrayed members of the society using a visual language clearly informed by these liberal commentators. Where the Daughters of the American Revolution were drawn as relics of a bygone era, clinging to outmoded values, Block depicted members of the conservative rightwing as an active threat to American society. He labeled them "Birchers," "Birchnuts," and "right-wing extremists," and caricatured them based on this assessment. Mirroring his depiction of white southerners, Block drew them as boorish thugs, with features designed to emphasize their presumed lack of education and propensity for violence, and directly connected them to some of his most common anticonservative themes. The first appearance of the John Birch Society in a Herblock cartoon depicted Welch conspiratorially whispering to Congressman Francis E. Walter, chair of the House Committee on Un-American Activities, "They're ALL Communists Except Thee and Me—" (fig. 22).[28] While Block intended this cartoon to mock the paranoia that he and other liberals believed lay at the heart of conservative ideology, his work also visualized the danger that the society's ideas seemed to represent for American security. A hint of this came in this initial appearance of Welch, which sought to illustrate the complete control Welch had over his organization by presenting

FIGURE 22. *Washington Post,* April 5, 1961

him in a Napoleonesque pose replete with his right hand tucked into his waistcoat. But Block soon dropped such subtlety and showed the society engaged in such activities as infiltrating and undermining the authority of the U.S. Army, working together with white supremacists, and acting as an ally to the communist leaders they purported to oppose.[29]

Block's depiction of the Birch Society belied its appeal to a growing number of Americans. Like much of the broader conservative movement, the group was well-funded by business interests committed to rolling back New Deal–era policies, which gave it some legitimacy.[30] The typical member was also the very definition of respectability: white, middle-class, well-educated Protestants who lived in the suburbs, predominantly in America's western states, and who saw themselves as patriotic Americans who stood ready to defend traditional values against the excesses of liberalism and its moderate Republican allies. The John Birch Society's propagation of paranoid conspiracies about communism's grip over the American government and claims that President Kennedy had been assassinated as part of a communist plot to discredit the rising influence of the conservative movement made it easy for opponents to dismiss it as no different from other right-wing groups such as the Ku Klux Klan and the Minutemen, which advocated and practiced violent action to overthrow the postwar political order. But members of the Birch Society resented comparisons to the extremism of the Klan and the Minutemen, arguing that they operated well within the acceptable confines of civic discourse. Their rhetorical tactics of choice included letter-writing, billboards, newspaper advertisements, and radio broadcasts, which gave their grievances a veneer of legitimacy that allowed them to attract ever more converts to their cause. The society also offered a sense of community and belonging to its members, allowing conservatives to come into contact with like-minded individuals and offer them the opportunity to participate in a grassroots movement, which further strengthened their commitment to the cause.[31]

There was nonetheless a lot of truth in the media's characterization of Birchers as right-wing extremists, especially from the perspective of members of the liberal establishment. The society was fully sincere in its belief that communism had infiltrated every level of the federal government, and one of its explicit goals was to end the federal social welfare programs and economic regulations that were central to liberal ideology. Furthermore, Welch's public speeches and writings revealed a basic hostility to democracy and democratic values, which he framed as a threat to America's founding principles. Democracy, he declared in the John Birch Society's original manifesto, "is merely a deceptive phrase, a weapon of demagoguery, and a perennial fraud."[32] In a 1961 speech titled "Republics and Democracies," he elaborated on the danger the liberal state, with its commitment to expanded rights and democratic principles, posed to the American republic. "We are being insidiously, conspiratorially, and *treasonously* led by deception, by bribery, by coercion, and by fear," he stated, "to destroy a republic that was the envy and model for all of the civilized world." The existential threat the patriotic American faced, he claimed, was the "dangerous tendency" of democracy to "enslave him through the tyranny of majorities and the deadly power of their opinion."[33]

Block likely never read these words, but there is little doubt he would have strongly condemned them if he had. In a 1963 speech at Columbia University, he asserted that in "thinking about democracy and good government we might also re-examine some of our ideas about cities, long regarded as centers of wickedness and corruption, and about rural areas, associated with God's great outdoors and virtues like early rising." These portrayals of urban and rural life, Block argued, may have been accurate at the end of the nineteenth century, when almost two-thirds of Americans lived in rural regions and the muckrakers "wrote of 'the shame of the cities.'" But at a time when almost two-thirds of American now lived in urban centers, he continued, "the shame of the cities today is largely the shame of the suburbs and the shame of rurally dominated state legislatures."[34] Block was thinking here of how America's cities were both underfunded and underrepresented in comparison to the nation's rural population. His belief that America's urban majority best reflected American values asserted itself in his depiction of rural Americans as uneducated thugs or selfish politicians, concerned only with their own special interests and the maintenance of their political power. Urban voters, on the other hand, were shown as respectable, middle-class workers who represented the selfless policies of postwar liberalism. This was seen, for example, in October 13, 1961's "If You Don't Like This Situation, You Can Cast Your Twentieth of a Vote against It," which portrayed a well-dressed man, labeled "Urban Majorities," lying bound and gagged while a weasel-like politician, labeled "Domination by Rural Minorities," sneers over him (fig. 23).[35]

Block's strong response against this opposing viewpoint was also seen in his treatment of conservatives' belief that liberalism was eroding the country's commitment to religious and moral values. The John Birch Society, for example, declared that its first principle, above even anticommunism and patriotism, was that "with very few exceptions," its members were "deeply religious people . . . [whose] never-ending concern is with morality, integrity, and purpose." Religion was therefore

FIGURE 23. *Washington Post,* October 13, 1961

not only the foundation on which both American families and the nation itself were built but also provided the moral authority for the fight against godless communism.[36] From this perspective, it was not enough for the federal government to treat religious devotion as a private activity. It must be actively protected and promoted and any effort to curtail those rights resisted. The high point in the campaign to assert the centrality of Christianity to American life arguably came with the 1954 insertion of the words "under God" into the Pledge of Allegiance. But many religious conservatives had become concerned that religious instruction was declining in public schools. In this context, there were two flashpoints in the early 1960s that antagonized religiously conservative Americans and suggested to them that the government was attacking their religious freedoms: federal support for religious schools and the role of religious recitations in public schools.

One of the Kennedy administration's priorities in 1961 was an ill-fated $2.3 billion bill to provide funding for the construction and operation of America's public schools and to increase teachers' salaries. The bill passed the Senate but floundered in the House thanks to the usual coalition of southern Democrats and Republicans that regularly blocked liberal priorities. Their opposition centered on two primary concerns. Some conservatives, including the Democratic Speaker of the House Sam Rayburn, objected to the bill's financial costs, finding the inclusion of funds to support teacher salaries especially troublesome. But others rejected the bill because of its focus on public schools and failure to provide commensurate support for America's parochial schools. The administration had excluded such support to adhere to the constitution's "clear" mandate of separation of church and state. For Catholic opponents to the bill, however, the issue was much more profound. With some 6.24 million children attending private schools, and all but 1 million of that total attending Catholic schools, opponents argued that parents would effectively be taxed twice to pay for their children's education. The result, opponents such as the archbishop of Cincinnati argued, was that these children would be "victims of discriminatory legislation."[37]

Block's cartoons had long supported America's public schools and teachers. In April 1947, for example, Block depicted public schools as a teetering pillar of American democracy that needed additional congressional funding to address the longstanding issues Kennedy's bill sought to resolve.[38] By January 1961, he had drawn over eighty cartoons for the *Washington Post* on the topic, frequently depicting dozens of children crammed into collapsing schoolhouses while members of Congress or the administration dispassionately look on.[39] He therefore greeted the initial submission of the school-assistance bill with cautious optimism with his February 21 cartoon, "This Little Kid's Got a Big Guy with Him," depicting a gang of "legislative dead-enders" rethinking their plan to assault a boy (labeled "1961 Education Bill") who was walking hand in hand to school with Kennedy.[40] But Block was also a lifelong sceptic of organized religion who wryly noted in his autobiography that his mother's failure to raise him Catholic had resulted in "a kind of mini church-state crisis at home."[41] He was sensitive to what he saw as a disconnect between what some religious leaders preached and what they practiced, suggesting that what was important to them was not the well-being of their parishioners. This was clearly seen in "Onward, 'Christian' Soldiers," published on October 23, 1960, in which Block depicted "Race Prejudice" and "Religious Bigotry" as two singers sharing a duet. One distributes "Hate Pamphlets" and the other a handbook marked "Religion for Politics and Profit."[42]

As resistance to the bill's passage intensified on religious grounds, Block made explicit to his readers what he viewed to be at stake in the legislative wrangling. March 8, 1961's "Here Little Boy. Pull the Nice Horsie in with You" depicted a lobbyist for parochial schools encouraging a schoolboy to accept the Trojan Horse that was government-supported religion. The message could not have been clearer. If the Kennedy administration acquiesced to the demands of the Catholic Church to provide funding to their schools, it would the open the gates to further erosion of the separation between church and state.[43] Predictably, readers took especial umbrage with this cartoon. One correspondent accused Block of suggesting that "Catholic taxpayers should not benefit from tax money," and that he was "emotionally" engaging in "anti-Catholic activity." Following a second cartoon on the same issue, another reader accused him of lacking "fairness and understanding."[44]

For all of the emotions the school aid bill evoked, they were nothing compared to the response to a pair of Supreme Court rulings that came down in 1962 and 1963 directly addressing the role religion should play in

American society. In *Engel v. Vitale,* the Court ruled that the New York public school system could not require students to read nonsectarian prayers in school. The following year's *School District of Abington Township v. Schempp* went further by declaring that mandatory Bible readings and recitation of the Lord's Prayer were breaches of the Constitution's separation of church and state. For conservative critics of the Court, these two rulings seemed to remove God from America's public schools, and in doing so affirmed all of their fears that the federal government and Supreme Court were pushing the country toward secularism.[45]

For Block, these rulings were simply commonsense interpretations of the Constitution and a continuation of the issues that had underscored the earlier controversy over Kennedy's proposed school bill. Two cartoons dealing with these rulings proved to be especially controversial and led to Block receiving letters from offended readers. The first depicted an irate senator pontificating on the Senate floor that "Leaving Religion to Private Initiative Is Un-American" as his colleagues look on aghast.[46] The cartoon provoked a correspondent from California to rebuke Block by insisting that all Americans like her wanted was "to be free to worship God." That being said, "Our free nation is founded on Christianity," and as such she did not want "the country to have freedom from religion."[47] A year later, Block's response to the *Abington Township* decision imagined a family's breakfast routine interrupted by the patriarch reading about the ruling in his morning newspaper and incredulously asking, "What Do They Expect Us to Do—Listen to the Kids Pray at *Home*?"[48]

In both cartoons, Block mocked what he saw as the hypocrisy of some of the Supreme Court's harshest critics, who, he argued in a 1963 speech, were "among those most eager to turn over so particularly personal a thing as religious training from family to state-supported educational institutions." These people "profess to be so concerned about the religious upbringing of children" but "are perhaps not concerned enough to take the children to church or Sunday School."[49] He further elaborated on this point in his 1964 book *Straight Herblock,* arguing that these Americans were "talking about . . . not their own children but *other* people's children" because they wanted "to make sure that everybody believes—no, that everybody *knows*—as they know." Block's worry was that they would not be satisfied until they had converted a "world struggle for individual freedom into a kind of 'holy war' in which the difference between us and the totalitarians would be not that we were free but that we were religious—forgetting that while free governments have protected religion, religious governments have seldom protected freedom—or freedom of religion."[50]

As the 1964 presidential election approached, each of these constituencies within the right-wing of the Republican Party—the religious conservatives who looked aghast at what they saw as postwar liberalism's increasingly successful efforts to remove religion from American life, the fervent anticommunists and isolationists of the Daughters of the American Revolution and the John Birch Society, and the movement's intellectual leaders—looked for a candidate who could repudiate the moderate Republicanism of Eisenhower and give legitimacy to their grievances. They found him in Barry Goldwater, a conservative politician who William Buckley specifically claimed credit for making "much more complete in [his] conservatism" than any other. Goldwater would become Block's most familiar and controversial target during the first half of the 1960s.[51]

Today hailed by conservative think-tank the Heritage Foundation as "The Most Consequential Loser in American Politics," the junior senator from Arizona first came to national prominence in March 1960 upon publication of his book *The Conscience of a Conservative.* In it, Goldwater denied the prevailing belief that conservatism was a spent force in American politics. "America is fundamentally a Conservative nation," he bluntly stated in the book's foreword. "The preponderant judgment of the American people, especially of the young people, is that the radical, or Liberal, approach has not worked and is not working. They yearn for a return to Conservative principles."[52] Goldwater advocated in moral terms for a smaller federal government and a systematic attack on some of the central tenets of postwar liberalism. He condemned the forced integration of America's schools in the name of states' rights, advocated to end subsidies for farmers, called for the establishment of a single tax rate that would apply equally to all Americans, and urged the deconstruction of the welfare state. As for the Cold War, Goldwater argued that the ongoing policy of containment was a failure that had in fact increased the Soviet threat. He instead advocated for an uncompromising escalation of military strength, opposing talk of test-ban treaties and arguing that the nation's leaders must never rule out the threat of nuclear war lest the Soviet Union be empowered to launch limited wars without fear of escalation. Underscoring it all was his assertion that conservatism derived its legitimacy from "the laws of God and of nature" and was therefore as relevant a political ideology to Americans in 1960 as it had ever been.[53] The book was a sensation and led to the mobilization of grassroots activists across the country in an effort to persuade Goldwater to pursue the 1960 Republican nomination. Goldwater ultimately declined to have his name put forward at the party's nominating convention, but Richard Nixon's subsequent loss to Kennedy reinforced Goldwater's position as the champion of conservative Republicans.

Throughout most of 1960, Block had ignored Goldwater's rise to national prominence, focusing instead on the Republican primary battle between Nixon and Nelson Rockefeller. Block's only direct reference to Goldwater during the election campaign came on July 28. Following the conclusion of both parties' nominating conventions and the renunciation of each's most conservative elements, Block depicted two school friends, one a member of the "Goldwater Republicans" and the other representing "anti–Civil Rights Democrats," as truants sitting despondently on a street curb while telling each other that "Sometimes I Feel Like Running Away, Too, but I Don't Know Where to Go." This cartoon, with its assumption that conservative values had no place within the existing party structures of consensus liberalism, anticipated what would become a theme in Block's depictions of both Goldwater and conservative values.[54] By positioning each of these groups as isolated from their respective parties, Block simultaneously positioned them as outsiders to the postwar liberal consensus while also suggesting that their political views were not that different and might one day combine into a dangerous new form of politics.

Following Nixon's defeat, leaders of the Republican Party struggled to determine which direction it should pursue to maintain political relevancy. On one side were the moderate Republicans who had backed Nixon's campaign in 1960 and favored the status quo; on the other were so-called Movement Republicans who supported the ideology of men like William Buckley and wanted to see Goldwater take on the mantle of the party's leadership. To liberal observers, who largely dismissed him as a politician without credibility whose ideas lacked broad support even within his own party, there was little doubt that Goldwater's staunch conservativism would quickly run afoul of the practicalities of modern party politics and the need to build a consensus within the Republican Party itself. Writing in November 1961, Alan Barth predicted that Goldwater would "be obliged before very long to choose between the support of the Rightists and the support of real Republicans who will not care to forsake the traditions of their party for a forlorn kind of fascism."[55] Six months later, Arthur Schlesinger described the Arizonian as being "too amiable a man [who] wants too much to be liked ever to commit himself to the radical Right." Goldwater, he concluded, "will always be betrayed by his own yearning for respectability."[56] The *Washington Post*'s Walter Lippmann posited a similar theory when he argued that Goldwater was not a "fanatic of the extreme right but an ambitious politician [who] is now reshaping himself for the political realities of the country."[57] Block, though, was unconvinced by these arguments against Goldwater's chances of emerging victorious from the Republican nomination process.

While Block abhorred the Republicanism of Richard Nixon, the growing influence of Goldwater over the party's direction was even more alarming. In particular, Block objected to Goldwater's unapologetic commitment to the principles of free enterprise and small government. As early as December 1960, Block made clear the direction he thought Goldwater was leading the Republican Party. "On to the Old OLD Frontier" dresses the senator as a caveman, pulling a reluctant GOP elephant into "Goldwaterland," a place where dinosaurs freely roam and economic aid for the needy is banished.[58] It was this latter point that Block again targeted in his July 1961 cartoon "I Don't Want My Tax Money Spent on Your Kind" (fig. 24). Drawn in response to Goldwater's endorsement of a conservative welfare program that had been implemented in Newburgh, New York, the cartoon shows a crazed Goldwater towering over a terrified and impoverished child. Among its most controversial aspects, the Newburgh plan denied any benefits to unwed mothers who had additional children and limited access to benefits to three months out of the year.[59]

To many of Block's readers, the "Red tinged" cartoon represented "the most vicious, distorted lying attack." Claiming that Goldwater was merely "trying to discourage bastardy, illegitimate breeding, and laziness," a correspondent from Chicago continued that "there was a time

FIGURE 24. *Washington Post,* July 25, 1961

when minorities were protected. But now that sanity and honesty have fallen into the minority category, you seem to want to squelch any trace or remnant of the former highly held virtues of honesty, morality, industry, and legitimacy." Another reader made the point clear when she tried to explain that the "problems that have arisen because of the people who do not wish responsibility of paying, literally, for their living has fallen to we people who do feel this responsibility and meet it. I too," she continued, "am sick of paying for some lazy prostitute's children. What gives her the right to guffaw at morals and raise as many children as she cares to conceive on my taxes."[60] In making this explicit connection between morality and personal and fiscal responsibility, these letter writers clearly articulated conservative fears over the perceived decline in traditional family values that Goldwater sought to exploit.

Undaunted by criticism, Block revisited this theme in a December 1961 cartoon that depicts Goldwater peering down at a mother with her three children huddled together in a slum neighborhood and, without irony, advising her, "If You Had Any Initiative, You'd Go Out and Inherit a Department Store" (fig. 25).[61] The cartoon again resonated with many of his readers, in large part because of the direct contrast it drew between Goldwater's seeming disinterest in helping the poorest of Americans and his status as heir to an Arizona-based department store chain. Correspondents declared it a "piece of cartoon genius" and a "masterpiece" that "hit the nail on the head" in "putting Mr. Goldwater in his proper perspective—most dramatically" and for creating a cartoon that "unquestionably imparts more meaning on 'the conscience of THE conservative' than any editorial prose."[62]

Beyond Block's own mailbox, national and international magazines raised the profile of the cartoon further. *Time* magazine decried it as "one of the lowest blows in [Block's] editorial-cartooning career," while *Pravda*, the official newspaper of the Communist Party of the Soviet Union, turned the cartoon into a propaganda piece by reprinting it with an explanatory note that described how "the rich man is advising the unfortunate Americans on how to become fully equal citizens of the United States."[63] California's *Sacramento Bee* received such a strong reaction to the publication of the cartoon that the newspaper printed a series of letters to the editor during December 1961 with correspondents engaging each other in an ongoing debate on its merits. One such reader accused the paper of having "reached a new editorial low" by printing the cartoon.[64] Another argued that it was "in bad taste and does not accurately reflect the political character of the senator portrayed" before presciently claiming that "the cartoon could have been made in the Pravda composition room."[65] And a third correspondent decried the cartoon as simply "appalling" and declared that it displayed "no sense of humor" in its portrayal of political leaders as "ridiculous morons trying to destroy the welfare and political structure of our democratic government."[66]

FIGURE 25. *Washington Post,* December 6, 1961

Defenders of the cartoon, by contrast, argued that its portrayal of Goldwater was relatively tame compared to earlier Herblock cartoons depicting Richard Nixon climbing out of the gutter.[67] While these Goldwater-themed cartoons may have appeared to be personal attacks to Block's critics, they just as clearly revealed his objection to Goldwater's policies. To some readers, conservatives protested the cartoon precisely because it all too accurately revealed that "the only freedom these conservatives are interested in is to be free to make money."[68] Nonetheless, the majority of the published responses came from conservatives outraged by Block's depiction of Goldwater. In seeking to explain why the cartoon struck such a nerve in himself and others, a conservative letter writer argued that it was representative of "a typical unhealthy attitude which liberals use to attack the sound philosophy of conservatives 'wondering if there is some clear cut alternative to an ever expanding welfare state.'" In a clear echo of Goldwater's own rhetoric, the writer concluded, "Man cannot be free if we take from him the responsibility to care for his material needs."[69] But the response that would have most resonated with California's growing conservative movement was the blunt retort: "This is liberalism? Bah!"[70]

As it became increasingly apparent that Goldwater would be a candidate for the Republican nomination in 1964, he and Block staked out positions for the election. Goldwater was unapologetic in the conservatism he extolled. The larger problem for the conservative movement was how to disassociate itself from the extremism of the John Birch Society while retaining the support and grassroots enthusiasm of its members. Leaders of the movement, including William Buckley, worried that if they failed to shed the label of "lunatic fringe," Goldwater would be unable to prevail over an East Coast, moderate Republican such as New York governor Nelson Rockefeller. Without winning the primary, victory against Lyndon Johnson was a moot point.[71] The solution was to draw a distinction between the Birch Society's founder and leader, Robert Welch, and its members, which Buckley did in a February 1962 *National Review* editorial that questioned how the society could be an "effective political instrument while it is led by a man whose views on current affairs are . . . so critically different from their own, and, for that matter, so far removed from common sense."[72] For his part, Goldwater had long refrained from criticizing the society but grudgingly acknowledged that the electoral prospects of both himself and the movement relied on this distancing. He urged Welch to resign lest the "emblem of irresponsibility . . . be attached to the conservative banner."[73] Even so, when he was asked about his views on the Birch Society during a January 1964 press conference to formally announce the launch of his presidential campaign, he equivocated. He was opposed to "any organization that wants to overthrow our government by violence or treason" but saw "no reason to take a stand against any organization just because they're using their constitutional prerogatives."[74]

As early as November 1961, Block had suggested that Goldwater's efforts to insulate himself from the more radical pronouncements of the

John Birch Society was a difference in semantics rather than principle. November 21's "Mind You, I Don't Put It Exactly That Way" sees Welch and Goldwater in an embrace, each holding signs with supposedly different messages. "The Government Is Full of Communists!" reads Welch's, while Goldwater's declares that "The Government Is Full of Dangerous Left-Wing Extremists!" A month later, Block imagined Goldwater as an undersized cowboy, timidly tip-toeing out of a western-style saloon and holding a flag of surrender emblazoned with Goldwater's own words, attempting to avoid denouncing the "merits of the Birch Society or its members." The other cowboys in the saloon look on, ironically observing, "Why, Sure Enough—It's Fearless Barry Himself." Block's response to Buckley's and Goldwater's denunciations of Welch made this clear. Published on March 6, 1962, the cartoon imagined a dejected Welch discovering his wife, labeled "Birchism," in a passionate embrace with the "GOP Right Wing," who insincerely tells the jilted husband, "Sorry, Old Boy, but Your Wife and I Feel You're Becoming an Embarrassment." The cartoon's message that the society's principles still had a place within the conservative movement could not have been clearer—or more accurate.[75] For his part, Goldwater was aware of the impact these cartoons was having on his public persona and lashed out against Block at least once. When accused in February 1962 of belonging to the Birch Society by the Reverend D. Duncan Howlett, Goldwater angrily retorted that "you frightened people amuse me when your knees tremble at the mention of an organization whose major sin is being against communism," before finishing the exchange with a rhetorical challenge: "Have you ever publicly condemned Herblock, the cartoonist of *The Washington Post,* for his character-destroying cartoons?"[76]

Block depicted the broader internal struggle between establishment and conservative Republicans as a war for the very soul of the Republican Party. Since his "On to the Old OLD Frontier" cartoon, Block had shown the rising influence of Goldwater as an effort to pull both the Republican Party and the nation back from its contemporary policies and alignment with postwar liberalism. He now redoubled these efforts. In cartoons such as June 25, 1963's "Tusk to Tusk" and May 6, 1964's "You Guys Think *You* Have Trouble?" Block used the visual shorthand of the Republican elephant to represent the modern, progressive wing of the Republican Party, while he employed a wooly mammoth to embody Goldwater and his policies.[77] The February 20, 1963, cartoon "Birchhead" was especially revealing. Drawn in response to the election of a member of the Birch Society as president of the California Young Republicans, the cartoon shows a Californian beach littered with the bodies of moderate Republicans as a caveman raises a flag to right-wing extremism over a Spanish Colonial Revival–style building. In a forced perspective, the cartoon's background depicts the skyline of New York City and a gathering of moderate "Rockefeller Republicans" looking on in horrified silence (fig. 26).[78] The dichotomy

FIGURE 26. *Washington Post,* February 20, 1963

between East and West, between moderate Republicanism and right-wing extremism, is stark but also makes plain Block's own assumptions about the legitimacy of political ideas outside of the eastern establishment.

During the early months of 1964, Block's cartoons on the Republican nominating process tended to favor the quixotic write-in candidacy of Henry Cabot Lodge, but as the campaign pivoted to a two-person race between Goldwater and Rockefeller, Block made clear his preference for the New York governor. To Goldwater's supporters, Rockefeller represented no more than a continuation of the liberal policies that they so despised and reaffirmed their idea that the Republican Party was dominated by an eastern elite who cared little for their priorities. This was the core thesis of Phyllis Schlafly's 1964 self-published book *A Choice Not an Echo*. But where Block sought to bolster the values of moderate and liberal Republicans as the lesser of two evils, Schlafly vilified them by arguing they were propped up by "secret Kingmakers" who collaborated with "left-wing" Democrats to profit from a weak foreign policy. This eastern establishment, assisted by the *New York Times* as their "chief propaganda organ," would never allow Goldwater to be the nominee because they recognized him as "a Republican they could not control."[79] Over half a million copies of Schlafly's book were distributed across southern California in the weeks leading up to that state's primary. The work helped mobilize an army of right-wing volunteers who canvassed on Goldwater's behalf and ultimately helped him beat Rockefeller by 51.6 to 48.4 percent, effectively securing the nomination.[80]

Liberals were disturbed by Goldwater's influence over the Republican Party. Perhaps the most influential critiques came from Richard Hofstadter, who argued that Goldwater's rise represented the takeover of the Republican Party by a minority fringe. In a June 1964 letter to the *New York Times,* he declared that Goldwater's views were "not representative of the rank and file" of the Republican Party and urged Dwight Eisenhower to intervene on behalf of the party's moderate wing and "challenge the Goldwater faction."[81] He elaborated further in an essay that appeared in the fall 1964 issue of *Partisan Review* as part of a forum reflecting on the significance of Goldwater's nomination. "Goldwater is something new," he wrote, "very new, in our politics." Explaining that a candidate normally secured his party's nomination for the presidency by winning broad support among party members and building a consensus with other party leaders, Hofstadter declared that Goldwater had done neither. Instead, Goldwater was "creating a party dominated by an uncompromising minority faction of uncommon discipline and dedication." With Goldwater as its leader, Hofstadter warned, the Republican Party was in danger of becoming "a front organization for a minority point of view."[82] Other contributors to the *Partisan Review*'s forum were even less circumspect about their fears. Harvard professor Daniel Bell, for example, argued that the "play-acting of Barry Goldwater has the elements of intellectual farce and sinister politics. It is the angry cry of a social stratum with its back to the world." Meanwhile, Hans Morgenthau, a German American scholar of international relations who was an advisor to the Johnson administration and an ADA board member, was perhaps the most dramatic when he warned that win or lose, Goldwater's candidacy "conjure[d] up a threat to the democratic order, that is, the threat of fascism in America."[83]

With the nomination secure, neither Goldwater nor Block held back their views. Block greeted Goldwater's victory with a graphic cartoon titled "An American Tragedy" that foreshadowed Hofstadter's fears about Goldwater's takeover of the Republican Party by depicting a right-wing extremist leaning over the side of a boat labeled "We're in the Mainstream of Republican Thinking" to drown Republican moderates.[84] Block made a similar point four days later by depicting Goldwater with a giant axe nonchalantly resting on his shoulder, having decapitated the GOP elephant and insisting, "Shake Hands—This Is a Time for Unity."[85] Meanwhile, Goldwater's campaign presented America with an uncompromising vision of conservative values. He promised to roll back the achievements of both the New Deal and postwar liberalism, to privatize public utilities such as the Tennessee Valley Authority, to oppose passage of the Civil Rights Act, and to pursue a more aggressive foreign policy against the Soviet Union. The high point of his campaign arguably came at the 1964 Republican National Convention held in California. In accepting the nomination before thousands of his most ardent and committed supporters, Goldwater declared that "extremism in the defense of liberty is no vice. . . . Moderation in the pursuit of justice is no virtue."[86]

Block was clearly horrified by what he was witnessing and shared his dismay with his readers. During the party's national convention, he depicted a Goldwater-supporting delegate declaring that Republicans "Stand upon Our Historic Principles—" while standing on a broken portrait of Abraham Lincoln.[87] The next day, Block doubled down on the theme. Adapting the title of Schlafly's book, which Goldwater had adopted as his campaign slogan, Block depicted the same angry Goldwater delegate declaring, "We Want a Choice—*a Choice*—Not an Echo—*an Echo*—." Shadowing him is a nineteenth-century slaveowner, whip in hand, who represented what Block viewed as the true Republican platform: inequality, antifederal government, violence (fig. 27). This, Block was arguing, was the politics not of 1964 but of 1864.[88]

In his book *Straight Herblock,* published several weeks before the presidential election, Block made clear his disdain for Goldwater and his conservative policies. Riffing on Khrushchev's reported disappointment that he was unable to visit Disneyland during his 1959 visit to the United States, Block introduced his readers to "Goldwaterland." While this was not the prehistoric world depicted in the "On to the Old OLD Frontier" cartoon, it was nonetheless a place rooted in the past. "Here, as in Disneyland, you enter via Main Street, and immediately you are back to the turn of the century. Here are old-fashioned stores and buildings," he continued, "everything delightful and good and nostalgic." This conservative fantasy appealed because the land's host, an unnamed Barry Goldwater, "knows that we all have a longing for the old days as we like to think they were." Thus, the architecture, prices, taxes, and moral standards of Goldwaterland may all hail from the early 1900s, but they nonetheless retain "modern miracle drugs and indoor plumbing" so that it mixes "the best of yesterday and today." And best of all, there is "not much government . . . to worry about" so that everybody is "well fed [and] nobody is ever ill." This conservative utopia was, in short, "Never-Was Land."[89]

Goldwater's crushing defeat in the 1964 election—he received only 27 million votes to Johnson's 41 million and lost the electoral college 486–52, winning only five southern states and Arizona—seemed to bring definitive closure to the question that lay at the heart of all of these issues: what values should define American society? For Block, the answer had been obvious all along and could be found in a federal government that actively sought to protect the rights of the most vulnerable Americans. This might mean equal protections under the law, the separation of church

FIGURE 27. *Washington Post,* July 15, 1964

and state, commonsense gun policies, or a cooperative foreign policy—in other words, a continuation of the liberal consensus and its postwar priorities. As for those who opposed these goals? Block was equally certain. In a December 1963 lecture at Columbia University he explained why he so adamantly rejected the rise of conservatism as a legitimate movement. "I'm inclined to wince every time I see the good old term conservative," he told his audience, "applied to extremists or to those who accept the support of extremists." Specifically calling out Goldwater's past support of McCarthyism and equivocation on the John Birch Society as proof of someone who was neither "conscientious [nor] a conservative in the tradition we have known in this country," Block went on to question whether it was even desirable to find common cause with such an ideology.[90]

And this was the heart of the issue. By depicting conservative ideology as antithetical to American democracy and its practitioners as dangerous extremists, Block helped persuade conservatives that liberalism was neither prepared for nor willing to listen to their concerns. A bumper sticker that soon started appearing on cars proclaimed that "26,000,000 Americans Can't Be Wrong," an explicit statement of defiance from conservatives unwilling to accept the defeat of their candidate and already looking toward the next election.[91] Actor Ronald Reagan made the same point in the pages of *National Review* less than a month after the election when he wrote that conservatives believed they "represent the forgotten American—that simple soul who goes to work . . . pays for his kids' schooling, contributes to his church and charity, and knows there 'just ain't no such thing as a free lunch.'"[92] This sense of isolation from the political establishment helped sustain the grassroots movement that had propelled Goldwater and conservative values to the forefront of the Republican Party. All they needed was a means of persuading moderate Republican and Democratic voters that they were not the extremists Block and other liberals had portrayed them as. Such conservatives found that cause in the growing number of political protests that not only seemed to threaten their values and security but also appeared to them to be the natural consequences of liberal policies. Motivated by such issues as opposition to the Vietnam War, frustration at the lack of racial justice outside of the South, and the expansion of gender-based rights, these social movements, as depicted by Block, further exposed the fractures within American society increasingly threatening the liberal order.

5

"I'M AFRAID TO LOOK"

Defending Liberalism from the Left

ADDRESSING THE NATION FROM HIS desk in the Oval Office on March 31, 1968, President Lyndon Johnson updated the American public on the state of the Vietnam War. Two months earlier the North Vietnamese had launched the Tet Offensive in an effort to trigger a popular uprising that would lead to the collapse of the South Vietnamese government and the withdrawal of American troops from the region. Early on January 31, some eighty thousand Viet Cong fighters had initiated coordinated attacks on cities across South Vietnam. Their targets included the U.S. embassy in South Vietnam's capital city, Saigon, where nineteen guerrillas seized part of the building before they were killed by American forces. Although the North Vietnamese were ultimately repelled, the Tet Offensive, and especially the brief occupation of the embassy building in Saigon, fundamentally changed the American public's perception of the war. According to opinion polls conducted in mid-February, a majority of Americans did not approve of Johnson's handling of the war, and more significantly, they did not believe it was a conflict America was likely to win as the administration's policy then stood. Even so, General William Westmoreland's request that another 206,000 troops be sent to Southeast Asia to help buttress American forces was widely expected to be fulfilled, at least in part.[1]

Johnson's speech confounded expectations. Not only would there be no major increase in the number of American forces being sent to Vietnam, he also ordered a halt to the bombing of over 90 percent of North Vietnam and called for the immediate commencement of peace talks with Hanoi. After making these announcements, Johnson shifted gear and talked about the cost of the war, both to the nation and to himself as commander in chief. Evoking his predecessor's inaugural address, he acknowledged that American soldiers had been asked to "pay any price, bear any burden, meet any hardship, support any friend, oppose any foe to assure the survival and the success of liberty." No one understood this better than himself. "I have lived—daily and nightly—with the cost of this war," he stated. "I know the pain that it has inflicted. I know, perhaps better than anyone, the misgivings that it has aroused."

And then he ended his address with a bombshell. Making reference to another assassinated president, Johnson looked at the bitter divisiveness caused by the war and used the words of Abraham Lincoln to warn that "a house divided against itself by the spirit of faction, of party, of region, of religion, of race, is a house that cannot stand." It was his responsibility, "as President of all the people," to prevent this. "I do not believe that I should devote an hour or a day of my time to any personal partisan causes or to any duties other than the awesome duties of this office—the Presidency of your country," he concluded. "Accordingly, I shall not seek, and I will not accept, the nomination of my party for another term as your President."[2]

Block did not hold back his delight at these announcements. His April 2 cartoon, titled "Gave Proof through the Night . . . ," depicted the American flag as fireworks exploded behind it in celebration of Johnson's decision both to deescalate the war and to not seek reelection, the patriotic and celebratory imagery reinforced by the title's quotation from "The Star-Spangled Banner" (fig. 28).[3] The cartoon represented a moment of catharsis as Block's frustration with Johnson's presidency found a release. Block believed, as he wrote later that year, that the administration had created a "credibility gap; a generation gap; the gap between hope and achievement; the cosmic gulf between space flight and the nearby slums; and the Grand Canyon between opinions on the Vietnam War."[4]

How had Block become so disillusioned? In the 1964 election, after all, Johnson had run on an unapologetically liberal platform and resoundingly

"Gave Proof Through The Night . . ."

FIGURE 28. *Washington Post,* April 2, 1968

beaten Barry Goldwater while the Democratic Party had added to its majorities in both the House and Senate. But the year 1968 looked very different to the world that Block and other liberals might have anticipated based on that overwhelming victory four years earlier. In the weeks leading up to Johnson's address, the nation was bracing itself for yet another summer of rioting as African Americans in the urban North sought the same improvements to their lives that the civil rights movement had appeared to have won in the rural South. Women, Latinos, American Indians, and gays and lesbians were similarly engaged in social movements agitating for an expansion of federal protections to their communities. And overshadowing every aspect of Johnson's presidency was the quagmire of Vietnam, which had launched an antiwar movement unprecedented in its scale. What connected each of these protest movements was their generational nature. As the activist group Students for a Democratic Society (SDS) made clear in their 1962 Port Huron Statement, many younger Americans had grown disillusioned with the politics of postwar liberalism, which they argued was complicit in the racial discrimination, economic inequality, and Cold War paranoia that blighted American society. While liberal policies had undoubtedly improved the lives of their parents, these campaigners—whether middle-class white students or African Americans not living in the South—were united in wondering what improvements liberalism would bring to their own lives.

The Voting Rights Act of 1965 was a landmark piece of legislation that marked the culmination of the civil rights movement's efforts to pressure the federal government to protect the voting rights of African Americans across the South. In signing it into law on August 6, Johnson declared the moment to be a "triumph for freedom as huge as any victory that has ever been won on any battlefield." After outlining the long history of injustices that necessitated this legislation, Johnson issued a warning and a challenge to the African American community and its leaders. It was not enough simply to have the right to vote, he admonished. That right must also be exercised. To do so could not "be met simply by protests and demonstrations" but must instead be achieved through education and outreach. Nonetheless, Johnson concluded, doing so was worth the effort to ensure that "the rights woven into law" might also be "woven into the fabric of our Nation."[5]

It was shocking to most Americans when the Los Angeles neighborhood of Watts erupted in five days of rioting just five days later. The violence ended only after 13,900 members of the National Guard came in to restore order. Thirty-four people were killed and hundreds injured, almost four thousand were arrested, and approximately $35 million in damage had been inflicted.[6] Members of the administration reacted with incredulity. Johnson asked after being told the news, "How is it possible after all we've accomplished? How could it be? Is the world topsy-turvy?" while Deputy Attorney General Ramsey Clark insisted, "That can't be. There must be a great distortion in the communication of the facts, and that just can't be."[7] These initial reactions from within the administration foreshadowed white Americans' broader uncertainty about how best to respond to the news of Watts. In public remarks after the riot had been put down, Johnson acknowledged that the residents of Watts were "imprisoned by the shadowed walls of hatred, coming of age in the poverty of slums, facing their future without education or skills and with little hope of rewarding work," and vowed that his administration would work harder to confront these inequities. Yet he also condemned the violence as a betrayal of American values. "Injustices of our society shall be overcome by the peaceful processes of our society," he declared before going on to assert that "there is no greater wrong, in our democracy, than violent, willful disregard of law. . . . To resort to terror and violence . . . strikes from the hand of the Negro the very weapons with which he is achieving his own emancipation."[8]

Most liberals agreed with this interpretation of the riot. The ADA, for example, echoed Johnson's statement in its monthly periodical *ADA World* by both reassuring its members that, no matter the underlying inequities, the rioting was to be "condemned not condoned" and urging the administration to do more to enforce the provisions of the Civil Rights Act and ensure racial equality.[9] But Watts was just the first of a series of riots that tore through the urban centers of America between 1965 and 1968. There were thirty-eight riots in 1966, killing seven and injuring a further four hundred. The following year witnessed an even higher number of urban riots. In the first nine months of 1967, there were some 164 disorders, 33 of which required the intervention of state police, while 8 culminated in the National Guard being mobilized. The two biggest riots, in Newark and Detroit, each lasted for almost a week and resulted in 23 and 43 deaths respectively. Finally, 1968 witnessed an estimated 155 outbursts, resulting in 75 deaths.[10]

Responding to this violence, President Johnson established the National Advisory Commission on Civil Disorders, better known as the Kerner Commission, in July 1967, which seven months later released its controversial conclusion that "white society is deeply implicated in the Ghetto. White institutions created it, white institutions maintain it, and white society condones it."[11] Later that same year, Block gave his own interpretation of the causes of the rioting. Approvingly quoting long passages from the Kerner Report, he wrote that the "white racism which has bred ignorance and all its attendant consequences among many Negroes has been the result of ignorance on the part of many whites. They haven't known what life in the ghettos is like. They haven't acted to correct the situations that create impossible pressures, poverty, crime and violence. They haven't been aware of 'what's happening' except when those conditions erupt in disorders."[12] In other words, if only whites had been fully cognizant of the conditions faced by African Americans living in urban centers, they would have acted to end those inequities and avoided the violence and deaths that characterized the summers of 1965, 1967, and 1968. Block was writing, however, with the benefit of three years' hindsight. In truth, his liberalism, with its conception of racial discrimination as fundamentally a moral issue that could be corrected through legislative reform, had left him unprepared for the wave of rioting that swept through northern cities during the mid-1960s. As a result, Block's work failed to connect the structural inequalities—such as unemployment, overcrowded schools, poor housing conditions, and higher rents—experienced by African Americans living in the industrial North's inner cities with the actions of these protestors.

Block explored all of these subjects in his cartoons at various points throughout the postwar period, but his treatment of them was almost exclusively from the perspective of their impact on whites. For example, between 1955 and 1965, Block's concern about the impact of inadequate school facilities on American society was dealt with a total of thirty-six times in cartoons such as January 31, 1955's "Emergency Alarm" and January 8, 1961's "It's Too Small to Play House. Let's Play School."[13] He depicted the issue in a variety of contexts, ranging from congressional inactivity to its importance to national security in the Cold War era, and from its impact on families to its presentation as a preferable option to the construction of new jails in urban planners' efforts to reduce delinquency rates. But the one constant was his depiction of white children as those who were being disadvantaged by the poor standard of educational facilities available to them. This is not to say that African American children were wholly absent from these cartoons, but Block sharply distinguished between the subjects in which it was appropriate for each to appear.

Whereas white children were seen in cartoons with potentially universal significance—teacher shortages, overcrowding, outdated facilities—Black children appeared only in cartoons that commented on issues specifically affecting the African American community, namely cartoons focused on segregation and the reluctance of whites to follow through on the Supreme Court's ruling in *Brown v. Board of Education.*[14]

By showing African Americans only in one context and making white children the default for all other education-related subjects, as well as other issues such as poverty, health-care access, and poor housing conditions that were identified as the priorities of qualitative liberalism, Block reinforced postwar liberalism's sequestration of segregation as a "Black" issue and everything else as "white" issues. He may have believed, and intended, that his cartoons commenting on the lack of educational resources were speaking to all Americans, regardless of their race. But his decision to codify educational issues along racial lines ultimately served to reinforce his readers' ignorance of the realities of the discriminatory practices that existed across the country and did nothing to expose the daily hardships faced by African Americans living in the urban North. In this regard, these cartoons were a reflection of the prevailing liberal framework that recognized the injustices faced by southern Blacks as a consequence of the legal edifice of Jim Crow, which could be dismantled through federal action, but struggled to see the same types of injustice in the North as anything more than the result of poverty or the exaggerated grievances of violent troublemakers.[15]

There were exceptions to this, such as a December 20, 1962, cartoon that critiqued the Kennedy administration's failure to follow through with a campaign promise of ending housing discrimination.[16] This was followed on May 30, 1963, by a cartoon captioned "Faster! . . . Here It Takes All the Running *You* Can Do, to Keep in the Same Place," a slightly adapted quotation from Lewis Carroll's *Through the Looking-Glass.* The cartoon imagines Carroll's Alice, labeled "Civil Rights Progress," and the Queen of Clubs, labeled "Moves for Racial Equality," flying over a chessboard together. In each of the board's white spaces are perfect examples of suburbia: middle-class homes surrounded by trees and open spaces. In the black spaces, however, almost invisible because of the dark shading that Block employed, are tenement buildings crowded into their squares and leaving little doubt as to the squalor they represent (fig. 29).[17] These two cartoons represented an astute depiction of the harsh differences that existed between life in the suburbs and the inner city that demonstrates Block's own awareness of these inequities and also likely exposed his readers to ideas to which they may have otherwise been unfamiliar. They also show a willingness on Block's part to critique liberalism's underestimation of the extreme poverty and pent-up anger and alienation that existed within these highly segregated neighborhoods.

Several of Block's cartoons similarly reveal that he was conscious that the more overt problems of racism and discrimination were not

FIGURE 29. *Washington Post,* May 30, 1963

limited solely to the former Confederacy and forced his northern readers to question the nature of their own prejudices. The most common subject Block used to illustrate this was imagining the continued efforts of many labor unions across the North to maintain segregated practices. As historian Thomas J. Sugrue argues in his important study of postwar Detroit, although the national leadership of unions such as the United Automobile Workers held a progressive stance on civil rights issues, white rank-and-file members "often abetted by local leaders, worked to protect the color line." As a result, African Americans faced limited job advancement opportunities, and their complaints about racial discrimination were ignored by the unions.[18] Over the course of four cartoons produced between March 1960 and June 1963, Block sought to draw the attention of his readers to the segregated nature of many local union chapters across the North. His cartoon of March 12, 1963, for example, imagined a member of the "Northern Jim Crow Local" standing beside a sign that reads "No Negroes Need Apply," and with a clearly bemused expression on his face, asking the reader, "What's the Matter? We Don't Say 'Niggers' Up Here."[19]

His most pointed and effective cartoon about the nature of northern prejudice was, however, unrelated to the working classes and instead targeted the very constituency most likely to be consumers of his cartoons: white-collar workers. This May 1963 cartoon showed a group of white, middle-class morning commuters waiting at a train station marked "North Suburbia," so there could be no question as to the cartoon's locale. To pass the time, they are reading a newspaper account of events occurring in Birmingham, Alabama, where Bull Connor, the city's commissioner of public safety, has authorized the use of high-pressure water hoses and police attack dogs against peaceful protestors, including young children. In a caption that perfectly encapsulated the many contradictions of liberal attitudes toward race, Block had one of his commuters indignantly ask his neighbor, "Those Alabama Stories Are Sickening. Why Can't They Be Like Us and Find Some Nice, Refined Way to Keep the Negroes Out?"[20]

It is therefore telling that when violence erupted in Watts, Block's response was to focus not on the underlying conditions and frustrations that existed within the neighborhood, and had built up over time until they found an outlet in the riot, but on the white racism and subsequent actions of the city's authorities. In this regard, he was repeating a model he had developed in response to white racism and violence in places such as Birmingham and Selma. The first cartoon he drew after the rioting began—August 17, 1965's "You Ugly Devil!"—showed a white man, labeled "Stupid Injustices" and with the brutish physical characteristics Block typically reserved for white southerners, staring into a pool of water and seeing his own reflection, labeled "Stupid Violence." He revisited Watts five days later in the cartoon "How Could Anyone Think We Might Have Any Responsibility for What Goes on Here?" which depicted Sam Yorty and William H. Parker, Los Angeles's mayor and chief of police respectively, incredulously denying that they bore any responsibility for the riots.[21] Although neither cartoon attempted to engage readers with insights into the motivations of Watts's residents, Block did anticipate the Kerner Commission's later conclusion that the rioting was caused by white racism. The images also stood in stark contrast to the dominant narratives the national media presented as to the riot's causes. The *Post,* like other newspapers, initially reported the rioting as a breakdown in law and order and used language that coded the rioters as violent criminals battling against the lawful representatives of government. In a front-page story printed on August 15, for example, the paper breathlessly reported that "Negro hoodlums [had] waged a guerrilla war with 5000 National Guardsmen and law officers in battle-scarred south Los Angeles." Elsewhere in that same issue, the *Post* printed a series of photographs depicting ruined streets that had become, in the words of their captions, a "hell for lawmen and property owners" in which "the rioters' rage turned to destruction," and looters "pelted firemen [with bricks] and forced them to withdraw." In this article, and others like it, the underlying narrative of the riot was framed as a minority of brazen criminals battling against heroic police officers and firemen trying to protect the broader, and law-abiding, community of Watts.[22]

Even after Watts, Block's cartoons only occasionally analyzed the experiences of African Americans in the urban North. July 17, 1966's "The Built-In Bomb," which imagined the "Slums" as a time-bomb sitting in the heart of America's cities, ready to explode at any moment, stands as the lone cartoon from this two-year period to make any sort of gesture in this direction.[23] Instead, Block once more focused on the importance of congressional action, connecting the poverty and violence in America's cities to the failure of Congress to pass Lyndon Johnson's proposed 1966 civil rights bill, which would have banned discrimination in the sale and renting of houses. In September 20, 1966's "Open Housing," for example, Block showed a member of the Senate nonchalantly lighting a cigar from a burning torch that had presumably been used only moments earlier to burn down the ruined building he is standing in front of, representing the recently defeated civil rights legislation.[24] It would not be until the summer of 1967 that Block began to make serious and explicit connections between the structural inequalities of inadequate housing, unemployment, poor schools, and white racism found in the inner city and the dangers of renewed rioting.[25]

At the same time, Block continued to assert that the solution to these problems lay primarily in congressional action and sharply criticized what he saw as politicians' misplaced priorities, especially the Republican Party's focus on passing legislation aimed at preventing "organized elements" and "outside agitators" from moving into urban communities with the express intent of provoking an otherwise contented group of residents to riot. Widespread claims that these agitators were actually acting out a communist plot to create instability in American society as a result of rising tensions between African Americans and whites gave this theory an even more sinister edge and were given a veneer of official credence by the white establishment.[26] High-profile figures such as former President Eisenhower, for example, hinted at the existence of a conspiracy, while newspapers breathlessly reported on Soviet attempts to leverage the riots for propaganda purposes. A grand jury blamed racial violence in Cleveland in 1966 on "a small group of professional radicals and Communists," and a major FBI investigation was launched specifically to determine if there had been any communist influence behind the rioting in Watts.[27] Indeed, according to a 1965 Gallup Poll, 78 percent of whites believed that the Communist Party of America had played at least some role in inciting racial disturbances. So prevalent was this theory, and so strong this belief among politicians, that the 1968 Civil Rights Act included language that explicitly prohibited interstate travel by those intending to incite a riot.[28]

Block's outright dismissal of the notion that organized groups such as the Communist Party played a role in inciting the riots was clearly seen in two cartoons drawn in July 1967. In "Keep a Sharp Lookout for Outside

Agitators," published on July 13, a member of Congress is depicted sitting on top of a pressure cooker boiling over representing "Slum Ghetto Condition" while eagerly looking out for the seemingly ubiquitous "outside agitators" that city and state leaders insisted were responsible for inciting the riots. In his eagerness to spot communists, however, the congressman is oblivious to the white racist, labeled "Anti-Equal Opportunity," who is happily feeding the fire with the fuel of "Slum Schooling," "Slum Housing," and "Unemployment." Twelve days later, Block drew Congress as the Roman emperor Nero, obliviously playing the tune of an "Anti-Agitators Bill" on his violin as America's cities burn in the background.[29] In both instances, the cartoons simultaneously revealed Block's disdain for the notion that the riots were in any way influenced by these alleged outside agitators but also reaffirmed his belief in the importance of strong congressional action to prevent future outbreaks of violence.

As such, he was reflecting the prevailing attitudes of the white liberal establishment, which largely sought to rationalize the rioting by ignoring its underlying causes and instead condemned the African American community for sabotaging their prospects for future civil rights reform. The *Boston Globe*, for example, declared the "Civil Rights Revolution Stalled by Extremists, White and Black," in an article that compared the rioting in Los Angeles to the murder of a civil rights worker in Hayneville, Alabama, while *Time* urged African Americans to practice "patience, to let the new laws work, to let elections bring about the change implicit in all the stress on voting rights, to let the courts strike at anyone who discriminates in housing or jobs."[30] Lyndon Johnson, meanwhile, publicly declared that "a rioter with a Molotov cocktail in his hands is not fighting for civil rights any more than a Klansman with a sheet on his back and a mask on his face."[31] Privately, Johnson was even more explicit in expressing his concerns over the impact the rioting would have on future legislative reform when he told his domestic affairs advisor that "Negroes will end up pissing in the aisles of the Senate . . . [and] will once again take unwise actions out of frustration, impatience, and anger."[32] Although he was never as crude as Johnson, Block's cartoons increasingly sought to reinforce these arguments in a visual form, reflecting both the president's public comparison between African American activism and white supremacists and his private fear that their militancy would sabotage future reform.

Block had written as early as 1964 about the rise of "demagogues among Negroes . . . who will seek to wrest control from responsible leaders," a warning that clearly stated his belief that a more militant form of African American protest than "responsible" leaders such as Martin Luther King advocated would not be embraced by the liberal establishment.[33] But, as the slogan "Black Power" rose to national prominence in the summer of 1966, prompting a so-called white backlash against civil rights reform, so too did the liberal media create a narrative that framed the Black Power movement as antithetical to the goals and achievements of the liberal-supported civil rights movement. In a July 1966 article titled "The New Racism" that began by celebrating the Supreme Court's 1954 ruling in *Brown v. Board of Education* striking down the doctrine of "separate but equal," for example, *Time* warned its readers against those "militant ideologues . . . impatient with what they consider the glacial pace of progress in civil rights" who now threatened to "perpetuate the very separatism against which Negroes have fought so successfully."[34] In a series of speeches given during the summer of 1966, Vice President Hubert Humphrey similarly decried "Black Nationalism" for its focus on "separation and exclusion as the remedy for racial injustice and evils of the past," and warned that the movement had "created a backlash of resentment among whites." The true victim of their violence, he concluded, was "the cause of social justice."[35]

Block's cartoons from the era were, in their own way, just as blunt in their condemnation of African American activists who rejected integration and nonviolent tactics in favor of Black nationalism and armed self-defense. In both September 20, 1966's "Open Housing" and September 30's "That's Showing Those Damned White Civil-Righters," for example, Block depicted "Black Power Demagogues" working together with "White Power Bigots" to undermine the efforts of white liberals to enact meaningful legislative reform.[36] In a similar vein, Block's memorial to Martin Luther King after his assassination in April 1968 was a cartoon that shows the civil rights leader as a ghostly figure cradling a book containing his ideals and nonviolent philosophy. But King is shown being menaced by two arms, one white and one Black, holding a smoking gun and a burning torch respectively. The cartoon's title, "Enemies of the Dream," connected the two sets of extremists—Black and white—and made them equally culpable for both King's assassination and preventing his vision of racial equality from becoming a reality. Two days later, Block made this connection even more explicit, drawing a cartoon that showed the hands of a white man and an African American grasped in friendship with the celebration of "The Work of Martin Luther King" threatened by a brutal club labeled "Wallace-Carmichael Racism" (fig. 30). The cartoon references both Alabama's staunchly segregationist former Governor George Wallace and the Black Power activist Stokely Carmichael, who had previously been a leader of the Student Nonviolent Coordinating Committee and whose presence in Washington, DC, the night of King's assassination was blamed by the news media for inciting the ensuing riots that rocked the city.[37] Cartoons

FIGURE 30. *Washington Post,* April 9, 1968

such as these, with their direct connection between the violence of white supremacists and Black nationalism, underscored Block's belief that the only acceptable form of African American protest against racial inequality was that endorsed by the white liberal establishment.

In other cartoons, Block sought to draw a contrast between the violent rhetoric and actions of the Black Power movement and the forms of nonviolent protest the liberal establishment found acceptable. On July 7, 1966, for example, Block depicted an African American, casually dressed in light-colored clothing and representing the very definition of respectability, being menaced by the cartoon's titular "Dangerous Genie" who is emerging from a container labeled "Black Power." The genie's muscular appearance, threatening arms, and fearsome expression combine in an unsubtle warning against what Block viewed as the potentially fatal appeal of militant actions to future civil rights progress.[38] The clearest example, however, is May 28, 1968's "Race," which depicts two African Americans—one labeled "Progress," the other "Violence"—engaged in a closely matched foot race (fig. 31). The cartoon is drawn to emphasize what Block saw as the moral stakes at risk from Black nationalism. Where the figure representing Progress is depicted in a white polo shirt and with a determined but kindly expression, the character Violence is drawn in darker shades and wearing a vest that emphasizes his poorer and less cultured background. But most notable are the facial expressions this Black Power figure has been given—an angry scowl, a set jaw, unkempt hair, and with the whites of his eyes prominently visible—that together serve to reinforce which of these characters Block's readers are expected to empathize with and to cheer on. Progress may be holding on to a slight lead in this race, raising hope for future reforms and gains in civil rights, but the unspoken assumption underlying this cartoon was that "Progress" is leading because he is playing by the rules laid out by the white establishment, and that the tactics of Black Power represented by the "Violence" figure had no role to play in the national civil rights movement.[39]

Block, like most other white Americans, was ultimately unable to view the Black Power movement beyond the context of its apparently inflammatory rhetoric, which was widely condemned in the media as antiwhite and a new form of racism. What is significant about his cartoons, however, is that victims of this "racism" were not shown to be the white

FIGURE 31. *Washington Post,* May 28, 1968

population who so feared the emergence of Black nationalism but instead the "respectable" members of the African American community. Indeed, his representation of this community remained essentially unchanged from the halcyon days of his depiction of the civil rights movement in the late 1950s and early 1960s when he imagined them as the passive, law-abiding victims of white racism. Now, however, these essentially identical actors became the victims of Black militancy. In his "Dangerous Genie" cartoon for example, the African American who has unleashed the titular genie has as little agency as Block had given the subjects of earlier civil rights cartoons such as "Somebody from Outside Must Have Influenced Them" and "Pray Keep Moving, Brother." Agency was instead given to representative members of the Black Power movement, who were universally portrayed in a negative light and, significantly, shown in opposition not to the white society that the media presented as threatening but instead to the broader African American community and the hard-won gains of the civil rights movement itself. With this portrayal of "good" African American civil rights activists engaged in a struggle against the temptation and violent nature of the "bad" proponents of Black Power, it is not hard to see cartoons such as "Dangerous Genie" and "Race" as prototypical examples of what historian Peniel E. Joseph has described as the consistent unwillingness of "historians and professional scholars... to research the movement on its own terms, preferring instead to characterize Black Power as the 'evil twin' that wrecked civil rights."[40]

The Black Power movement was just one of several social movements—including the Chicano movement, the gay rights movement, and the American Indian movement—to emerge during the 1960s in an effort to win a wide range of rights and new legal protections. But the most prominent was the women's rights movement, which was a reaction against the image of domesticity expected of women as part of the conformist postwar society. Betty Friedan's 1963 book *The Feminine Mystique* first articulated for many American women the frustration and unfulfillment they felt with their lives, which Friedan dubbed "the problem that has no name" and which she argued was caused not by women themselves but by the constraints and expectations placed on them "to be perfect wives and mothers" at the expense of their own dreams and ambitions.[41] Although many rejected Friedan's thesis, the book inspired an increasing number of women to call for greater reproductive rights, equal responsibility in the home for housekeeping and child-rearing, an end to domestic violence, protections in the workplace against sexual harassment and the "glass ceiling" that limited job opportunities, and an end to official legal inequalities. In many ways, the growing movement was remarkably successful at achieving its goals. The right to use birth control was affirmed by the Food and Drug Administration in 1960 and again by the Supreme Court in 1965's ruling *Griswold v. Connecticut.* The Equal Pay Act of 1963 abolished wage disparity based on sex, while Title VII of the Civil Rights Act of 1964 prevented discrimination based on sex in the workplace. But as members of the civil rights movement had learned, passing laws was one thing, enforcing them was something else entirely. In particular, the inability of the Equal Employment Opportunity Commission to enforce the Title VII provision inspired a group of women, led by Friedan, to form the National Organization for Women (NOW) in 1966. Intended to replicate the success of the civil rights movement, the leaders of NOW declared that it was time "to take action to bring women into full participation in the mainstream of American society now" and to "endeavor to change the false image of women now prevalent in the mass media . . . [that] perpetuate contempt for women by society and by women for themselves."[42]

Despite all of this activity, the women's rights movement was essentially absent from Block's cartoons throughout the 1960s. Of the movement's priorities, the one issue he directly engaged with was birth control, which is seen in two 1968 cartoons that critiqued the Catholic Church's opposition to the contraceptive pill.[43] The broader fight for women's equal rights was depicted just once, in a January 1967 cartoon drawn to mark the victory of Lurleen Wallace, George Wallace's wife, in Alabama's gubernatorial election. The cartoon imagines George, who was prevented from running for a second term because of term limits, wearing an apron and glaring over his shoulder at three people—a Black male activist, a white man, and a white woman—who are together holding a sign advocating for equal rights and innocently asking the arch-segregationist, "Would You Care to Join the Movement, Brother?"[44] This is the closest Block came in his cartoons during the 1960s to declaring his support for the women's movement. Yet his inclusion of a woman advocating for her own rights was clearly intended to highlight the reversal of gender roles that Wallace was experiencing, contrasting it with his longstanding and virulent opposition to civil rights, rather than as a commentary on the importance of women's equality as an issue in its own right.

Block's relative lack of attention to women's rights was not a statement about his views on those issues but instead a reflection of postwar liberalism's own lack of interest in the question when compared to the seemingly more pressing concerns of civil rights. This is not to say that women did not appear in Block's work. On the contrary, women were a regular feature within the scenes he imagined but Block only rarely drew cartoons related to subjects that might have been considered of specific interest to women. More typically, women were depicted in what could best be described as gender-specific roles and rarely given any agency of their own. When not simply included as part of a crowd or to complete the depiction of a family, women were typically shown as housewives, mothers, and shoppers and were depicted in scenarios that emphasized and reaffirmed these roles. Even on the rare occasions that women were given a professional occupation, it was as teachers, nurses, and secretaries, all positions that the male-dominated society of the postwar era deemed appropriate for women to possess. These were, in other words, the very type of "false image" that NOW decried and urged the media to stop propagating.

In other cartoons that included depictions of women, Block relied on three major tropes: dangerous seductress, innocent victim, or as a symbol of American values. Typical of the portrayal of women as seductresses was June 24, 1956's "I've Been Deceived and I'm a Lonesome Little Girl," which cast a woman dressed in a cleavage-baring, skin-tight dress as a proxy for "Communist Leaders Outside Russia." Block depicted this character sitting on a park bench attempting to seduce a perplexed-looking middle-class man who represents noncommunist political parties across Europe, while Soviet leader Nikita Khrushchev looks on from the bushes.[45] Meanwhile, Block's depiction of women as helpless victims is seen in numerous cartoons. Its earliest use was to highlight the growing humanitarian crisis in Europe that followed the end of the Second World War, when Block drew a series of cartoons depicting an emaciated girl in situations that contrasted her plight with the wanton consumption of postwar American society, and continued into the 1970s with cartoons such as December 10, 1972's "Tell Us about the Voices That Speak to You," which portrays America's news media as a woman sitting in chains while being questioned by a medieval court.[46] But one of his most graphic uses of this trope occurred on March 23, 1948. In "Going! Going!—," drawn as tensions in Palestine were quickly escalating into a crisis that would erupt only weeks later in the 1948 Arab-Israeli War, Block imagined the United Nations and its efforts to avert war as a naked woman standing on an auction block as the oil interests of Great Britain and the United States sell her to a group of leering sheikhs.[47] The cartoon might have powerfully illustrated Block's anger at how national and corporate self-interests were undermining the UN's efforts to resolve the crisis, but it also underscored the problematic ways in which he depicted women within his work.

By far the most common of these tropes, however, was Block's use of women as a representation for such concepts as "Peace," "Liberty," or "Justice." In this regard, he was hardly alone as cartoonists had been ascribing these values with feminine characteristics since at least the early nineteenth century.[48] Thus, the Statue of Liberty appears in cartoons such as October 9, 1946's "What Happened to the One We Used to Have?" when Block sought to comment on threats to American civil liberties, while Lady Justice was regularly employed as a visual representation of the American judicial system.[49] Block, however, regularly subverted the values encoded in these characters by placing them in positions in which they were vulnerable or victimized. In February 4, 1949's ". . . Not Much Change in Temperature . . . ," for example, a woman labeled "Peace" is shown dressed in rags and shivering in the middle of a snowstorm as a visual metaphor for the state of relations between the United States and the Soviet Union. More graphically, May 11, 1965's "Hung Jury" depicts a group of Klansmen celebrating the lynching of Lady Justice, her scales discarded at her feet. And June 1, 1947's "I Don't See Any Danger of Fascism" sees the Statue of Liberty lying trampled underneath a member of the House of Representative's Committee on Un-American Activities.[50]

Block's lack of interest in depicting women outside of these narrowly defined tropes is further revealed by the absence of real-life female figures from his cartoons. Across the thirty-year period that began on January 1, 1946, and ended December 31, 1975, Block drew only thirty-six cartoons that involved a public female figure. Furthermore, of the nineteen women depicted in these cartoons, only six appeared more than once. Of those six, only Margaret Chase Smith, a moderate Republican senator from Maine who publicly opposed fellow senator Joseph McCarthy and his anticommunist activities in the early 1950s, was depicted in a positive light or setting. The Indian prime minister Indira Gandhi, meanwhile, was regularly depicted in the mid-1970s as both a dictator and terrorist and placed in situations where she was shown to be undermining democratic principles.[51] Closer to home, four of the five appearances of Ovetta Culp Hobby (President Eisenhower's secretary of the U.S. Department of Health, Education and Welfare) aligned with cartoons critiquing the state of America's school system. In each of these cartoons, Block labeled Hobby with the derogatory title "Dept. of Not-Too-Much Health, Education, and Welfare," reflecting his belief that the Eisenhower administration was uncaring and not doing enough to improve access to and increase the quality of education across the country. To underscore this point, Hobby was depicted, for example, daintily dabbing her eyes at the plight of 8 million illiterate Americans and shooing away a stork carrying news that the American population had surpassed 160 million souls instead of fixing the dilapidated and overcrowded school shown in the cartoon's background.[52]

Block perhaps assumed that women were not the primary audience for his cartoons and was unconcerned at how they would respond to their portrayal. Indeed, many contemporary newspaper editors assumed that women were only interested in reading articles focused on so-called women's issues—primarily stories about fashion, high society, and lifestyle—and dedicated specific sections to these subjects to leave the "serious" news and editorial pages for men.[53] Both the letters page of the *Post* and Block's own correspondence belied this notion, however, and it is clear that women were as interested and engaged in consuming Block's cartoons as men.[54] The relative invisibility of women in his work reveals both Block's assumptions about the traditional roles he expected them to play in American society and his lack of understanding of the changes that were already underway. In the postwar period, women were barraged with media images that asserted their place was in the home as wives and mothers while their husbands went out to work and earned a living.[55] Block's cartoons reinforced this stereotype and made no attempt to portray women as individuals who had lives distinct from how they were defined in relation to men.

This lack of representation of women and feminist issues carried over to the other rights-based movements that emerged in the 1960s, none of which were addressed in his cartoons from the period. He did not explicitly cover the struggle to pass an equal rights amendment until November 1977, while his first cartoons focused on abortion and gay rights did not appear until December 1978 and January 1993 respectively.[56] These gaps in Block's work were hardly surprising. Given the pressure of creating a new cartoon on an almost daily basis, Block chose to prioritize other issues he considered more urgent or more appropriate for his imagined male readership. But it does also suggest that he was unwilling to engage with movements that critiqued the patriarchal institutions and cultural practices of postwar liberalism. The same commitment to protecting those interests informed his reaction to the antiwar movement, which sought to end America's involvement in Vietnam, even though Block himself shared many of the same concerns as the students who protested the war.

Vietnam had long been a topic of concern for Block. His earliest cartoons on the region appeared during the Truman administration and depicted Vietnam as a place that could soon become problematic in America's fight against communism. This portrayal became more explicit during the Eisenhower administration, as the country fought for, and won, independence from France in 1954. Vietnam then fell off Block's radar, not appearing again until August 1959 when he imagined Khrushchev preparing for his visit to the United States. In the background are two maps, one depicting East and West Berlin, the other Vietnam and Laos, with the clear message that the Soviet Union was hoping to expand its influence westward.[57] Throughout the Kennedy administration, Block portrayed America's growing involvement in Vietnam as a necessary, albeit unfortunate, buffer against the spread of communism. On October 15, 1961, for example, he depicted North Vietnam as a Soviet thug, punching the peaceful South Vietnam over a cliff and declaring, "Remember, It Would Be Unfriendly to Strike Back."[58] Such depictions of Soviet aggression were tempered by a recognition that America and its South Vietnamese allies did not share the same values. In a series of cartoons published between July and October 1963, Block showed South Vietnamese president Ngô Đình Diệm and his sister-in-law Trần Lệ Xuân violently oppressing their country's Buddhist population.[59] Recognizing that American policy in the region was, at best, contradictory, as late as October 22, 1963, just ten days before Diệm's assassination, Block showed how important the partnership between the two countries was by imagining an American soldier urging two South Vietnamese soldiers to stop assaulting a Buddhist monk and redirect their aggression toward the communist war to the north.[60] These cartoons cumulatively served the dual purpose of highlighting the extent to which America was propping up an authoritarian regime while still suggesting that there was some justification for that policy.

Block's equivocation over America's moral responsibility to be involved in Vietnam as a means of curtailing communist expansion ended in February 1965 with Lyndon Johnson's order both to bomb targets regularly and extensively in North Vietnam and to deploy American ground troops in retaliation for a Viet Cong attack on two American bases. He initially celebrated the American retaliatory strikes as potentially turning the tide of the war, recalling in his 1968 book *The Herblock Gallery* that they "seemed—on the basis of general information at the time—to be a proper response." These cartoons weren't without criticism in the moment, as shown by a letter to the *Washington Post*'s editor that lamented how "Herblock, whom I had found a gentle wit, is shrieking as loudly now for war as many of the Goldwaterites of whom he was contemptuous."[61] But by the end of the month, following another coup in South Vietnam, the tone of Block's cartoons had begun to change. His February 23, 1965, cartoon played on the widely accepted "domino theory," which justified American intervention in Vietnam by positing that if one country fell under the influence of communism, its neighbors would soon follow in a domino effect. Warning about the possible consequences of America's continued involvement, he imagined Vietnam's successive leaders as a series of collapsing dominoes, with the last man in the line an American soldier.[62]

Block was not alone in having doubts about the consequences of this decision. Many liberals viewed the escalating conflict as an appropriate response to communist activity in the region and feared that a prolonged national debate would damage the prospects of Johnson's domestic agenda. But for other, especially younger liberals, Vietnam represented an unwelcome intervention in a part of the world that seemed to hold little strategic importance.[63] At the University of Michigan, for example, students and faculty members organized an eleven-hour "teach-in" at which they participated in lectures and discussions to learn about the historical context of the conflict. Although those in attendance heard arguments both for and against America's continued involvement in Vietnam, the event was interpreted as an antiwar demonstration, and by the end of the night the majority of participants had endorsed an American withdrawal.[64] These teach-ins soon spread to other campuses across the country, leading to a national teach-in event in Washington, DC, attended by thousands, including members of Congress and McGeorge Bundy, special assistant to the president for national security affairs, who defended the administration's policies. Block took notice of this event, drawing a cartoon that negatively depicted both the administration and the leaders of the teach-in movement as arguing professors, each unyielding in their positions.[65] Even so, the burgeoning antiwar movement largely escaped Block's attention with the only other reference being a cartoon drawn after the Easter March on Washington in April that lampooned what to him appeared to be the never-ending series of overwrought protests then occurring in the nation's capital.[66] Yet Block's own views on the war were clearly evolving at this time, a change that was beginning to be reflected in his cartoons.

The clearest indication of this came in two cartoons published a week apart following announcements that ten Americans had been killed in Vietnam with more missing or wounded, and that in March the administration had authorized American troops to engage in regular combat operations when appropriate. Even so, a White House statement claimed, there had been "no change in the mission of United States ground combat units in recent days or weeks."[67] The cartoons Block drew in response to these developments made use of the same iconography to suggest the changing nature of America's involvement. June 10's "The Other Ascent into the Unknown" depicts an American soldier climbing a fog-filled staircase, uncertain of what awaits him at the top. This was followed a week later with a depiction of Johnson and an aide standing on an escalator. As the mechanism, labeled "Viet-Nam escalator," moves the two men upward, Johnson declares that "Our Position Hasn't Changed at All" (fig. 32). These two cartoons used the same motif—a climb toward an unknowable future—to make two very different points about the administration's policies. In the first, Block highlighted both the uncertainty of what lay ahead for American forces, while emphasizing the personal risks those soldiers were being asked to make. In the other, he exposed the meaninglessness of the administration's insistence that nothing had changed, even as they ordered expanded bombing raids and mobilized more and more men to the region.[68]

While these two cartoons are often held up as evidence of Block's early doubts about the war, the truth is more complicated. Block was neither the first nor the last American to express these concerns, but with the benefit

FIGURE 32. *Washington Post,* June 17, 1965

of hindsight both cartoons look prescient. But neither cartoon outright condemned American involvement in the war or even Johnson's military strategy. Nor did these cartoons necessarily represent a complete split with the liberal establishment. Block was actually highlighting both the uncertainty of what would come next and the fallacy of claiming that an expansion of troops on the ground would have no impact on the nature of the war. As such, while they were expressing a clear sense of discontent with the direction the president was leading the country, their main purpose was to offer a warning about the danger of unintended consequences, especially as they related to American lives. The two cartoons also conspicuously placed Block in opposition to the editorial stance of his home newspaper. On June 10, as he highlighted the uncertainty that lay ahead for American soldiers, the *Post* argued in an editorial that the "basic policy" of the Johnson administration had not changed. Instead, the paper's editorial board claimed, the administration had "merely indicated in more explicit terms that it is following a somewhat flexible policy . . . [and] reaffirmed its determination not to abandon South Viet-Nam to Communist conquest."[69] With this in mind, his June 17 cartoon can be read as a rebuttal not just of the administration's rhetoric but of the *Post*'s as well.

Where Block's own break with the Johnson administration first became undeniable was in his depiction of the war's negative impact on the liberal agenda and especially Johnson's program of Great Society reforms. Launched to great fanfare in 1964, the Great Society was a series of domestic programs designed to eliminate poverty and racial injustice. It included legislative accomplishments such as the Civil Rights Act (1964), the Voting Rights Act (1965), the Elementary and Secondary Education Act (1965), and the Social Security Act (1965), which established Medicare and Medicaid. The Great Society also established national endowments for the arts and the humanities, introduced consumer protections over a wide range of industries, and created over a dozen environmental laws and programs. All of these were elements of Arthur Schlesinger's qualitative liberalism and were longstanding priorities for Block that had been appearing favorably in his cartoons well before Johnson assumed the presidency. Environmentalism, for example, was the theme of Block's very first professionally published cartoon in 1929, and Block's concern over such wide-ranging environmental issues as air pollution, deforestation, and even the impact of tourism on America's national parks and wilderness were issues with which his cartoons regularly engaged. But these policies also required the appropriation of billions of tax dollars, and as the cost of the war grew exponentially, Congress became increasingly unwilling to spend the money necessary to continue to expand the Great Society.[70] As the impact of the war on liberalism's domestic achievements became clearer, Schlesinger spoke for many liberals when he wrote in 1966's *The Bitter Heritage* that "the Great Society is now, except for token gestures, dead. The fight for equal opportunity for the Negro, the war against poverty, the struggle to save the cities, the improvement of our schools—all must be starved for the sake of Vietnam."[71]

The first indication of Block's concern for the survival of the liberal agenda came on the eve of Johnson's 1966 State of the Union address. In what became a recurring theme, Block imagined "The Vietnam War" and "Domestic Problems" as observers of Johnson's speech. Both figures are oversized, but the militaristic representation of the war is significantly larger and taking up more space than the domestic civilian struggling for room in the aisle.[72] But the most devastating critique came in August 1967, when Block depicted Johnson arm in arm with a voluptuous woman, dressed in a cleavage-revealing dress, mink stole, and heavy makeup. Labeled "Vietnam War," Block made sure that there could be no doubt as to what she represented, replacing her bracelets, necklace, and earrings with shell-casings. Looking on aghast at this scene is a thin, malnourished woman dressed in rags, labeled "U.S. Urban Needs." Johnson is shown to be distracted by her just long enough to reassure her that "There's Money Enough to Support Both of You—Now, Doesn't That Make You Feel Better?" (fig. 33).[73] In capturing the bitter dilemma in which the president found himself, Block inadvertently anticipated how Johnson would later justify his decisions. "I knew from the start that I was bound to be crucified either way I moved," Johnson later claimed. "If I left the woman I really loved—the Great Society—in order to get involved in that bitch of a war on the other side of the world, then I would lose everything at home."[74] It was this same concern for how Vietnam would impact the administration's ability to fulfill the liberal agenda that informed Block's response to the antiwar protests which started on America's college campuses in 1965.

Despite his own disillusionment with America's involvement in Vietnam, Block was not a supporter of the antiwar movement and its tactics. In particular, he drew a clear distinction between those activists, most of whom were students and other young Americans, who *dissented* against the war, and those who *protested* against it, mirroring the manner in which he supported what he saw as the legitimate tactics of the civil rights movement but condemned the protests of Black Power. One sign of the war's growing unpopularity was the increasing number of young men who symbolically turned in or burned their draft cards as an act of resistance against the government. Such action was already illegal because the law

"There's Money Enough To Support Both Of You — Now, Doesn't That Make You Feel Better?"

FIGURE 33. *Washington Post,* August 1, 1967

required all draft-eligible Americans to carry their draft card with them at all times, but in 1965 Congress passed the Draft Card Mutilation Act, which introduced stiff penalties for destroying a card. Block's cartoons, while not explicitly supporting the actions of those who destroyed their draft cards, nonetheless strongly denounced the backlash from politicians and others as both an overreaction and an infringement of the students' constitutional rights. The first such cartoon appeared on September 2, 1965, and depicts Congress and a draft dodger as petulant children, each trying to outdo the other in their childish behavior. More bluntly, May 7, 1967's cartoon shows two sets of protestors: a pair of students opposing the draft standing opposite several members of the House Armed Services

Committee, including South Carolina's L. Mendel Rivers and Louisiana's F. Edward Hébert. The action of each group mirrors the other. Where the students are burning a copy of the Draft Card Mutilation Act, the congressmen are holding a sign declaring, "Let's Forget the First Amendment" and burning a copy of the Constitution. To further emphasize the cynicism of the cartoon's caption—"We'll Teach You Patriotism and Respect for the Law"—and the anti-American values that Block was ascribing to them, the congressmen, all southern Democrats opposed to civil rights legislation, were shown clutching a Confederate flag.[75] For Block, the right to burn a draft card, which was not an action without consequence for those who protested in that fashion, was something that should be protected no matter how much opponents disagreed with it.

But in the same way that he opposed the actions of the Black Power movement, Block was not so accommodating in his portrayal of those who took more direct action to protest the war. In November 1966, for example, members of the SDS confronted Defense Secretary Robert McNamara after he gave an address at Harvard. The incident was the inspiration of Block's cartoon "Harvard, Unfair Harvard," which depicts a calm and collected McNamara surrounded by a crowd of heckling male Harvard students.[76] Block later highlighted this incident as an example of how many antiwar protestors went too far as they "expressed their devotion to freedom by howling down anyone who attempted to speak for the Administration's position on the war."[77] Similarly, May 5, 1968's untitled cartoon, which was drawn in the midst of a series of student protests that shut down Columbia University, further revealed the limits that Block placed on what he considered legitimate forms of protest. The demonstrations, which saw students occupy multiple university buildings for a week, were intended to force the university to end its involvement in government programs that supported the war in Vietnam and to protest the university's purchasing of buildings and land in the nearby African American neighborhood of Harlem. Although Block had previously critiqued the government's activities on university campuses, it was clear he had little sympathy for the student activists, even after the New York Police Department violently ended their protest. Block's cartoon on the events imagined an Ivy League student writing a letter to his mother. After describing how he and his friends had "seized five University buildings, held the Dean prisoner, wrecked the office and rifled the personal papers of the Pres[ident]," the student expresses his incredulity that the police were called, "just as if we were ignorant kids who didn't know what we were doing." Further highlighting what Block saw as the self-centered privilege of these protestors, he had the student sign off his letter with a request "to send some extra money, as we are fighting to close down this thoroughly rotten University."[78]

This disregard for the grievances of student protestors, and the implicit assertion that they should express their discontent in less radical ways, became even clearer in later cartoons. By 1968, while antiwar sentiment was still an important cause of unrest, student activists had broadened their grievances to more directly reject the societal underpinnings of the postwar liberal establishment. Castigating these protestors as belonging to the "Students for Demolishing Society," Block repeatedly depicted them as violent terrorists determined to shut down college campuses and disrupt the orderly running of society for their own purposes, an effort in which they were aided by irresponsible faculty members. In December 1968, for example, Block showed a member of the organization, replete with goatee, a broken bottle, and an "SS" armband, comparing his record in closing universities with an anthropomorphic representation of the seasonal flu, which was especially serious that winter. The following month, he depicted another student working in concert with a faculty member to hijack a plane representing Americans colleges.[79] It is certainly true that in 1968 the SDS began to pursue more radical and disruptive forms of protests. But just as his cartoons often acknowledged the reality of the racism and injustices that motivated the Black Power movement while failing to recognize the movement's activities as appropriate forms of protest, Block similarly refused to give legitimacy to a movement that rejected the underpinnings of postwar liberalism despite agreeing with their antiwar sentiments.

The tensions that each of these protest movements revealed within the Democratic Party came to a head in the 1968 presidential campaign, during which it must have seemed to Block as though the continued legacy of postwar liberalism was at stake. Lyndon Johnson, whose status as the Democratic nominee had seemed unassailable a year earlier, was now a decidedly flawed candidate whose handling of the war in Vietnam was opposed by a majority of Americans, regardless of their political allegiances.[80] Highlighting the challenges faced by Johnson from the political left, student antiwar groups launched a "Dump LBJ" movement in the summer of 1967 in an effort to prevent his renomination as the Democrats' presidential candidate.[81] While much of the liberal establishment—including politicians, leaders of the labor movement, and members of the media—continued to support Johnson, a determined group of liberals decided to try to force the Democratic Party to adopt a peace platform at its upcoming nominating convention. The most dogged was arguably ADA member Allard Lowenstein, who took it upon himself to identify a potential candidate to run against Johnson in the primary and, if not beat the sitting president, at least push him further left. After being rejected by such men as Robert Kennedy and George McGovern, Lowenstein convinced John Kenneth Galbraith and Joseph Rauh, the ADA's chair and vice chair, who both believed in the need to withdraw from Vietnam, to persuade Senator Eugene McCarthy of Minnesota, himself a former member of the ADA, to challenge Johnson on an antiwar platform.[82] Many of the same student protestors that Block had assiduously vilified for undermining the liberal agenda soon flocked to McCarthy's campaign, going so far as to cut their hair and shave their beards to present a respectable image as they sought to persuade Democratic voters to turn against Johnson.

On the Republican side, Block was concerned about the continuing battle between moderates and conservatives over control of the party. This had been a recurring theme of his cartoons since Goldwater's defeat in the 1964 election, and as the next cycle came closer, his despair over the increasingly likely nomination of Richard Nixon over a more moderate Republican such as Nelson Rockefeller or George Romney became palpable. Block's first cartoon of 1968 made this clear, depicting the Republican elephant, wounded from the result of the 1960 and 1964 elections, sliding toward a cliff face while trying to escape from the "Nixon-Goldwater Rut."[83] At the same time, George Wallace, the former governor of Alabama who infamously declared "segregation now, segregation tomorrow, segregation forever," had launched a third-party bid for the presidency. Wallace's intent was to win enough electoral votes to force the election into the House of Representatives, thereby giving southern segregationists an opportunity to win concessions regarding federal desegregation policies. Given all of these developments, it was no wonder that one of Block's last cartoons of 1967 depicts a voter worriedly declaring, "I'm Afraid to Look" while anxiously covering his face so that he can't see what is in store for the upcoming year in a fortune-teller's darkened crystal ball.[84]

Block had treated the news that McCarthy was challenging Johnson for the Democratic nomination as a quixotic campaign with little chance of success. On December 3, 1967, for example, he pictured McCarthy in a jousting competition, hopelessly lining up in a regular car against the Johnson campaign's armored tank.[85] Yet this portrayal underestimated McCarthy's growing support, which included endorsements from such celebrities as the actor Paul Newman and the television writer Rod Serling. Within the ADA, a debate raged on whether or not to endorse his candidacy. On the one hand, the ADA had historically benefited from its close connections with Democratic administrations and still had strong ties with members of the Johnson administration. On the other, the ADA's leadership had been instrumental in persuading McCarthy to declare his candidacy and strongly supported his antiwar message. The stakes could not be higher. Advocates of endorsing McCarthy believed that such a move would open the doors to tens of thousands of new, young, and enthusiastic members who would galvanize the ADA's political fortunes. Opponents feared alienating older, more traditional, and blue-collar members who had been part of the ADA's coalition since its founding. In the end, the pro-McCarthy faction emerged triumphant, passing a resolution that supported the "ideas" McCarthy represented but precipitating the resignation of several labor leaders from the organization.[86] The symbolic nature of the ADA—a prominent and influential liberal organization—endorsing McCarthy helped galvanize his campaign, and he defied expectations by winning 42 percent of the vote in the March 1968 New Hampshire primary. Block captured the result's impact on the Johnson campaign by revisiting the setting of his December 3, 1967, McCarthy cartoon, now depicting the Minnesotan's lance piercing Johnson's tank to stop it in its tracks.[87] McCarthy's success completely changed the dynamics of the campaign. Four days after New Hampshire, Robert F. Kennedy, the former attorney general and brother of the still-popular John F. Kennedy, announced that he was planning to enter the race, also on an antiwar platform. McCarthy's followers were outraged, accusing Kennedy of political opportunism, a sentiment captured in Block's cartoon reacting to Kennedy's announcement. Block imagined McCarthy as a nineteenth-century prospector working by hand in "Lonesome Gulch" who has just discovered gold. But in the background approaches Kennedy, spyglass in hand and followed by modern digging equipment, ready to steal the fruits of McCarthy's hard work.[88]

Following Johnson's unexpected withdrawal from the campaign in March, Vice President Hubert Humphrey also declared his candidacy. Confident in his position as the campaign's frontrunner, Humphrey spent the campaign winning endorsements from establishment figures within the party such as Lyndon Johnson, former President Harry Truman, and Chicago mayor Richard Daley, while McCarthy and Kennedy competed for votes in the primaries. Through April and May, Block's cartoons reflected what he depicted as the foregone conclusion of the race. Humphrey was shown standing above the fray, allowing McCarthy and Kennedy to fight between themselves for whatever other support was left to them. On April 26, for example, Block showed the two antiwar candidates fighting over the Democratic donkey, only to suddenly realize that Humphrey is calmly leading it away. A month later, just days before the primaries in California, New Jersey, and South Dakota, the artist showed Humphrey joyfully playing with a basket full of puppies, representing conference delegates, while scratched and bedraggled McCarthy and Kennedy appear outside, trying to rescue a feral cat, labeled "Primaries," from a tree.[89]

The assassination of Robert Kennedy following his victory in the California primary on June 5 changed the dynamics of the campaign once again. Humphrey was now able to enter the Democratic National Convention, held that year in Chicago, certain he would leave as the party's nominee for the presidency. But the divisions within the party had only hardened over the course of that summer. Running as the *de facto* incumbent had allowed Humphrey to build relationships with party insiders and cultivate the votes necessary to secure the nomination from delegates in nonprimary states—indeed, he did not win a single primary—but it also tied him to the policies of the Johnson administration.[90] This was especially true when it came to Vietnam, over which hawks and doves alike were pressuring Humphrey to stake out a position closer to their own. This tension was aptly captured on the eve of the convention in Block's cartoon "Politics of Happiness in Street without Joy," which shows Humphrey sitting in a car sandwiched between the tank of "Rule-or-Ruin Hard-Liners" and the hippie-mobile of "Rule-or-Ruin Doves."[91]

The antiwar wing of the party was especially unwilling to let Humphrey claim the nomination without first winning concessions. McCarthy determined to push for a plank to the party's platform that called for an unconditional end to the bombing in Vietnam, an effort that quickly descended into chaos as delegates hurled insults and expletives at each other.[92] Block captured the turbulence in two cartoons created during the convention depicting the Democratic donkey first as a casualty of the Vietnam War being awarded the posthumous "Vietnam Issue" medal by Lyndon Johnson, and then as a badly injured boxer being led away from a ring where the Republican elephant confidently relaxes.[93] Yet all of this turmoil paled next to the violence that erupted on the streets of Chicago as the city's police brutally put down a peaceful antiwar demonstration. In scenes broadcast on national television, armed police in riot gear beat and arrested hundreds of protestors who had gathered in the city's Grant Park. As the violence continued, it flowed into the Hilton Hotel, where many delegates were staying and were consequently caught between the two opposing forces. In the aftermath of all of this, Block demonstrated his lack of sympathy for the antiwar movement by pointedly not including them in a cartoon that depicted the delegates and members of the media as the sole victims of the Chicago police's violence.[94]

After the convention McCarthy refused to endorse his opponent, instead calling on his supporters to work to reform the Democratic Party.[95] This was a significant blow to Humphrey's prospects, and Block quickly moved to make clear the importance of Democratic unity for the party's chances in the election. Immediately after the convention, he drew the "Democratic Party Turmoil" turning the nomination into a poisoned chalice. The next day readers saw Humphrey as a pharmacist mixing together the medicine of "Unity" and "Peace" in an effort to heal a barely alive Democratic Party. And then on September 5, Block repurposed the iconography of Charles Schultz's popular *Peanuts* cartoon to highlight the challenges that lay ahead for Humphrey. Recasting him as the hapless and hopelessly optimistic Charlie Brown, Block placed Humphrey on a pitcher's mound attempting to rally a disinterested Lucy and Linus, identified as McCarthy supporters, to his cause.[96] The tone of these cartoons soon changed to depict the New Left as an active threat to Humphrey, every bit as dangerous as his electoral opponents.[97] As antiwar protestors hounded Humphrey at campaign rallies, chanting such slogans as "Dump the Hump" and "We Want Gene," Block felt compelled to respond in graphic form. Set at a Humphrey campaign event, Block drew a raucous group of hippies—all replete with untamed facial hair; wearing t-shirts, jeans, and necklaces; and holding signs with such slogans as "Dump the Hump," "Hell with Anything Humphrey Has to Say," and "We'll Decide Who Can Speak in This Country"—pushing up against a group of middle-class Humphrey supporters. Observing all of this, an angry voter, clearly articulating the artist's own views of what any respectable American should do, declares to a friend, "I've Decided to Protest Too—I'm Gonna Vote for Humphrey and Free Speech!"[98]

As November approached, Block's anger at the refusal of McCarthy's supporters to back Humphrey became palpable. On October 10, he imagined McCarthy high on glue surrounded by flower petals as campaign badges proclaimed McCarthy's grievances over how he had been treated by the liberal establishment during the campaign.[99] A little over a week later, Block depicted McCarthy as an Olympic athlete assessing the impossibly high hurdles he was being asked to clear in order to please the liberal judges accompanying him.[100] And in two separate cartoons, he showed McCarthy supporters actively hoping that Humphrey would be defeated so that the Democratic Party could be reconstituted around their agenda.[101] Taken together, these cartoons clearly illustrated the limits Block was willing to place on protest in America. Any group protesting against the liberal establishment, in this case Block's preferred candidate for the presidency, was to be condemned.

Block's fears were ultimately realized as Humphrey convincingly lost the election to Richard Nixon by an electoral vote of 301 to 191, while George Wallace claimed 46 electoral votes from southern states. In the aftermath of Humphrey's defeat, Block drew a series of cartoons that made clear where Block thought the blame should fall for Humphrey's defeat. On November 8, he depicted two members of the New Left lying in the trash while listening to a bipartisan crowd applaud Humphrey's effort in the election. With signs reading "Dump the Hump" and "Humphrey Will Get Clobbered and We'll Pick up the Pieces," one of the protestors confusedly tells the other, "That's Odd—Somehow I Get the Feeling That We Didn't Win."[102] Four days later, Block showed a minuscule McCarthy holding a sign that read, "Alas—If Only Humphrey Had Said Just the Right Magical Words at Just the Right Magical Moment, Perhaps . . . ," and wielding a bloody dagger while two nearby voters comment, "He Really Shrinks on You, Doesn't He?" (fig. 34).[103] These cartoons, with their blunt assertion that Humphrey lost the election because McCarthy and his supporters

FIGURE 34. *Washington Post,* November 12, 1968

failed to support the Democratic candidate, provoked a strong response from Block's readers. A common theme was a sense that it was Block himself who had betrayed not only the liberal cause but their trust in him as someone who shared and articulated their values. One correspondent wrote that "as a great admirer over many years of your value system and artistry, I take exception with your efforts to belittle Senator McCarthy."[104] Another explained that while Block's cartoons "over the years have been such a delight that I think of you as a good friend," his "He Really Shrinks on You" cartoon, with its denigration of McCarthy's character, "was a real shock."[105] A resident of London decried "the vile spite" of the cartoon and argued that Humphrey did nothing to earn the support of McCarthy's followers. "Can you not understand his continuing responsibility to those young people," she asked rhetorically, "who would feel most wretchedly let down if he supported Humphrey on any but his own terms?"[106] "Perhaps Herb Block can live with hypocrisy and spinelessness," another reader informed him, "this family can't."[107]

Block though was unmoved by these complaints and again revisited the campaign on December 3, this time depicting Humphrey with a bandage wrapped around his head and reading the conclusion of the official report into the violence which had marred the Democratic Convention earlier that year: "The Victims Were Often 'Persons Who Had Broken No Law, Disobeyed No Order, Made No Threat. . . .'"[108] As an indictment of the New Left and the damage Block believed it had caused to the liberal order, the cartoon had at least one fan. That same day, Hubert Humphrey wrote to Block congratulating him for producing "the most succinct, accurate and revealing analysis of what happened in the campaign that I have ever seen. Thanks for the diagnosis and analysis," he concluded. "Please prescribe the treatment."[109] As Richard Nixon prepared to move into the office that he had long coveted, Block was left with no answer.

6

"THAT SON-OF-A-BITCH HERBLOCK"

Taking on Nixon

IN DECEMBER 1972, RICHARD NIXON gave a rare interview with the Associated Press.[1] Coming just six weeks after his landslide victory in an election that saw the Democratic Party in complete disarray, a reader might have expected to learn about Nixon's goals and agenda for his second term in office. The interview, however, had been granted on the condition that the president not be asked "substantive questions about public issues but would seek only to elicit his personality and mood." As such, the resulting profile was an explicit effort on the part of the administration to recast Nixon's public image, transforming him from a battle-hardened campaigner into a strong, thoughtful, and experienced leader.[2]

The early part of the profile focused on Nixon's health and exceptional ability to run the country. His doctor testified to his remarkable physical condition, revealing that Nixon's weight and blood pressure rarely fluctuated and claiming that the president was the only man he had ever met who had never suffered a headache. According to this doctor, "Aside from graying a little [Nixon] shows less change accelerated by his office than most of his predecessors . . . [and is] probably one of the healthiest Presidents we've ever had." As the profile progressed, others vouched for his character. Aides especially lamented the dichotomy between Nixon's public and private personas, speaking of a fierce intellect that was hidden from public view lest he alienate a general audience who could only be reached "through the lowest common denominator." A quote from his daughter Julie made the same basic point. But the most insistent testimony came from Nixon himself, who recast himself as a more mature, calmer, and more considered politician than he had been earlier in his career. "Years ago, when I was a young congressman, things got under my skin," he admitted. "Herblock (the cartoonist) got to me. . . . But now when I walk into this office I am cool and calm."[3]

This seemingly casual mention of the *Washington Post*'s editorial cartoonist was no accident. In an interview that had clearly been carefully stage-managed by Nixon's aides, the reference to Block was calculated to address the concern that Nixon allowed himself to be emotionally affected by these cartoons. Block was among Nixon's fiercest and most consistent critics, and by the time of his reelection, the perception that Nixon could not bear to look at the daily Herblock cartoon had become deeply ingrained in the public's consciousness. Block's portrait of Nixon, which accentuated his dark jowl, heavy eyebrows, and ever-constant five-o'clock shadow, was so powerful, insistent, and persuasive that it is the Herblockian Nixon that is frequently invoked when commentators describe the former president's physical characteristics.[4] Activist Ralph Nader, for one, once admitted that "I can't think of Nixon without thinking of Herblock," while Nixon biographer Herbert S. Parmet wrote that Block's cartoons made Nixon appear to be "the devil incarnate," going on to position Block as Nixon's "principal nemesis, the cartoonist whose caricatures became engraved in the minds of a generation of liberals."[5]

In public, members of the Nixon administration attempted to downplay the impact of Block's cartoons. A February 1969 profile of the then new president in *Life* magazine, for example, quoted an anonymous cabinet member's declaration that he had "never seen [Nixon] more relaxed. He doesn't get upset about the things that used to bother him. . . . Herblock's cartoons don't irritate him."[6] Nixon himself, while swearing in Walter J. Hickel as his secretary for the interior, jokingly thanked his new cabinet member for having "rendered service far beyond the call of duty. In the first four days of this administration he, rather than I, has been the subject of the Herblock cartoons. I am grateful for that."[7] Nixon's chief of staff, H. R. (Bob) Haldeman, revealed the administration's true feelings toward Block's cartoons in an August 1971 interview when, with characteristic bluntness, he dismissed political cartoons in general as "brutality for the sake of brutality," and claimed that "Herblock wouldn't exist if he didn't have nasty cartoons of Nixon."[8] And in a January 1972 interview granted as part of *Time*'s coverage of Nixon as their "Man of the Year," the president famously declared, "I wouldn't start [the morning] by looking at Herblock."[9] But, as with so many other topics he wished to keep out of the public eye, Nixon was most candid about his true feelings when speaking in what he believed was a private space. Thus, on April 29, 1971, Nixon was captured on the Oval Office's recording system congratulating his secretary of the treasury John Connally for a speech he had given two days earlier at the Houston Chamber of Commerce. "The other thing that made me think you'd really come across is that son-of-a-bitch Herblock finally took notice of you," Nixon said. "Let me tell you this . . . Herblock took me on 23 years ago in the [Alger] Hiss case, and he's been against me ever since. And when he took you on, I said, 'By God, Connally's my man.'"[10]

As a man who has been described as "the dominant politician of the age of image-consciousness," it is no surprise that Nixon was so obsessed with his depiction in Block's cartoons.[11] Block took Nixon's physical characteristics—his posture, his complexion, his hairline, his features—and, through the tools of the cartoonist's craft, transformed them into an indictment of a political system run amok, one where selfish politicians routinely engaged in corrupt and illegal activities and ignored the needs of their constituents. This chapter shows how these cartoons played a critical role in defining the American public's perception of Richard Nixon. From the time Nixon first appeared on the *Washington Post*'s editorial page in a Herblock cartoon in May 1948 through his resignation of the presidency in August 1974, Block both created and reinforced an image of Nixon that focused readers' attention on the most unsavory aspects of his character. Block's cartoons played a critical role in transforming a young congressman from California who was admired by his supporters for both his good looks and his principled stance against communism into an archetype of corruption, a chameleon whose positions on the issues of the day changed based solely on political expediency and whose features became synonymous among liberals with the abuse of power and corruption of the presidency.

At the outset of his congressional career, Nixon enjoyed a reputation in the media as a young, handsome war hero who had unexpectedly beaten the popular five-term Democratic incumbent, Jerry Voorhis, to win California's 12th District in a 1946 congressional election marred by Nixon's allegation that Voorhis was a communist sympathizer.[12] A profile published in the December 5, 1948, edition of the *Washington Post* was typical of the prevailing view of the congressman when it described Nixon as "a bright young man, intensely earnest, serious, and sincere." He was, the profile's author reported, "strong-jawed," "tall, dark, and—yes—handsome," and "generally considered a restraining influence on the often-spectacular operations of the House Un-American Activities Committee."[13] Block's earliest depictions of Nixon would have done little to challenge this view. The first Herblock cartoons to feature Nixon were drawn as a response to his sponsorship of the Subversive Activities Control Act of 1948, popularly known as the Mundt-Nixon Bill. This legislation required communist organizations and their members to register with the Justice Department; prohibited such individuals from applying for, renewing, or using American passports; and implemented steep penalties for any "subversive" activities. Published in the *Post* on May 16, 1948, "We Got to Burn the Evil Spirits out of Her" remains a powerful indictment of the threat that Block felt this proposed legislation posed to basic American freedoms (fig. 35).[14] The cartoon depicts Nixon and Representative Karl Mundt dressed as Puritans gathering wood under the direction of HUAC chair J. Parnell Thomas as they build a pyre on which they have tied the Statue of Liberty as though she were a witch. Despite the resonance of the imagery found in the cartoon, Nixon is the least important of its depicted figures, his identity only confirmed by Block's ever-present use of labels. His back is to the viewer and his face almost entirely obscured by the large, Puritan-style hat he is wearing, leaving only a small portion of his clean-shaven chin visible to the reader. Indeed, Nixon's presence in the cartoon is primarily to make clear that the target of Block's anger was the Mundt-Nixon Bill.

Block's decision to deemphasize Nixon in this cartoon was hardly a surprise. At the time of its publication Nixon was still little known to

"We Got To Burn The Evil Spirits Out Of Her"

FIGURE 35. *Washington Post,* May 16, 1948

most Americans, and it was not until August 1948 that the Californian first gained a degree of national attention when, as a member of HUAC, he insisted on continuing an investigation into accusations that former State Department official Alger Hiss had been a Soviet spy. But despite the prominence and ultimate validation of his role in the investigation, Nixon was completely absent from the small number of cartoons Block drew about the Hiss case. Nor did Nixon feature heavily in Block's cartoons over the next several years, even as the Californian's national profile continued to rise thanks to his increasingly vociferous anticommunism and his election to the Senate in 1950 when he defeated the liberal favorite Helen Gahagan Douglas. The stories that emerged during his Senate campaign, which included the Nixon campaign's publication of a so-called Pink Sheet that compared Douglas's voting record to that of New York representative and accused communist Vito Marcantonio, appalled many liberals but barely made an impact on Nixon's image with the broader American public.[15]

Despite this growing acrimony within liberal circles, Block directly depicted Nixon in only five cartoons and referenced him in a further two that were published between that first appearance in May 1948 and the summer of 1952. These cartoons show that Block was still experimenting with how to portray Nixon. In particular, although the infamous five-o'clock shadow makes its first appearance in the second cartoon that Block drew featuring Nixon—June 27, 1948's "Anybody Got a Good Idea for a Summer Show?"—this was not yet a standard part of Block's caricature of Nixon as the stubble was absent in Nixon's next Herblock appearance.[16] Any negative sentiment Block's readers would have felt toward Nixon would thus have come not from the politician's physical depiction but from the circumstances in which he was placed. In the handful of cartoons that did feature him, Nixon is included as just one of several members of HUAC, who are consistently shown to be desperately looking for new ways of ensuring that they remain in the public spotlight.[17] Furthermore, in *The Herblock Book*, written and published in 1952, Block made no mention—specific or otherwise—of Nixon in his commentary, despite reproducing four cartoons that at least referenced him.[18] Contrary to Nixon's recollection of the origins of Block's animosity toward him, then, it is clear that, although Block drew cartoons critical of Nixon and his public actions during this period, the artist did not "take on" Nixon in a serious or sustained fashion during the latter's congressional career.

When Block did first take on Nixon was after the Californian's unexpected selection as Dwight Eisenhower's running mate on the Republican ticket in the 1952 presidential election. Nixon had been chosen in large part because he represented the center of Republican politics. On the one hand, Nixon supported scaling back, rather than completely dismantling, the New Deal's social protections and was hostile to the isolationist stance favored by some of the most conservative Republicans. On the other, his experience as a member of HUAC and public support of Joseph McCarthy made clear his staunch anticommunist credentials. Many liberals found it hard to attack Eisenhower's character during the 1952 election; he was after all a war hero, and they themselves had unsuccessfully courted him to run as a Democrat during the 1948 presidential election. Nixon, though, was a different matter, and liberals saw his inclusion on the ticket as an indication of the Republican Party's true ideology. Indeed, the ADA likely spoke for many like-minded liberals when it issued a statement declaring that Nixon's selection made it impossible for them to consider ever supporting Eisenhower.[19] For his part, Block rarely drew cartoons focused on vice presidential nominees—he never drew a cartoon depicting John Sparkman, Adlai Stevenson's running mate in 1952, for example—but Nixon's record of smearing his liberal opponents as communists, dating back to his first congressional victory in 1946, and his continued support of McCarthy's activities in the Senate was always likely to garner Block's attention during this campaign.

Nixon's return as a subject of Block's pen, published on August 25, 1952, saw two versions of Nixon walking down a street hand in hand while holding signs that read "Support of McCarthy" and "—Without Necessarily Indorsing McCarthy's Views."[20] The cartoon's title, "Middle of the Road," was primarily a reference to the Eisenhower campaign's strategy of appealing primarily to moderate Republicans but also served to underscore the contradictions Block saw in a campaign that sought to appeal to traditional American values while refusing to condemn the excesses of McCarthyism.[21] This cartoon also captured Block's perception, which would not gain widespread traction within liberal circles until later that decade, that Nixon presented multiple versions of himself depending on the audience at hand. But it was a scandal that erupted the following month and threatened to end Nixon's political career which came to define his image in the minds of conservatives and liberals alike, both for the duration of the 1952 campaign and for much of Nixon's future political life.

On September 18, 1952, the *New York Post* published a story revealing that Nixon had a private political "fund" containing $16,000 that had been donated to him by wealthy Californian supporters, ostensibly to reimburse him for political expenses. The report quoted Dana C. Smith, Nixon's attorney, justifying the fund "because Dick Nixon is the best salesman against socialism . . . and governmental control of everything in the country."[22] After the story broke, Democrats, newspaper editorials, and even some Republicans called on the Eisenhower campaign to drop

Nixon from the ticket. The *Washington Post,* which had already endorsed Eisenhower's candidacy, printed an editorial on September 20 bluntly titled "Nixon Should Withdraw." It spoke of a "man of basic decency with laudable aspirations for public service," but argued that there was no alternative to seeing this "promising career cut short" since Eisenhower's ability to "clear the air in Washington of the poison of scandal and corruption" would be "gravely handicapped if his running mate exemplifies the unethical conduct that he is denouncing."[23]

That day's Herblock cartoon, titled "Death of a Salesman," also offered an opinion on Nixon's political future. Clearly inspired by Smith's description of Nixon as a salesman, Block recast the disgraced candidate as Arthur Miller's eponymous character Willie Logan. But the figure that Block portrayed was far from the essentially honest and decent man who made a tragic error of judgment as described in the *Post*'s editorial. Instead, Nixon is depicted as a defeated figure, shown with hunched shoulders and heavy stubble and carrying suitcases packed with brooms to symbolize his past efforts to sweep up corruption and communism and the $16,000 that made up the contents of his secret fund.[24] This cartoon was followed three days later by one depicting the Republican elephant contemplating both Richard Nixon and the party's campaign slogan from the 1946 election: "Time for a Change."[25] That same evening, Nixon went on national television to defend and justify the existence of his expense account in an effort to garner public support in what popularly became known as the "Checkers Speech," named after the cocker spaniel given to his family by a supporter that Nixon emotionally described to sway public sentiment in his favor. Nixon's *mea culpa* ultimately saved his political career after an avalanche of supportive mail received by the Republican National Committee persuaded the party leadership to retain him as Eisenhower's running mate, but it did little to appease liberal detractors such as Block, whose response to the staged broadcast was to draw Nixon literally exiting stage left.[26]

The controversy and the Checkers Speech itself gave Block—and many of Nixon's other critics—plenty of ammunition with which to attack Nixon for the remainder of the campaign.[27] Block's original appropriation of Smith's analogy was soon echoed by other liberal commentators who by the end of the decade were regularly describing Nixon as a salesman in an attempt to imply that his career was, at least partially, the result of his ability to sell the American public a bill of goods.[28] Meanwhile, Block began to prominently feature the dog Checkers in several more of his cartoons as a representation of both the candidate's corrupt activities and the questions that Block believed were left unanswered in Nixon's speech. The October 13 cartoon, "Sic 'Im, Checkers," for example, shows Nixon hiding in the bushes, urging a small spaniel to attack a large bloodhound investigating the "Unanswered Questions about Nixon Finances."[29] But Block's more powerful—and controversial—anti-Nixon cartoons during the campaign were those that focused on his similarities to Joseph McCarthy.

Throughout the campaign, Block had made no apologies for his opposition to the Republican ticket and his support of Adlai Stevenson. Given Stevenson's impeccable liberal credentials and the controversy that continued to swirl around Nixon's presence on the ticket, this stance was unsurprising even though it was a position that proved something of an embarrassment to the Eisenhower-supporting *Post*.[30] Yet for much of the campaign, Block's cartoons had followed the lead of other liberals by avoiding what could be perceived as personal attacks against Eisenhower. Instead, Block showed his own political leanings by using either bemused voters or the Democratic donkey and Republican elephant as surrogates for the candidates themselves. As the campaign reached its climax, however, Block's cartoons attacked the Republican ticket by increasingly focusing on the party's vice presidential candidate. Nixon was depicted in half of the final ten cartoons that Block drew prior to election day.[31] Checkers the dog was featured in two of these cartoons, but the most significant cartoons drawn during the final week of campaigning illustrated Block's anger over Nixon's support for McCarthy, which while not entirely endorsed by Eisenhower was tacitly encouraged by the candidate's steadfast refusal to condemn the senator for fear it would alienate his supporters.[32] Block's frustration was clearly expressed in his October 29, 1952, cartoon "Naughty Naughty." Nixon and McCarthy are pictured as two smear artists with buckets and dripping paint brushes in hand. Eisenhower, meanwhile, is standing over the two figures, gently chastising them for painting over a Stevenson campaign poster as though they were little more than errant children—indeed, both Nixon and McCarthy are drawn noticeably shorter than Eisenhower (fig. 36).[33]

This cartoon, however, did not appear in the October 29 edition of the *Washington Post*. Although it had endorsed Eisenhower for president and consistently supported him in its editorials, the *Post* had to this point provided Block with the freedom to draw cartoons that clearly supported Stevenson. This arrangement was lauded by other newspapers around the country, such as Pennsylvania's *Beaver Valley Times*, which pointed out that, although "most cartoonists for papers that have endorsed one candidate or other must make cartoons coincide with the paper's editorial policy," the *Post* still allowed Block "complete freedom

FIGURE 36. Syndicated cartoon, October 29, 1952

of choice in his subjects."[34] Internally though, Block's public defiance of the *Post*'s editorial stance was leaving Phil Graham, the paper's publisher, "incensed."[35] The final straw came when he saw the "Naughty Naughty" cartoon, leading Graham to take the decision to stop printing Block's cartoons altogether until after the election. Block publicly presented the decision as his, claiming in an interview that he had wanted time off to visit his family in Chicago and had simply drawn "a few ahead of time and turned them in" to his syndicate for publication. They did not appear in the *Post* because he simply "hadn't offered them" to the Washington paper. But he hinted at the true reason for his cartoons' non-appearance when he went on to state that he "didn't submit them because I don't think they would have fit in completely with the *Post*'s policy."[36]

The reaction to Block's removal from the *Post*'s editorial page was swift and came from readers and other newspapers alike. Reginald Valles, for example, was no doubt looking to score political points in his capacity as the ADA's executive secretary when he wired the editorial page, curious as to why they were refusing "the week before [the] election, cartons [*sic*] by Herblock the man you hail as 'America's Best Cartoonist.'"[37] The *Washington Daily News*, the *Post*'s major local rival, gleefully ran the headline, "Where's Mr. Block? One of D.C.'s Top Draw-ers Is Missing."[38] The public outrage was so strong that Block's cartoons returned to their customary place on the *Post*'s editorial page on November 1. In the end, his cartoons were absent for only three days, but the initial decision to remove them created a controversy that reaffirmed Block's status as one of the most important and influential liberal commentators of the day.[39]

Following Eisenhower's convincing victory in the election, Nixon disappeared from Block's cartoons for the entirety of 1953. This is likely the result of Nixon being sent on a two-month goodwill tour of Asia and the Middle East early in the administration and Block having no particular desire to draw the vice president. As the midterm election cycle geared up again in the spring of 1954, though, Nixon once again became a regular subject of Block's work. Concerned with maintaining his own avuncular public persona, Eisenhower increasingly deployed Nixon as his proxy in support of Republican congressional candidates, allowing Nixon to besmirch their Democratic opponents with accusations of communist sympathies. In turn, Block's attacks against Nixon became increasingly vicious, almost personal in their ferocity. Block returned to themes that he had first developed during the 1952 presidential election to portray Nixon as the new spokesman for McCarthyism, while Eisenhower's refusal to condemn Nixon's smear tactics was depicted as a tacit sign of his approval and support.[40] Ultimately, Nixon had visited so many cities across the country, smearing Democratic candidates with his false or over-charged accusations, that Block came to think he was "figuratively criss-crossing the country by sewer," a realization Block later claimed was the inspiration for one of the cartoons with which Nixon is most closely associated, and which is often regarded as one of Block's most biting and astute.[41]

In truth, the catalyst for "Here He Comes Now," which was first published on October 29, 1954, more likely lay in Democratic National Committee chair Stephen A. Mitchell's angry accusation of October 22 that Republicans, led by Nixon, were engaging in a "desperate, last-minute 'gutter campaign.'"[42] But even if this was the case, the cartoon demonstrates that Block's work had potentially a far greater impact on the public's imagination than the original accusation could ever have achieved. Nixon's response to the cartoon, which depicts him climbing out of a sewer as a local welcoming committee and marching band rush to greet him, was to cancel his subscription to the *Washington Post* (fig. 37). Although he later claimed that he did this primarily to protect his daughters from seeing their father characterized as "the perennial bad guy of American politics," the cartoon clearly left a lasting impact on Nixon. In his memoirs, he wrote about how much he "resented being portrayed . . . as the sewer-dwelling denizen of Herblock cartoons. . . . As the attacks became more personal, I sometimes wondered where party loyalty left off and masochism began."[43]

For his part, Block had no regrets about drawing the cartoon and later commented that from the summer of 1973, when the Watergate scandal was at its peak, he received a growing number of requests for copies or reprints of this cartoon because his readers felt it had once again become especially pertinent.[44] The cartoon proved so effective that Block drew two "sequels" to it. The first appeared during Nixon's 1962 campaign for the governorship of California and showed him and his long-term campaign strategist Murray Chotiner climbing out of a sewer beside a movie theater in Hollywood. The second appeared in 1970, when Nixon had become president, and depicts him showing his own vice president, Spiro T.

"Here He Comes Now"

FIGURE 37. *Washington Post,* October 29, 1954

Agnew, the route into the sewer.[45] Had Block's cartoon never been drawn, Mitchell's original statement about gutter politics would likely have been quickly forgotten, dismissed as political partisanship and posturing during a contentious election cycle. But Block's depiction of Nixon as a gutter politician gave the metaphor a life of its own that struck a chord among liberals and helped to popularize this negative image of the vice president in the public consciousness.

Block also used his cartoons to associate Republicans more broadly with Nixon's brand of smear politics and to imply that these methods were a standard piece of the party's political playbook. This was seen in cartoons such as January 14, 1955's "Sweetest Little Feller—Everybody Knows—," which imagines Nixon as a baby laying in a pram and holding a hatchet and a bucket of tar while being sung a lullaby by Eisenhower and Leonard Hall, the Republican National Committee chair.[46] Both of Nixon's props in this cartoon are significant: the bucket of tar reflected Nixon's familiar tactic of casting unfounded accusations at his enemies in the hope that something would stick, while the hatchet showed Block's growing assessment of Nixon as Eisenhower's hatchet man, the person to whom the president delegated his dirty work lest it tarnish his carefully cultivated image of being above the political fray. Through this and similar cartoons, Block turned Eisenhower's tactic of deploying Nixon around the country on its head, using Nixon as a proxy through which Block could attack and reveal the hypocrisy of both Eisenhower and the Republican Party.

It was during the mid-1950s that Block began to characterize Nixon as being in constant need of a shave, harking back to his portrayal of Joseph McCarthy, with Nixon's dark jowls and heavy eyebrows serving to suggest the very image of the sinister—the archetypal Herblockian Nixon. It was also around this time that Block began to give Nixon different faces depending on the vice president's political position of the day. In part, this was certainly an effort to highlight what Block viewed as Nixon's hypocrisy. This was first seen in August 25, 1952's "Middle of the Road," with its depiction of two Nixons walking hand in hand down a street and offering two contradictory statements on Nixon's support of McCarthy. The cartoon clearly anticipated liberal rhetoric from later that decade which sought to portray Nixon as a changeable cipher espousing whatever rhetoric was most politically expedient at the time.[47] During the 1956 presidential election, commentators began to talk about a "'New' Nixon"—a Nixon, in the words of the *Christian Science Monitor,* who on the campaign trail now "eschewed sharp partisanship and kept his own address on the same high statesmanlike level as the President's."[48]

Adlai Stevenson, however, was speaking for the liberal establishment when he declared in September 1956 that Nixon was simply wearing a "new face," and "you have to be awed by the lack of conviction which makes so swift a transformation possible." He went on to declare that he knew "of no instance in which a man has so energetically tried to convince the electorate that everything he has said and done in past years bears no relation to himself, and that, until further notice, he is a new man."[49]

Arthur Schlesinger made much the same point during the 1960 presidential campaign when he argued that Nixon was, "in his own way, a serious political personality" who "stands for almost nothing" and "lacked an identifiable political philosophy." Nixon's appeal instead rested on his political malleability, his ability to constantly change "his public face" and take whichever political position was most advantageous in the moment. He was "neither reactionary nor radical, neither conservative nor liberal." Instead, Schlesinger concluded with obvious disdain, Nixon was obsessed with "appearance rather than with the reality of things, obsessed above all with his own appearance, his own image, seeking reassurance through winning, but never knowing why he is so mad to win or what he will do with his victory."[50]

Block, though, had passed judgment on Nixon's continuing efforts to reinvent himself and cast aside the "old Nixon" before either Stevenson or Schlesinger. Cartoons such as February 15, 1956's "Let's See—What'll I Wear Today?"—which preceded Stevenson's comments by seven months and depicts Nixon in his underwear choosing from a selection of outfits labeled "Dead-End Gang," "All-American Boy," "Look, Folks—I'm a Salesman," and "Political Pitchman"—suggested to readers the multiple characters that Nixon had portrayed throughout his career depending on what persona was most politically expedient in the moment. Similarly, October 26, 1956's "Now You Kids Beat It" imagines Nixon trying to shoo away a group of trick-or-treaters who are each carrying a bucket of paint and wearing a ghost costume representing Nixon's past electoral campaigns.[51] The cartoon suggested both the frequency with which Nixon had changed his political persona and the lengths to which he would go to disavow himself from his early rhetoric. Together, these cartoons, and others like them from the period, made the case that Nixon had not changed at all. This was made explicit in 1960 when Block began to draw Nixon wearing, for lack of a better description, a "Nixon mask" to hide the dark jowls that were now a distinguishing characteristic of Block's caricature of the vice president and to indicate that the "old" Nixon was still there underneath the new facade.[52]

Throughout the 1960 campaign, Block again made no effort to conceal his opposition to Nixon's candidacy, first during the Republican Party's nomination process and then in the general election. The tone was set by his very first cartoon of that year, which also marked his return from a four-month absence from the *Post*'s editorial page that had been enforced by a minor heart attack he suffered in September 1959. "Mirror, Mirror, on the Wall, Who's the Fairest One of All?" depicts Nixon, replete with his by now obligatory five-o'clock shadow, as a wicked witch lifted straight from the fairytale Snow White preparing a poisoned apple and speaking into a mirror framed by the Republican elephant (fig. 38).[53] Such a brazenly provocative image inevitably caused a strong reaction. The *Post*'s owner, Phil Graham, ever worried about unnecessarily exposing his newspaper to criticism, was concerned that the cartoon was too brazen in its

FIGURE 38. *Washington Post,* January 2, 1960

declaration, "I have returned."[54] *Time* magazine, meanwhile, commented that Block's return from illness had resurrected "the liberal Democratic image of Vice President Richard M. Nixon as a jowly, blue-jawed villain with a ski-jump nose" that in recent years had "receded in the light of his growing stature and achievements." Describing it as a "slashing assault on Nixon," the magazine confidently predicted that Block's cartoon would "set the style for the liberal Democrats' 1960 campaign."[55]

The response from Block's readers was even more polarized. On the one hand, a reader from Maryland wrote to Block professing the "wonderful, irreverent, damning glory" he felt on realizing that Block's cartoons had returned to the *Post*'s editorial page. A feeling of joy was only heightened as the reader imagined "Richard's face as he was properly putting it in order for the day, practicing that professional pall bearer's smile," when he saw that he was the subject of Block's first cartoon of the year.[56] On the other hand, a resident of Evanston, Illinois, was compelled to write to the *Chicago Sun-Times* to express how "extremely offensive" he found the cartoon. Decrying the "pictorial mudslinging" and depiction of Nixon as a "combination unshaven Joe McCarthy and Capone hood," this correspondent went on to wonder why Block found it "so necessary to make a bogieman out of Nixon in order to get his point across."[57]

Following Nixon's defeat in the presidential election, he next ran for governor of California in 1962, losing by just 297,000 votes out of 6 million cast. The next morning, he held a disastrous news conference in which he announced to the assembled press that "you won't have Nixon to kick around any more. . . . Just think how much you're going to be missing."[58] After this, many commentators wrote political obituaries, concluding that "barring a miracle, Richard Nixon [could] never hope to be elected to any political office again."[59] As if anticipating that this was not the end of Nixon's public career and reluctant to give him unnecessary attention, Block made no comment on this apparent retirement. This assessment indeed proved correct because in 1964, Nixon positioned himself as the unifier of the Republican Party and worked hard for the Republican cause throughout the campaign, even though he must have known the futility of the Goldwater effort.[60] Nixon's reappearance on the national stage provided great potential for commentary from Block, an opportunity that the cartoonist happily accepted. Portraying Nixon alternatively as a vulture or, more frequently, an undertaker, Block showed Nixon maneuvering himself into a position whereby he could step into the gap if no candidate emerged as a clear winner at that year's Republican Party National Convention.[61]

The portrayal of Nixon as an undertaker was one that Block continued into the former's successful 1968 campaign for the White House. In March 24's "Everything's Coming up Roses," for example, Nixon is seen in a graveyard overgrown with roses beside the final resting place of the "Rockefeller Candidacy."[62] In fact, throughout this period Block continually drew cartoons that evoked memories of those he had drawn during Nixon's earlier career. Thus, the September 18, 1968, cartoon "Come Out, Come Out, Whoever You Are!" found seven different Nixons, all wearing masks last seen in the 1960 campaign, hiding under a bed while holding the contradictory signs of Nixon's political past. "The Apt Pupil," which appeared on September 11, 1968, harked back to the old McCarthy-era cartoons in which Nixon was portrayed as a smear artist. Indeed, this cartoon was merely a reworking of the 1952 cartoon "Naughty Naughty," except that in this new version it is Nixon's running-mate, Spiro T. Agnew, who is the one covered in paint, while Nixon, far from mirroring the mildly reproachful look the original had given to Eisenhower, looks on approvingly. Nor was there any reprieve in the physical characteristics with which Block portrayed Nixon. He was now given a slightly hunched back, the jowls hung lower, and the five-o'clock shadow was, if possible, darker than ever. The overall effect was alternately to make Nixon even more sinister, especially when he was drawn as an undertaker, or else to make him appear especially tired, as though the effort of running his campaign was draining him of all energy.[63]

The message of these cartoons was clear. If, in the words of columnist Walter Lippmann, the Nixon of 1968 was "a new Nixon, a maturer and mellower man who is no longer clawing his way to the top . . . who has outlived and outgrown the ruthless politics of his early days," Block, through his cartoons, begged to differ.[64] For him there was no doubt that the old Nixon was still lurking under the surface, biding his time for an opportunity to reappear. For Block's readers, however, these cartoons only served to confirm their belief that not only was Block unfair in his treatment of Nixon but he was being deliberately provocative. Writing from Macon, Georgia, a correspondent looked at Block's anti-Nixon stance during the campaign and accused him of having "made a revolting smear career out of vilifying Nixon."[65] An anonymous reader who accused Block of having "spent a lifetime engendering hate, mistrust and malice" echoed these sentiments. Signing his note "A. Kruschev [*sic*]," the correspondent went on to urge Block to "please continue your envenomed assault on this country, its presidents, . . . those rotten American traditions, laws, virtue in women, the profit and loss system—and carbohydrate metabolism."[66] "Your extreme bias toward Richard Nixon expressed in your scurrilous cartoons has convinced me that I should vote for Nixon. There must be lots of good in anyone you hate so much," declared another reader. "But keep it up—you will promote more votes for Mr Nixon from others who will be sickened by your savage vindictiveness."[67] Even in victory, Nixon's supporters were far from magnanimous. One reader from Quincy, Massachusetts, for example, wrote to Block the day after the election, wishing him her "very worst regards" and taunting him to "sharpen your pencils, Buster. I'm sure you'll find ample targets for smear over the next few years!"[68] An anonymous correspondent informed Block that he had "better start learning how to draw your favorite sewer rat as president!"[69] Another simply wrote, "Boo! You lost."[70]

It was not just Nixon's supporters who had grown frustrated with Block's depiction of the Republican candidate during the campaign. As Block focused ever more strongly on the darker aspects of Nixon's character, newspapers across the country became increasingly concerned that he was abandoning any pretense at impartiality and instead becoming too personal in his attacks, leading some to refuse to print several of his cartoons. Coming under particular scrutiny was Block's continued emphasis on Nixon's five-o'clock shadow, which by this point had become synonymous with the candidate. This was clearly articulated by Meriden, Connecticut's *Morning Record*, which declined to publish several Herblock cartoons during the campaign explicitly because the stubble Block gave to his portrait of Nixon was "offensive" and "prejudicially unfair," making the candidate "look like a thug."[71] Block's correspondents also expressed these concerns. One Nixon supporter, for example, angrily described Block as a "sadist" for having picked the "most unflattering aspect of a person's appearance and then play[ing] it up, as if it were something that person could help if he tried."[72] Another complained that "for years I have found your 'sewer-hog-portrayal' of Nixon pretty sickening, to the degree that I have assiduously avoided your editorial page altogether. But now that he is elected President of these United States," she continued, "let us show a little more respect by shedding some of that psychopathic muck-raking."[73]

Concern over Block's cartoons existed even among the *Post*'s management. Russ Wiggins, the paper's former managing editor and Lyndon Johnson's ambassador to the United Nations, pointedly sent Block a razor and poem during the campaign to suggest it was time to change the portrayal of Nixon by giving him a figurative shave.[74] When the matter was raised at an editorial meeting, however, Block produced a photograph of Nixon, printed in that day's edition of the *Post,* which clearly showed a heavy growth of beard to be one of Nixon's most distinguishing characteristics. He went on to argue that the five-o'clock shadow was as "fair game for a cartoonist" as any other feature would be.[75] Following Nixon's victory in the election, the *Post,* which had supported Democrat Hubert Humphrey without formally endorsing him, wrote in an editorial that Nixon had earned from "those of us who have opposed him over the years—a *tabula rosa,* a fresh scorecard, you might say, or as Herblock would have it, a clean shave."[76] To accompany the editorial, Block imagined his own office as a barber's shop replete with a sign on the wall that reads, "This shop gives to every new President of the United States a free shave. H. Block, Proprietor" (fig. 39).[77] When he showed a sketch of this cartoon to Katharine Graham, who became the *Post*'s owner after her husband's death, she revealed how much criticism her paper had been absorbing because of Block's depiction of Nixon and the relief she now felt by "let[ting] out a whoop and [throwing] her arms around" the cartoonist in delight.[78]

Graham was not the only person excited and relieved by Block's decision to give Nixon a shave. The *Meriden Morning Record* wrote an editorial to accompany its publication of the cartoon that noted its "pleasure" at Block's change to his caricature.[79] Other Nixon supporters, such as William W. Gullett, the mayor of College Park in Maryland, wrote to Block to say that the cartoon "forces me to make a reappraisal" of the cartoonist's work. "Perhaps he has expressed the them[e] of 'bring us together,'" Gullett continued, "even more eloquently than the president-elect himself!"[80]

FIGURE 39. *Washington Post,* November 7, 1968

The *Post* printed several letters from readers congratulating Block for his "gesture of grace to Nixon."[81] Indeed, "If Herblock can agree to exhibit some degree of civility toward Richard Nixon," wrote another correspondent, "everybody ought to be able to get along with one another."[82]

Despite these platitudes, the cartoon also served to reinforce the partisan anger many Americans felt Block was at least partially responsible for fostering. "Please take the same razor," wrote one anonymous reader from Arlington, Virginia, in a telegram to Block, "and cut your own throat and kooky Katherines [*sic*] too."[83] Another reader, this time from Bayonne, New Jersey, took the opportunity to gloat over the outcome of the election. "I did not know that Blockhead had the intelligence to be a barber," he wrote below a clipping of the "One Free Shave" cartoon. "How did you like the socking the Hump got from Nixon? Without love and with lots of hisses."[84] Yet the very fact that the depiction of a five-o'clock shadow within a cartoon created such public debate is testimony to both the effectiveness and pervasiveness of the Herblockian image of Nixon. Through these seemingly simple cartoons, Block created an image of Nixon that entered the public consciousness and became a frequent touchstone for Nixon's detractors when discussing the fundamental flaws of his character.

Although the "One Free Shave" cartoon was first published in the *Post* on November 7 and syndicated across the country over the course of the next several days, readers did not see Block's new depiction of Nixon until after the inauguration. The cartoonist instead teased his audience until then by drawing Nixon on only two occasions, and only in situations in which his chin was obscured.[85] When Block did finally unveil the newly clean-shaven Nixon on January 21, 1969, it was deemed so important that the *Post* celebrated with an editorial on the subject, hyperbolically writing that the cartoon marked "an historic occasion and a watershed, a threshold as well as a turning point and a crossroads, though not, perhaps, a full-fledged rubicon."[86] It was also no coincidence that the cartoon in question, titled "Post-Inaugural Parade," illustrates Nixon sitting at his new desk in the Oval Office contemplating a line of heavily stubbled men representing four of the most pressing issues facing the president: domestic problems, the question of nuclear arms controls, the Middle East, and Vietnam.[87] Nixon's five-o'clock shadow might be gone, Block was saying, but that did not mean he would give the president a pass on his new responsibilities. Nor did it mean he would not denounce any recurrence of Nixon's old style of smear politics. Indeed, although Block had ultimately been prepared to make this change because he felt that "an incoming president, particularly at a time of national division and crisis, was entitled to his chance to lead," he was also well aware that his readers would probably realize Nixon's old face continued to lurk beneath the new facade.[88]

Evidence of the darker side to Nixon's character reemerged in the lead-up to the presidential election of 1972. As the electoral cycle started once again, Block increasingly drew his readers' attention to two scandals involving Nixon and his reelection campaign. The first appeared remarkably mundane. Early in 1971, the Department of Agriculture had announced that there would be no increase to the federal subsidies paid to dairy producers to support the price of milk, a policy Nixon himself supported. But after a March 23 meeting between Nixon and representatives of the dairy lobby, the administration announced that there would indeed be an increase in the subsidy. In what became popularly known as the "Milk Fund Scandal," it soon became apparent that this reversal occurred only after the dairy lobby began making contributions, which ultimately totaled $2 million, to Nixon's reelection campaign. The second scandal involved a $400,000 donation that the International Telephone and Telegraph Corporation (ITT) made to help pay for the Republican National Convention in 1972 in return for the Justice Department's settling an antitrust suit.[89] Block regularly featured and commented on both of these scandals, frequently connecting them to each other to establish a pattern of corruption and illicit activities that, in Block's view at least, lay at the heart of Nixon's presidency. In November 25, 1971's "Think of Yourself as Contributing to 'The New Prosperity,'" for example, Block depicts a Nixon campaign worker shaking down a federal employee to force them to make a cash donation to the president's reelection fund. April 13, 1972's "Isn't There Some Simple Word for All That?" is even more explicit in its connection of the Nixon administration to corrupt and illegal activities. Drawn at the height of public awareness of the ITT scandal, the cartoon shows John Q. Public confronting a Department of Justice official holding a sign that reads, "We merely covered up 'highly improper' conduct to preserve an image" with the dictionary definition of "corruption."[90]

The connection that Block was making between the Nixon administration—not to mention Nixon specifically—and these activities did not go unnoticed by his readers. As early as August 1969, the cartoonist began to receive requests from across the country to restore the five-o'clock shadow to his depiction of Nixon. "I for one would be much happier to have the 'old Nixon,' stubble and all, to deride each morning" was a typical sentiment expressed by his readers. Reacting to an April 10, 1970, cartoon drawn in response to the Senate vote not to confirm Harrold Carswell to the Supreme Court, another correspondent wrote to "suggest that in the interests of all of us that we be rid of him on January 20, 1973 . . . you allow the famous five o'clock shadow to begin to show bit by bit until the vintage Nixon has reappeared in Herblock. Knowing his fondness for you," the writer continued, "I am sure there is no surer way to diminish his enthusiasm for Washington and the job."[91] Block never did restore the stubble, but with his cartoons intent on associating Nixon with these scandals and the smear tactics of his past, Block was predisposed to connect a seemingly random break-in at the headquarters of the Democratic National Committee (DNC) to the highest levels of the White House.

The *Washington Post* greeted the news that arrests had been made following an attempted break-in at the Watergate complex early on Saturday morning, June 17, 1972, with the nonchalant headline, "5 Held in Plot to Bug Democrats' Office Here."[92] There was little in the accompanying report to suggest the ultimate significance of the story. With few facts in the case available by the time it went to press, the story's focus was on a description of the arrests with an emphasis on the Cuban origins of three of the would-be burglars.[93] At this early stage, of course, it was unlikely that anyone could have foreseen how this break-in could possibly be linked to the highest levels of government; as Nixon himself later wrote, the whole story "sounded preposterous."[94] Sensitive about the danger of leaving itself open to a charge of pursuing a vendetta against the administration, especially after White House press secretary Ron Ziegler offered a pointed warning that "certain elements" would try "to stretch this beyond what it is," the *Post*'s initial coverage of the break-in was careful to report only on verifiable facts.[95] From the outset, however, Block refused to dismiss the break-in as the "third-rate burglary" Ziegler tried to frame it as, instead maintaining an almost relentless assault on the Nixon administration and instinctively recognizing that the break-in was to have greater repercussions than anyone else immediately realized.[96] As Chalmers M. Roberts, the *Post*'s official historian, later wrote, over the course of the ensuing scandal and investigation, Block was to rain "hammer blows at Nixon and his crew, drawing some of the most powerful cartoons of his career."[97]

With the initial arrests occurring on a Saturday morning, the first opportunity for Block to publish a cartoon commenting on the break-in was not until Tuesday, June 20.[98] Block did not hesitate to link Nixon directly to the crime. Captioned "Who Would Think of Doing Such a Thing?" the cartoon features Nixon, holding a suitcase marked "Nixon Fund Violations of Corrupt Practices Act," and his two attorneys general, John Mitchell and Richard Kleindienst, standing outside the DNC Headquarters. As they attempt to look innocently on, one of the arrested burglars is led out of the DNC offices by a security guard (fig. 40). Given that Mitchell and Kleindienst are seen holding briefcases containing tape recorders, one of which is labeled "Unconstitutional Tapping & Bugging," the question asked by the cartoon's caption was clearly rhetorical and made explicit to Block's readers his view that Nixon, together with his most intimate circle of advisors, had sanctioned the break-in and attempt to bug the DNC headquarters.[99]

The following day, Block went even further, drawing a cartoon that anticipated the White House's efforts to cover up the scandal. Captioned

FIGURE 40. *Washington Post,* June 20, 1972

"Remember, We Don't Talk till We Get a Lawyer," the cartoon pictures the same three men featured in the previous day's cartoon, all of whom were lawyers, holding a door in the White House closed while surrounded by newspaper headlines of the various lawsuits that the administration was facing at the time.[100] The most pointed of Block's initial Watergate cartoons, however, appeared on June 23, 1972, the same day that Nixon and his chief of staff, Bob Haldeman, conspired to have CIA Director Richard Helms inform Acting FBI Director L. Patrick Gray that the FBI's investigation into the break-in impinged on a CIA operation. Block's cartoon depicts two investigators examining footprints representing the Nixon fund scandals and the Watergate bugging, which lead directly to the front door of the White House. The caption reads, "Strange—They All Seem to Have Some Connection with This Place."[101] In this way, Block had within days of the break-in already linked it to the highest level of government in the country, well in advance of any news story even suggesting that Nixon might have been directly involved. Furthermore, and in line with both the paper's caution about over-aggressively reporting negative stories about the president and Block's unique position of editorial freedom, these three cartoons represented the first occasion on which the *Post*'s editorial page featured *any* mention of the break-in.

Block's ability to immediately see and depict the underlying truth of the Watergate break-in is not surprising. After all, by the time these cartoons were drawn, arrested burglar James McCord's association with the Nixon administration's Committee to Re-Elect the President had already been made public. Given that the unlabeled burglar in the "Who Would Think of Doing Such a Thing?" cartoon has a sheet of paper in his coat pocket marked "$1200 A Month From G.O.P.," we can assume that Block was responding at least partially to this news item and that his intent was to depict McCord in this cartoon. The *Post*'s June 20 story "White House Consultant Tied to Bugging Figure" had also suggested a tenuous connection between E. Howard Hunt, whose name was mentioned in a notebook seized from one of the burglars, to Charles Colson, a White House special counsel and one of Nixon's inner circle of advisors.[102] Furthermore, Block had long been outraged by the growing number of controversies emanating from the Nixon White House, dedicating a growing number of his cartoons to such issues as the ITT case and the Milk Fund scandal.

Evidence pointing to some level of administration involvement in the break-in therefore already existed by the time Block drew his first cartoons on the subject. But no major newspaper had published a story or editorial that made the connection as explicit, while the cartoonist's concerns over the ethics of Nixon's administration—although certainly popular with liberals—had yet to gain widespread credence from the general public. For Block, the Watergate scandal was initially just one more example in an ongoing litany of illegal activities, and throughout 1972–74 he incorporated these earlier scandals and allegations of corruption into the cartoons he drew about the unfolding Watergate scandal. He had also associated John Mitchell with government wiretaps since February 1971 and suggested Nixon's involvement in the cover-up of corrupt or illegal activities as recently as March and April 1972.[103] In this context, it was logical for him to make an explicit link between the White House and Nixon to the break-in. By doing so, Block presented a position that went further than the *Post*'s headlines, its editorials, or the rest of the mainstream media were prepared to go at this early stage of the story. Years later, Carl Bernstein, one of the two reporters who led the *Post*'s reporting of the unfolding scandal and who have become inextricably linked to the news media's coverage of the scandal, admitted that Block grasped the significance of the break-in far more quickly than anyone else in the *Post*'s newsroom, commenting that Block "had an understanding before the facts [came out] of where [the story] was going to go."[104] Similarly, Block's instinctive response to the break-in led Katharine Graham to declare that his cartoons were "well ahead . . . of the news side of the paper['s]" own understanding of the break-in's ultimate significance.[105]

After these three June 1972 cartoons, however, Block's attention reverted to more pressing issues. During July and August, most of his cartoons were focused on the 1972 election campaign and Vietnam, with only seven of the forty-four cartoons drawn over this two-month span having any relation to the scandal. Nevertheless, Block did attempt to ensure that his readers across the country remained familiar with the break-in by connecting it to some of these other events. On July 14, for example, Block drew a cartoon showing a delegate to the Democratic National Convention leaving a hotel room that very obviously had every item of furniture bugged by the Republicans.[106] Block's tendency at this time to focus primarily on other events was also seen five days later in a cartoon that clearly reacts to a news story published on July 11 in the *Post* reporting on claims from the Nixon campaign that "'Bug' Hearings Would Hurt [Their] Campaign." The cartoon is nonetheless prescient in a way that Block could not have possibly anticipated as its depiction of a campaign worker caught up in reams of tape while attempting to prevent a judge from accessing his recordings foreshadowed Nixon's own future battles with the courts for control of his Oval Office recording system.[107]

Of the five Watergate-related cartoons drawn during August, two demonstrated Block's uncanny ability to see straight to the heart of the matter. August 25's "The Dark at the Top of the Stairs" shows Nixon stopping an attempt to investigate the break-in by physically assaulting a public investigator, while "Keep the Lid on till after the Election," first published four days later on August 29, instinctively recognized the fear that existed within the administration that the scandals might begin to unravel and threaten Nixon's reelection bid.[108] What is significant about both of these cartoons is their explicit depiction of Nixon's active involvement in the administration's efforts to block the initial investigations into Watergate. Although later revelations revealed the accuracy of this charge, it was a stance few other commentators were yet willing to take in such a public forum. After August, Block began to give greater prominence to Watergate until the crisis came to dominate his cartoons. Although there were undoubtedly some cartoons that had greater relevance with knowledge of later developments, until Nixon's resignation Block tended to simply follow the story rather than anticipate it. This was made clear in some of the captions to his cartoons, including October 1's "Latest Item Pulled out of the Swamp," which remarks on the revelation from two days earlier that John Mitchell had controlled a secret fund used to gather information about the Democrats. The cartoon's vivid depiction of a safe, labeled "Attorney General of the United States Secret Republican Fund for Political Espionage," being hauled out of the swamp of "Administration Corruption" might have graphically reminded his readers of the corruption Block believed permeated every aspect of the Nixon administration, but its caption also served to highlight the reactive nature of Block's work.[109]

At the time, though, there was little in the way of breaking news for Block to comment on. With the election quickly approaching, Block's interest clearly lay in reminding the public about the general corruptness of the administration in the hopes of peeling voters away from the incumbent. Nixon's opponent in 1972 was South Dakota senator George McGovern, who had won the Democratic nomination despite not being supported by the party's establishment. Instead, he built a grassroot movement that attracted many of those who had supported Eugene McCarthy four years earlier—and took advantage of changes to the convention's rules that had been implemented since 1968, resulting in an increase to the number of delegates who were women, minorities, and young people—to win the nomination. Considered the most liberal of the various Democratic candidates, McGovern ran on a progressive platform that reflected many liberal priorities from the time, including support for a guaranteed minimum wage for the poor, endorsement of the Equal Rights Amendment, and the promise of an immediate end to the Vietnam War coupled with a scaling back of the nation's military capacity. More important than McGovern's actual positions, though, was the public's perception of what he stood for. In the heat of the battle for the nomination, an anonymous Democratic senator, later revealed to have been Missouri's Thomas Eagleton, was quoted saying, "The people don't know McGovern is for amnesty, abortion, and legalization of pot. Once middle America—Catholic middle America, in particular—finds this out, he's dead." The truth was more complicated, and while he did support offering pardons to draft dodgers, McGovern's pro-choice views on abortion were shared by millions of other Americans, including many Republicans, and he considered drug legalization to be an issue for individual states to decide. Nonetheless, McGovern was never able to escape the charge, leveled at him first by Humphrey supporters and then Nixon supporters, that he stood for "amnesty, abortion, and acid," and the electorate overwhelmingly rejected him in a landslide defeat, leaving liberals to consider how their ideas had fallen so far outside the political mainstream.[110]

Throughout 1972, Block's Watergate cartoons tended to fall into one of three categories. Some dealt with specific incidents, which generally proved to be of little consequence in the context of Nixon's overall corruption.[111] Others depicted the administration attempting to prevent investigations into various scandals.[112] A very few showed Nixon intimately involved either in the wrong-doings or in the attempted cover-ups.[113] Block's success in painting a picture of an administration that would do anything to win the election led one reader to credit him in a letter to the *Post*'s editors for "exposing the highly questionable dealings of the Nixon administration."[114] In total, Block drew 139 cartoons between June 17 and December 31, 1972. Of these, 27—or almost one in five—commented on the Watergate break-in in some fashion. In contrast, over the same set of dates, the *Post* wrote only 17 editorials on the topic, a significantly lower level of engagement and interest, which illustrates the greater focus Block placed on the scandal in the months immediately following the break-in.[115] There was also no discernible pattern linking the cartoons to the editorials. In 1972, it was certainly more common that when the *Post* printed an editorial commenting on Watergate, Block's daily cartoon would focus on, for example, the state of the economy or Vietnam, rather than both editorial and cartoon focusing on the scandal.

With the start of Nixon's second term in January 1973, the pattern changed as Block increasingly gave more attention to the crisis. Not only did these cartoons become more powerful and outspoken against Nixon but they also clearly began to imply it was only a matter of time before the scandal caught up with him and caused permanent damage to his presidency. April 27, 1973's "Somebody Has to Think about Tomorrow" depicts a Republican congressman frantically building an ark designed to shelter two Republican elephants from the increasing floodwaters of the "Watergate Scandals" that are already beginning to overwhelm the White House.[116] This cartoon, with its clear implication that rank-and-file Republicans were beginning to abandon the president to the inevitability of his fate was drawn in response to comments from Republican National Committee Chair George H. W. Bush that Watergate was undermining the Republican Party which were reported on the front page of that day's *Post*.[117] As Block increasingly responded to the *Post*'s own headlines, he also took advantage of his close proximity to the paper's lead reporters on the scandal, Bob Woodward and Carl Bernstein, who helped him stay abreast of the story and ensured that his cartoons accurately reflected the latest developments in their reporting. This ranged from fact-checking details, such as "the correct amounts of the secret stash in the safe of

Maurice Stans and John Mitchell," to keeping him abreast of "which things were definite and which were not yet nailed down" so that Block could ensure his cartoons reflected the most accurate and up-to-date version of the publicly available story as possible. As Block wryly commented in his autobiography, "This was as close to the horse's mouth as a person could get without lodging in its deep throat."[118]

As Block devoted more of his work to the unfolding crisis, he gave greater attention to each stage of the revelations, frequently drawing sequences of cartoons inspired by a single event that served to both highlight different aspects of the story and reinforce in his readers' minds the points he advocated. During February and March 1973, for example, he drew a series of cartoons commenting on Acting FBI Director L. Patrick Gray's confirmation hearings in the Senate to make his appointment permanent. The first of these, titled "Shadowed," appeared on February 27—a day before the hearings even opened—and depicts the integrity of the FBI compromised by Gray's willingness to defer to the political ambitions of the Republican Party. As the confirmation hearings progressed, and Gray's early cooperation with John Dean in seeking to limit the scope of the investigation into the break-in became more apparent to the general public, so too did Block's cartoons more directly show Gray turning a blind eye to the obviously illegal activities of Nixon's closest aides, a group that Block began to collectively refer to in his cartoons as the "White House Gang."[119]

Block also increasingly drew more general cartoons on the scandal, which represented Nixon's ever more desperate efforts to find a way out of the crisis. "Obstacle Course," published on February 19, 1974, shows Nixon pushing over representations of executive privilege and national security concerns in an effort to impede a pursuing Lady Justice, while March 6's "Streaking" depicts a naked Nixon running from the protection of one attempt to cover up the scandals to another.[120] Yet another frequently used motif was a portrayal of the scandals as rising floodwaters threatening to engulf the administration. Block first introduced this imagery in April 1973 in a cartoon that imagined water lapping at the door of the White House, and he employed it throughout the crisis, showing Nixon frantically holding on to his desk as the water burst through into the Oval Office at the time of Dean's testimony in June 1973 and again in March 1974 when seven of Nixon's former aides were indicted, until finally

Nixon threatened to be swept away by the strength of the evidence against him in July 1974.[121] By returning to and reinforcing his own iconography in this way, Block ensured his readers received familiar visual cues that connected the illegal activities of the administration to the break-in and ensuing cover-up.

A subtle change in Block's depiction of the scandal occurred in May 1973. Whereas many of his earlier Watergate-themed cartoons had depicted Nixon, or one or more of his aides, trying to hide evidence from investigators, Block began to show Nixon hiding *himself* from both investigators and the American public. This motif first appeared in a cartoon published in the *Post* on May 3. In it, Block imagined Nixon hiding behind his Oval Office desk while holding a sign in his right hand that reads, "The man at the top must bear full responsibility. About a special prosecutor—see my next attorney general." With his left hand, Nixon is frantically gesturing away from himself, while on his desk is a nameplate that sardonically declares, "The Buck Passes Here."[122] This change in emphasis was most vividly seen, however, in May 27's "National-Security Blanket," which depicts Nixon wrapping himself in the national flag while surrounded by the evidence of his political corruption, including piles of illegally acquired cash, wiretapping equipment, and stolen and forged documents.[123] The change is important because it indicated to Block's readers the culpability of the president while also reflecting the shifting emphasis of the administration itself, which by this point was heavily focused on protecting Nixon from being implicated directly in the quickly escalating cover-up.

Block's unwavering focus on exposing what he saw as Nixon's inherent criminality inevitably provoked a strong reaction from readers of his cartoons. One reader, for example, wrote to the *Middletown Times Herald Record* in February 1973 demanding that the New York–based newspaper stop printing Block's "vicious cartoons." Arguing that Block "nurtures a personal hate 'hang up' against President Nixon," the letter writer took solace in the notion that "Herblock is able to work off his frustrations and aggressions through his syndicated cartoons instead of resorting to writing poison pen letters or making obscene phone calls as an outlet for his neurotic behavior." This letter clearly struck a chord with some of the *Times Herald Record*'s readership, compelling a different reader, who was angry at Block's willingness to use his platform to promote a political ideology the letter writer did not share, to suggest that "Herblock devote one cartoon to a caricature of himself so that the readers may absorb his Holier Than Thou Image." Demonstrating the fierce partisanship that Block's cartoons engendered, however, yet another reader defended the cartoonist. "If Herblock's penthrusts can provoke such anguished screams of affront from 'red-blooded' Americans who voted for Richard the Fist [*sic*]," this third correspondent wrote, "then he is doing his job and earning his keep. . . . He is a man whose feeling for liberty and honesty runs closer to the mainstream of American ideology than the overheated superpatriotism of some of your readers could ever dimly comprehend."[124] Even Block's colleagues at the *Post* at times became angered by what they viewed as the blind partisanship of Block's cartoons. At a dinner hosted by W. Averell Harriman in April 1974, Block became embroiled in an argument with the *Post*'s syndicated columnist Joseph Alsop, who accused the cartoonist of having contributed to the hyperpartisan environment that surrounded the elections of 1968 and 1972 and was therefore "one of those who had helped to elect [Nixon]." In a written apology to Block, Alsop expressed his anger at those critics of the president who, in his opinion, were "behaving like hyenas around a corpse" but nevertheless argued that no matter what his crimes, Nixon demanded respect because, "after all, he is our President, son of a bitch 'though he may be."[125]

Throughout the Watergate period, particularly as it approached its dénouement, Block created a visual arsenal of uncompromising cartoons that clearly demonstrated his anger at the abuses of the Nixon administration. Among the most powerful of these was an ongoing series in which he portrayed the symbol of Lady Justice—a personification of the moral force that underpins the judicial system—being victimized by Nixon and his aides. The first appeared as early as November 1, 1972, in a cartoon that juxtaposes the landslide victory polls were predicting in the presidential election later that week with the sight of Justice teetering on the verge of an abyss as the ground collapses around her due to the instability caused by the Nixon scandals and the administration's efforts to cover up its involvement. A later appearance, on July 12, 1973, depicts John Mitchell standing bloody-handed over Justice's dead body innocently telling the American public that "In Retrospect, Looking Back, and with Hindsight—."

The following month, Block showed her being tied and gagged by Nixon and his close aides Bob Haldeman and John Ehrlichman. On October 23, 1973, as a response to Nixon's dismissal of independent special prosecutor Archibald Cox, and the subsequent resignations of Attorney General Elliot Richardson and Deputy Attorney General William Ruckelshaus—an event that became known as the "Saturday Night Massacre"—Block depicted Nixon "Mugging" Justice (fig. 41). The final appearance of Lady Justice in a Watergate-themed cartoon, published on July 21, 1974, is just as graphic: she is seen tied to a post awaiting the firing squad as Nixon stands ready

FIGURE 41. *Washington Post,* October 23, 1973

to give the order. Meanwhile, an onlooker asks, "How Can They Say He Hasn't Faithfully Executed the Laws?"[126] For readers, the impact of these cartoons would have been clear and unequivocal. Richard Nixon, president of the United States, was seen to be metaphorically destroying America's deepest values.

The cartoon that most successfully captured the moment of Watergate, however, was published on May 24, 1974. It shows Nixon precariously hanging between two reels of tape on which the words "I Am . . . a Crook" appear. In Nixon's mouth is a clipped piece of tape on which is written the single word "Not" (fig. 42).[127] In a single powerful graphic, Block managed to synthesize the most salient details of the events that led to the collapse of Nixon's political career. During a news conference on November 17, 1973, Nixon had declared that "in all of my years in public life, I have never obstructed justice. . . . People have got to know whether or not their president is a crook. Well, I am not a crook."[128] The cartoon, which was drawn in the wake of Nixon's decision to release only edited transcripts from the Oval Office's taping system, turns this declaration of innocence on its head. Block had referenced this speech in three earlier cartoons—on two occasions showing the president holding a sign that declared "I Am Not a Crook" and once depicting two men listening to the White House tapes and imagining that they can hear him repeating the phrase over and over again like a mantra.[129] But in this cartoon, Block transformed the assertion from a passive statement into an active act of illegality by Nixon that perfectly captured both the ongoing cover-up and the desperation that pervaded the administration as it made one final effort to avoid Nixon's culpability from coming to light.

From the very beginning, Block had grasped the importance of Watergate far sooner than the rest of the editorial team at the *Washington Post,* and throughout the twenty-six-month period that culminated in Nixon's resignation, Block gave proportionately more space to it than the paper's editorial writers. Because of the complete editorial independence that he enjoyed with the *Post* at this point in his career, Block was also able to concentrate his cartoons on those aspects of Watergate he considered most important. This allowed him, earlier than the majority of other observers, to anticipate later developments, such as Nixon's direct involvement in efforts to cover up the scandals. September 17, 1972's

FIGURE 42. *Washington Post,* May 24, 1974

"There You Are, Boy—Nice Bone—" was an early example of Block's effort to tie the president to the scandals. It shows Nixon pointing to a small bone, representing the indictments of the burglars, in an effort to deflect an investigative bloodhound's attention from a room overflowing with administration scandals.[130] The cartoon clearly predicted Nixon's tactic of making scapegoats out of his aides and offering compromises to the Senate Select Committee on Presidential Campaign Activities, which was established in February 1973 to investigate the Watergate break-in and subsequent cover-up of criminal activity, in an effort to deflect blame from himself and satisfy the committee's enquiries. With Block's belief that political cartoons should act as an independent voice within the *Post,* and that he had a responsibility to not simply illustrate that day's editorial, he picked the subjects of his cartoons and was able to focus his readers' attention on issues that did not necessarily capture as much coverage in the national press as other developments in Watergate.[131] He was very concerned, for example, about revelations regarding the use of taxpayer money to renovate Nixon's home in San Clemente and his evasion of income taxes. Block's outspoken concern for such topics—which he depicted in his cartoons long after any initial media attention on them had moved on to other concerns—is revealing as, generally speaking, it was only staunch liberals who considered these to be significant offenses.[132]

Block's early and sustained coverage of the unfolding drama ultimately made him as prominent a political and journalistic presence during the crisis as Woodward and Bernstein. This fact was recognized in May 1973 when the *Post* was awarded the Pulitzer Prize for distinguished public service for its coverage of Watergate. The accompanying citation praised the paper for how it "mobilized its total resources for a major investigation" and specifically named both the work of its "two first-rate investigative reporters . . . and [the] editorial cartoons drawn by the two-time Pulitzer Prize winner Herbert A. [*sic*] Block (Herblock)."[133] In the heady days following Nixon's resignation, accolades such as this led the news media to claim credit for their role in driving the process forward, a sentiment that journalists and the general public have echoed ever since.[134] Indeed, the notion that Nixon's resignation was the result of a "liberal witch-hunt" led by the press surfaced long before he left the White House in disgrace and has since become a mantra within conservative circles.[135] As early as June 1972, columnist David B. Wilson was able to allude to this notion when he asked his readers to imagine "a candidate supported by Herblock, Shirley MacLaine and the New York Review of Books, and suppose that candidate's administration had [achieved what Nixon's administration did during its term]. . . . The Left would be hailing him as the savior of the country."[136]

In the aftermath of Nixon's resignation, several reviewers of Block's 1974 cartoon anthology *Herblock Special Report* even seemed to suggest that if only the rest of the press had been as willing as Block to fearlessly take on Nixon and reveal the corruption that lay at the heart of his character, he would never have been elected president in the first place.[137] Nixon himself certainly believed that he was ultimately a victim of media bias and increasingly saw his chances of surviving in the White House to the end of his second term as coming, in his words, "down to a race for public opinion: in other words, a campaign."[138] In truth, the media's role in Watergate was not as important as these commentators claimed. But the *Post,* and other newspapers and media outlets across the country, did influence the ways in which the public and, to a lesser extent, politicians thought about and defined the basic facts of the case as they were revealed and reported. By doing so, the media forged an underlying current of opinion that enabled the judicial and legislative branches of the federal government to move their cases against Nixon forward.

Whatever role the press, and the *Post* especially, had in Nixon's downfall, Block played an integral part in helping to influence and shape the public's view of Watergate. He recognized earlier than anyone else that, as he later wrote, "Watergate was not just an isolated incident. It was the place where events and the law finally caught up with a group of criminals operating under a corrupt official at the very top of the government."[139] Block's role in influencing public opinion was also magnified by the vast reach the syndication of his cartoons gave him. With his work regularly appearing in over 200 newspapers around the world, his cartoons were seen by a far larger audience than the approximately 530,000 who were regularly reading the *Post* at this time.[140] Even the notion that Watergate played out as a political witch-hunt connects to Nixon's earliest Herblock appearance in the cartoon "We Got to Burn the Evil Spirits out of Her."[141] Katharine Graham, meanwhile, was certain that his cartoons had a more "immediate impact" than the *Post* on "the way people came to think about Watergate."[142] In a twenty-four-page retrospective of Nixon's career that made almost no mention of the media's role in pursuing the Watergate story, the *Post* nevertheless dedicated a full page to Block's long record of attacking Nixon in his cartoons. The cartoons were printed under the same words that Nixon had used just thirty months earlier to prove to the American people he had grown as a politician and a man: "Years ago, when I was a young congressman, things got under my skin. Herblock the cartoonist got to me. . . . But now when I walk into this office I am cool and calm."[143]

Ultimately, Block was so successful in getting "under Nixon's skin" because of his unerring ability to take seemingly off-the-cuff descriptions of Nixon first made by others—from the use of Checkers the dog to the depiction of Nixon emerging from a sewer, from Adlai Stevenson's description of the then vice president's "new face" to the beleaguered president's own defiant declaration "I am not a crook"—and repeat them in graphic form as the basis of not just one cartoon but multiple sequences of cartoons that created a narrative around the politician that became lodged in his readers' minds. As a result, Nixon became irrevocably identified across liberal circles with this Herblockian archetype. The "Herblock Nixon" became a visual and literary shorthand that could be invoked by liberal writers and others when they needed to conjure a particular image of Nixon that presented him as a sinister, untrustworthy criminal who, after cheating his way into power through his unabashed use of smear and gutter politics, treated the presidency as his own personal fiefdom. This was, in short, a visual representation of what Arthur Schlesinger described in his 1973 book *The Imperial Presidency* as the "expansion and abuse of presidential power" that had begun under Johnson and "constituted the underlying issue . . . that Watergate raised to the surface."[144] It was not just liberals, however, who used Block's caricature of Nixon for their own purposes. Conservatives also invoked the specter of the Herblock Nixon as a shorthand with which to rally their supporters. But in their hands, the imagery became a metaphor not for the dangers of unfettered power but of liberal hubris run wild. The sagging jowls, ski-jump nose, and heavy five-o'clock shadow all became evidence of the lengths to which liberal ideologues, and especially the liberal-controlled media, was prepared go to discredit and remove from power the president of the United States.

Block's depiction of Richard Nixon and later of his administration and the Watergate scandal therefore highlighted a deep partisan split that was becoming all too evident across the country. His cartoons were not the cause of this increasingly acrimonious atmosphere, but they provided an important rallying call for the agendas of both sides of the country's political divide.

EPILOGUE

"A Watchman in the Night"

WHEN RICHARD NIXON RESIGNED ON August 9, 1974, Block was sixty-four years old and enjoying a renewed level of influence and popularity. Just six days later, the cartoonist took a month-long vacation from his duties at the *Post* to write the book that would cement his reputation as one of the first and most powerful critics of Nixon's life and career. A celebratory account of Block's long and antagonistic relationship with Nixon, *Herblock Special Report* noted that Nixon partisans, dating back to his tenure as vice president, had stated that critics "who questioned Nixon's fitness for public office had some mysterious quirk. The problem was not with him—it was with us." Repudiating that claim, the book outlined the litany of offenses committed by Nixon against the American people. It reveled in the irony that a man whose career had been launched to expel "subversive" elements from American government had himself been condemned for actions "subversive of constitutional government." Reminding his readers that while America may have been built on "a government of laws, not of men," Block ended his book with a call to action, stating that those laws "don't enforce themselves." To keep the abuses of government in check, the "public has to be a watchman in the night, keeping such a sharp lookout that public servants find it easier to do the right thing than the wrong thing."[1] Reviewers of *Herblock Special Report* lavished praise on Block and his cartoons, noting his prescience in opposing Nixon so early. "It is the public's good fortune that Herblock was where he was when he was and the public's good fortune that he put together this record," one declared. "Long after [the names of various Watergate actors] have receded behind the curtains of time, this book will be consulted by our descendants who will want to know what it was all about."[2]

Over the next several months, Block fielded a steady stream of invitations for interviews and personal appearances. Ever a proponent of an engaged press that would stand up for what was right, in the few interview requests he granted Block urged his fellow citizens and journalists to remain ever vigilant against the next threat to American democracy despite criticisms they faced from those whose corruption and misdeeds they were pursuing. "Every fight is a new fight," he declared in a December 1975 speech delivered at a fundraiser for the liberal publications the *Nation* and the *Progressive,* "and each time the non-complacent part of the press is viewed with suspicion." He decried the increasingly common trend of massive corporations purchasing local newspapers and replacing their news and editorial content with syndicated material that both served to commoditize the news and reflected the often-conservative biases of those new owners. "In the United States today," he complained, "there are many states in which there are no competing newspaper ownerships in any city. If you travel around the country, you come across newspapers which publish columns that run the gamut from pro-Reagan to pro-Ford."[3]

Just as Block cautioned that journalistic consolidation would endanger the liberal roots of American democracy, he also tried to embolden individual citizens to fight for the nation's founding principles. The postwar liberal order, so vividly articulated in Block's cartoons, had attempted to leverage the resources of the federal government to create a better society that protected the welfare of all Americans. But liberalism was largely shattered by the political disorder that saw the solidification of conservative power in government with 1976's election of Jimmy Carter as president. A conservative Democrat who ran as a political outsider, Carter promised to cut wasteful spending and limit the size of the federal government. The combined trauma of Vietnam and the Watergate scandal had compromised many Americans' faith in the ability of the government to act in the best interests of the people. The fall of Saigon in April 1975, which precipitated the panicked withdrawal of American personnel from Vietnam, highlighted the conflict's cost in terms of American lives and led some to question the purpose of continuing to fight the Cold War. The Russian invasion of Afghanistan and the ousting of the American-backed Iranian government by Islamic fundamentalists in 1979 punctuated the impotence of American foreign policy. Closer to home, Gerald Ford's decision "to firmly shut and seal" the Watergate scandal by pardoning Nixon only succeeded in inflaming the passions of many Americans who were incensed that the cover-up seemed to be continuing. New revelations regarding the intelligence and national security communities' abuses in the fight against communism, including revelations of the CIA's participation in efforts to assassinate foreign politicians and domestic spying against civil rights leaders, further eroded Americans' confidence in their government. As that faith in government crumbled, so too did the prospects of postwar liberalism's survival as a meaningful ideological force, whether the New Deal liberalism that underscored the era's consensus politics or the qualitative liberalism that informed the Great Society. Both had been sustained by a combination of Cold War anxieties and the widespread belief that the government should act to improve society. The failure of government to protect its citizens and enforce its foreign policy stimulated liberalism's decline.

Other developments in the 1970s further undermined liberalism's viability as a political ideology. Liberal-leaning political organizations such as Americans for Democratic Action struggled to maintain both relevancy and members as the coalition of moderate Democrats and Republicans, southern Democrats, and labor unions that had originally forged the postwar liberal consensus fractured. Southern Democrats abandoned the party during the campaign for civil rights. Conservative activists successfully purged the Republican Party of its more moderate members, who were targeted as unfaithful to the party's priorities. White working-class men, meanwhile, became disillusioned with what they perceived as liberalism's dismissal of their concerns and grievances. They increasingly saw liberalism's most prominent spokespeople and leaders as out-of-touch elitists. Adding to this was the faltering and then collapse of the booming economy that had enabled many of the federal programs championed by liberals. Brought down by a combination of deindustrialization and the rising cost of oil, the economy experienced significant inflation and rising unemployment. News reports and popular culture portrayed America's biggest cities as crime-infested dystopias. Politicians, from the federal administrations of Ford and Carter down to local municipal officials, were supposedly unwilling and unable to do anything to fix urban issues. In tandem, the nation's commitment to equality for all seemed more tenuous. The court-mandated busing of students to reduce racial segregation in schools drew impassioned protests across the country. Many white Americans hastened their flight from the cities to new suburbs where they could live in homogenous communities that excluded people of color. The Supreme Court's 1973 ruling in *Roe v. Wade* that women have a constitutional right to an abortion was a significant victory for the feminist movement. But conservative activists led by Pat Buchanan politicized the issue, drawing an increasing number of southerners, Catholics, and senior voters to the Republican Party. Feminists were dealt an even heavier blow when conservatives, led by the activist Phyllis Schlafly, defeated the Equal Rights Amendment just as it was on the cusp of winning ratification. The efforts of gay and lesbian activists to draw attention to their own lack of equal rights before the law similarly incensed self-proclaimed defenders of traditional American values.

Collectively, these factors contributed to the fracturing of postwar liberalism and played a role in the victory of Ronald Reagan in the 1980 presidential election. Running as the standard-bearer of conservative Republicanism that Block had spent much of the 1960s attacking, Reagan promised a complete renunciation of liberalism and its politics. "Government is not the solution to our problem," he famously declared during the campaign. "Government is the problem." In his effort to shrink the size of the federal government, Reagan persuaded Congress to pass sweeping tax cuts that reduced the rate paid by those in the highest tax bracket from 70 to 50 percent. Coupled with soaring defense spending that resulted in unprecedented federal deficits, Reagan advanced policies that limited the government's responsibility for social problems, opposed efforts at racial justice, and eased the regulation of private business. Compounding this unraveling of the liberal state was the administration's disdain for the news media, which it accused of pushing a liberal bias in its reporting.

Although there was little evidence that this was true, the repeated complaints had an impact on the profession. Ben Bradlee, the *Washington Post*'s editor, admitted that his paper, in reporting on the first "really true conservative" presidential administration and aware of its reputation "as the great liberals," had "been kinder to President Reagan than any President I can remember."[4] Whether the *Post* employed different standards when reporting on Reagan than it did with his recent predecessors, it was a policy that was assuredly not followed by the paper's political cartoonist.

After spending the previous administration frustrated at Carter's indecisiveness and unwillingness to pursue a liberal agenda, Block greeted Reagan with a full-blooded assault that emphasized the new president's disregard for social and racial equality. He attacked the callousness of Reagan's push for indiscriminate spending cuts to social programs, which impacted the poorest and most vulnerable of Americans. In one March 1981 cartoon, Block depicted Reagan's head as a wrecking ball set to tear down social protections such as Medicaid, family planning, and job training initiatives as part of the administration's twisted version of the War on Poverty. Six months later, he showed Reagan cheerfully telling a malnourished schoolgirl that her glass of milk was still half full after a round of cuts to school-lunch funding.[5] As the decade progressed, Block increasingly critiqued the divide between rich and poor that became ever larger during the 1980s. He condemned the vast tax cuts that favored the wealthiest Americans, contrasting the riches lavished on defense and military spending with the austerity imposed on domestic programs. He explicitly questioned the priorities of an administration that seemed to be increasingly influenced by a religious right that advocated for socially conservative policies over policies for economic and social justice.[6] At the same time, Block reinforced the continuing importance of the type of programs that had characterized the qualitative liberalism proposed by his old friend Arthur Schlesinger. Cartoons advocating for stronger environmental protections became a regular feature of Block's work, as did cartoons lamenting the lack of progress toward meaningful civil rights legislation. He also pushed for greater gun controls, regularly critiquing the influence of the National Rifle Association on national policy.

Overwhelmingly, though, the theme that Block repeatedly returned to was his belief in Reagan's willingness to mislead the American public without remorse or repercussion. In January 1983, for example, Block highlighted the administration's frequent need both to clarify presidential statements and blame the media for its own shortcomings by depicting Larry Speakes, Reagan's deputy press secretary, angrily telling the White House Press Corps, "Damn Media! You Should Know Better Than to Report All the Dopey Things He Says." A year later Reagan was shown in a frozen landscape preparing to address the nation on his achievements in office over the last three years while standing next to space heaters and in front of a backdrop depicting a warm, sunny climate.[7] Block used similar visual metaphors to highlight the devastation that Reagan's policies had wrecked on the achievements of postwar liberalism. In his December 1, 1981, cartoon, Block imagined a series of government agencies, ranging from the Environmental Protection Agency to the Consumer Product Safety Commission, as a series of buildings being torn apart by a construction crew of "Reagan's Wreckers" while the president himself eagerly tells the foreman, "Leave the Facades—It'll Be Just Like Hollywood."[8] Block argued in 1984 that "Reagan differed from his predecessors . . . because to him there was apparently no distinction between delivering statements as president and delivering lines as an actor—*it didn't matter* whether the words were factual."[9] His cartoons reinforced this point, depicting Reagan and his administration as having less credibility than the movies in which the former actor once starred.

Block was well aware that his views were not shared by the majority of Americans. He would later describe Reagan's presidency as eight years in which "the country became involved with a former actor and entered into an era when fact, fiction and fantasy, reality and silver-screen make-believe, all blended together."[10] The cartoon that best captured Block's incredulity about the Reagan administration's dismantling of the liberal state was published on June 3, 1984. Inspired by both Lewis Carroll's *Alice through the Looking Glass* and the marketing for the 1982 movie *Poltergeist*, the cartoon depicts a young girl stepping into a television set that is broadcasting coverage of Reagan (fig. 43). For Block, and the liberal establishment that he represented, the country had truly passed "Through the Looking Glass," into a dimension where everything, including logic, had been reversed.[11] But where Carroll had once imagined a fantasy, for Block this alternative world was a place of horror. How else could one

FIGURE 43. *Washington Post,* June 3, 1984

explain the rise of Reagan and the conservative movement which stood antithetical to the liberalism of postwar America?

Some four decades later, Block's cartoons stand as powerful testaments to the priorities of postwar liberalism. By drawing liberalism, his cartoons helped shape and popularize liberal ideology by creating symbols and imagery that resonated with his readers to reinforce their own beliefs and prejudices. Like most liberal intellectuals of his generation, Block understood the primary makers and influencers of history to be political leaders and those in charge of the government's institutions and bureaucracy. As a result, his cartoons tended to privilege the actions of the nation's white establishment—the president, the legislature, the Supreme Court, and the governors—and to portray them as the men primarily responsible for change in America. Block believed, though, that it was his responsibility as an editorial cartoonist to stand up against forces that would subjugate the rights of ordinary Americans for their own benefit and self-interests. The hero of his cartoons therefore remained the average, middle-class American who represented what Block saw as commonsense liberal values.

Block ultimately placed his faith in America's future in the willingness of its people to "do the right thing" and guard against corruption, guided by a free and vigorous press. But the twenty-first century is a very different media environment to that of the postwar world in which Block lived. The emergence of dedicated twenty-four-hour news channels and, especially, the internet has transformed how Americans consume the news. Between 1970 and 2018, the number of daily newspapers in the United States fell from 1,748 to 1,279. Far more dramatically, the paid circulation of these newspapers dropped from 62.82 million in 1970 to only 24.29 million in 2020.[12] These developments have had a profound impact on how newspapers are operated, with twenty-five companies now owning more than half of the newspapers still being published, editorial decisions enforced by corporate interests, and the number of staff in a newsroom slashed. The *Washington Post* itself has been impacted by these changes, with the Graham family selling its controlling stake in the newspaper to Amazon.com founder Jeff Bezos for $250 million in 2013. At the same time, the industry has been politicized with news organizations constantly fending off charges of liberal bias and, since 2016, of being peddlers of "fake news."

Block's profession has been especially hard hit. According to a 2011 report compiled by the Herb Block Foundation, whereas "at the start of the 20th century, there were approximately 2,000 editorial cartoonists employed by newspapers in the United States," by the time of the report there were "fewer than 40 staff cartoonists, and that number continues to shrink."[13] Indeed, in the decade since, the *Arizona Republic, Houston Chronicle, Indianapolis Star, Pittsburgh Post-Gazette,* and *New York Times* are just some of the more prominent newspapers to eliminate their staff cartoonists, relying instead on syndicated material.[14] This dramatic decline can, in part, be explained by the same cost-cutting measures that have resulted in dramatically smaller reporting staffs at newspapers across the country. But the result has been a homogenization of the opinions expressed by cartoonists, with fewer references to local news stories and less willingness to engage in the full-throttled attacks on political figures that helped secure Block's reputation and legacy.

Block's liberalism was the defining characteristic of his career, making him a celebrated defender of Americans' rights to those who shared his sensibilities and a hated and vindictive purveyor of lies to his detractors. Even today, two decades after his death from pneumonia in 2001 at the age of ninety-one, Block's cartoons continue to raise partisan hackles. In June 2013, the American Film Institute hosted a gala reception in Washington, DC, to mark the release of the documentary film *Herblock: The Black and the White.* Interviewed in the film, and providing glowing commentary of Block's cartoons, were such media figures as television journalists Bob Schieffer and Tom Brokaw, the *Washington Post*'s Carl Bernstein and Bob Woodward, fellow cartoonist Jules Feiffer, and television satirists Jon Stewart and Lewis Black. Although reviewers were uncertain about a narrative device in which an actor portrayed Block and provided a linking narrative that was based primarily on extracts from Block's autobiography, the film was generally well received by critics. Typical was *Time*'s David Von Drehle, who declared that "Block belongs on the short list of the greatest journalists of the 20th century, even though he rarely wrote more than a few words at a time and worked in a cluttered office far from distant battlefields."[15] Others, however, were less complimentary. Despite unintentionally highlighting the impact that his cartoons had by pointing out that many commentators considered Joseph McCarthy to be "ruggedly handsome" until Block began to portray him as "a perpetually sweaty ape-man," the *New Republic,* for example, deplored what it described as the efforts of the filmmakers to "deify" a man for whom "maliciousness was [at] the very heart and soul of his creativity." The *Weekly Standard,* meanwhile, used its review of the film as an opportunity to dismiss Block as a talentless "court jester to a class of complacent and powerful people who pretended to value the outrageous, the irreverent, the fearless, . . . [whose] only genuine qualification was that he hated the right people."[16] That his work is still able to generate such impassioned responses is testament both to the enduring visual impact of Block's cartoons and to the continued need for the type of commentary he provided.

Speaking in January 1976 at the opening of an exhibit of political cartoons depicting the American presidency, Block recalled an exchange he had had with Art Buchwald, a fellow satirist at the *Washington Post,* in the wake of Nixon's electoral victory in November 1968. Perhaps looking for a silver lining, and unaware of how right he would prove to be, Buchwald commented that a Nixon presidency "should provide plenty of material" for satirists like himself and Block. When Block replied that he would prefer to have an administration he trusted to act in the best interests of the country, Buchwald shot back: "Herb, you've got to stop putting the country ahead of your work." In recounting this anecdote, Block went on to reflect on his own legacy and the importance of his work. "If the millennium should arrive when we have the brotherhood of man—or the brotherhood and sisterhood of persons—if the time should come when political figures and all the rest of us should sprout angel wings," he ruminated, "there will still be some differing views about the best way to flap those wings. . . . And there will still be something funny about a halo that's worn a little askew." But even in this imagined utopia there was still a need to be vigilant, and Block declared that he "would like to still be around and still drawing cartoons," using his work to defend against those who would abuse their power. After all, he concluded, "I wouldn't want to see any head angel throwing his weight around."[17]

NOTES

INTRODUCTION

1. Arthur M. Schlesinger Jr. to Herbert Block, March 1, 1951, Box 70, Folder 7, Herbert Block Papers, Manuscript Division, Library of Congress (hereafter HBP).
2. Chester Bowles to Herbert Block, March 5, 1951, Box 7, Folder 4, HBP. See also Box 33, Folder 61, Chester Bowles Papers, Yale University Library.
3. The literature on postwar liberalism is extensive. See, for example, Bell and Stanley, eds., *Making Sense of American Liberalism;* Boyle, *The UAW and the Heyday of American Liberalism;* Brinkley, *The End of Reform;* Delton, *Rethinking the 1950s;* Ericson and Green, eds., *The Liberal Tradition in American Politics;* Hamby, *Beyond the New Deal;* Hamby, *Liberalism and Its Challengers;* Kamen, "Rethinking Postwar Liberalism"; Mattson, *When America Was Great;* McAullife, *Crisis on the Left;* Pells, *The Liberal Mind in a Conservative Age;* Rossinow, *Visions of Progress;* Sandbrook, *Eugene McCarthy;* and Wall, *Inventing the "American Way."*
4. Schlesinger, *The Vital Center.*
5. Trilling, *The Liberal Imagination,* xv.
6. The margin of Eisenhower's victory in 1956 was even wider, winning 57.4 percent of the popular vote and the electoral college by a margin of 457 votes to 73.
7. See, for example, Delton, *Rethinking the 1950s;* Hodgson, *America in Our Time;* McClenahan and Becker, *Eisenhower and the Cold War Economy;* and Weisbrot and Mackenzie, *The Liberal Hour.*
8. Hodgson, *America in Our Time,* 67. The term "liberal consensus" traces its origins to Higham, "The Cult of the 'American Consensus.'" Hodgson is highly critical of consensus liberalism, condemning it as a "strange hybrid,

liberal conservatism [that] blanketed the scene and muffled debate." Hodgson, *America in Our Time*, 73.

9. Hodgson, *America in Our Time*, 76. See also Chafe, *The Unfinished Journey*. These tenets of postwar liberalism were also an expression of American exceptionalism.
10. Hofstadter, *The American Political Tradition*, xxxvi.
11. Scholars have challenged the homogeneity of postwar liberalism on a number of fronts. For discussion of women and gender roles, see Cuordileone, *Manhood and American Political Culture in the Cold War;* Eisenmann, *Higher Education for Women in Postwar America;* Hartmann, *The Other Feminists;* May, *Homeward Bound;* Meyerowitz, ed., *Not June Cleaver;* and Mittelstadt, *From Welfare to Workfare*. For critiques of liberalism's racial politics, see Averbeck, *Liberalism Is Not Enough;* Dudziak, *Cold War Civil Rights;* Gerstle, "Race and the Myth of the Liberal Consensus"; Hirsch, *Making the Second Ghetto;* and Sugrue, *The Origins of the Urban Crisis*. On industry's challenge to postwar liberalism, see Fones-Wolf, *Selling Free Enterprise*, and Phillips-Fein, "If Business and the Country Will Be Run Right."
12. On the collapse of liberalism and rise of the conservative movement, see Brands, *The Strange Death of American Liberalism;* Brinkley, *Liberalism and Its Discontents;* Gerstle and Fraser, eds., *The Rise and Fall of the New Deal Order;* Kimmage, *Conservative Turn;* Lassiter, *The Silent Majority;* Lowndes, *From the New Deal to the New Right;* McGirr, *Suburban Warriors;* Phillips-Fein, *Invisible Hands;* and Schulman and Zelizer, eds., *Rightward Bound*.
13. Bradlee, *A Good Life*, 286; Graham, *Personal History*, 169; Spiro T. Agnew, quoted in Block, *Herblock: A Cartoonist's Life*, 226; Long, "Cartoons without Humor," 22.
14. "Truman Answers Press Query by Citing Herblock Cartoon," *Washington Post* (hereafter *WP*), June 17, 1949. The cartoon in question was "Okay—Now to Find Somebody That Can Read," originally published in the *Washington Post* on June 18, 1949. The cartoon depicts two members of the committee staring at an avalanche of textbooks that have been sent to them from across the country.
15. Quoted in Block, *Herblock: A Cartoonist's Life*, 201–2.
16. DeSousa and Medhurst, "Political Cartoons and American Culture," 85–89.
17. Block, Joseph Pulitzer Memorial Lecture, February 22, 1957, Box 184, Folder 14, HBP.
18. Michelmore, "Old Picture in New Frames," 37; Shaw, "Drawing on the Collections," 742.
19. Edwards, *Political Cartoons in the 1988 Presidential Campaign*, 19.

20. Press, *The Political Cartoon*, 62.
21. Keller, *The Art and Politics of Thomas Nast*, preface.
22. Halloran, *Thomas Nast*, 119–20.
23. For examples, see Fischer, *Them Damned Pictures*, 2; Michelmore, "Old Picture in New Frames," 37; Lamb, "Drawing Power," 717; and Navasky, *The Art of Controversy*, 43. Fiona Deans Halloran argues, however, that the story is "probably a distortion of a private comment" rather than an actual demand for action from members of his political machine. Halloran, *Thomas Nast*, 132.
24. Shikes, *The Indignant Eye*, 311; Fischer, *Them Damned Pictures*, 26.
25. Halloran, *Thomas Nast*, 205–10.
26. Sayer, "Art and Politics, Dissent and Repression," 55.
27. Wallis, ed., *Killed Cartoons*, 117–19.
28. Block, "A Letter from Herblock to Brezhnev," *WP*, July 14, 1969; Block, *Herblock: A Cartoonist's Life*, 251–52.
29. Anderson, *Imagined Communities*, 6, 35–36.
30. Schneider, "Stop Them Damned Pictures"; Forker, "The Use of the 'Cartoonist's Armoury'"; Mikailova, "Intellectuals, Cartoons, and Nationalism"; Göçek, "From Empire to Nation."
31. Gitlin, *The Whole World Is Watching*, 7.
32. Drucker, "Not Sound," 242.
33. The Herb Block Foundation, "Biography," http://www.herbblockfoundation.org/herb-block/herb-biography.
34. Quoted in White, *The Making of the President*, 266.
35. Kercher, *Revel with a Cause*, 36–49.
36. Bradlee, *A Good Life*, 114, 285–86, 369; Downie, *All about the Story*. Katharine Graham's autobiography does include more discussion of Block's role at the *Post*, with its index indicating thirteen total references to him. Graham, *Personal History*, 633.

1. "AN UNINHIBITED VOICE OF LIBERALISM"

1. Block, "The Cartoon," 151.
2. See, for example, Beth Bogart, "An Interview with Herblock." *Princeton Forerunner*, February 15, 1976, Box 187, Folder 7, HBP, and Block, Remarks at the Opening of "The American Presidency in Political Cartoons: 1776–1976" Exhibit, University of California, Berkeley, January 13, 1976, Box 187, Folder 5, HBP.
3. "The Barbed Pen," *Newsweek*, February 29, 1960, 92.
4. *Herblock: A Cartoonist's Life*, 9–14; Katz, "Herblock's History," 11.

5. "They Rival Roentgen: Startling Claims Made by David Block and William F. Hild of Chicago," *Chicago Daily Tribune,* January 26, 1896; "Keeps Record of Light," *Chicago Daily Tribune,* March 26, 1900.
6. Block, *Herblock: A Cartoonist's Life,* 11.
7. See "Chicago Ward 20, Cook County, Illinois," *Thirteenth Census of the United States, 1910* (Washington, DC: National Archives and Records Administration, 1910), Roll T624_263, Enumeration District 0883; "Chicago Ward 25, Cook County, Illinois," *Fourteenth Census of the United States, 1920* (Washington, DC: National Archives and Records Administration, 1920), Roll T625_341, Enumeration District 1419; "New Trier, Cook County, Illinois," *Fifteenth Census of the United States, 1930* (Washington, DC: National Archives and Records Administration, 1930), Roll 503, Page 21B, Enumeration District 2224.
8. Block, *Herblock: A Cartoonist's Life,* 2.
9. Guglielmo, *White on Arrival,* 14.
10. Tuttle, *Race Riot,* 75–76; Pacyga, *Chicago,* 207–12.
11. Katz, "Herblock's History," 15.
12. Block, *Herblock: A Cartoonist's Life,* 7–8.
13. Ibid., 3, 6–7.
14. Lamb, "Herblock Talks about Life as a Cartoonist," 33.
15. Jack Star, "Herblock's Golden Key," *Look,* February 26, 1963, 62–65, Box 199, Folder 11, HBP.
16. Block, "There Would Be Few Successful Flights If Airmen Were Selected Like This—," *Senn High Paper,* September 24, 1925; Block, "It's All Very Well to Speed the Parting Guest but Why Not Give Some Attention to the New Arrival?" *Senn High Paper,* October 1, 1925. For more of Block's cartoons drawn while a student at Senn High see the digital resource "Senn High School, 1924–1926" in Johnson and Katz, eds., *Herblock.*
17. In 1963, Block nominated Harris for the American Association of School Administrators' Golden Key award, given to the teacher who most influenced him. Jack Star, "Herblock's Golden Key," *Look,* February 26, 1963, 62–65, and "Golden Key Awards," *Maryland Teacher,* February 1963, Box 199, Folder 11, HBP.
18. Block, *Herblock: A Cartoonist's Life,* 23–24. For Chicago's strong tradition of public humor and background to the "A Line o' Type or Two" column, see Williams and Duffey, eds., *Chicago's Public Wits,* especially 205–10.
19. The text of this column reads, "SIGN IN CORNER DRUG STORE QUOTE DRINK CANADA DRY UNQUOTE STOP CANT DRINK CANADA DRY STOP TOO DAM BUSY DRINKING UNITED STATES DRY." "A Line o' Type or Two: Ah, Yes, It's Quite a Task These Days," *Chicago Daily Tribune,* August 30, 1926.

20. Block, "Evanston Streets, Now—and When?" *Evanston (IL) News-Index,* August 13, 1928; Block, "Exaggerated? Not Very Much," *Evanston News-Index,* August 18, 1928; Block, "Get Ready for the Cleanup," *Evanston News-Index,* October 6, 1928.
21. Block, *Herblock: A Cartoonist's Life,* 33–34.
22. Block, "This Is the Forest Primeval—," *Chicago Daily News,* April 24, 1929. The cartoon's title references the first line of Henry Wadsworth Longfellow's 1847 poem "Evangeline," which goes on to describe in vivid detail the beauty of ancient forests. Block juxtaposed this literary allusion with his own image of a barren vista of tree stumps, all that remains after the site has been gutted of its natural beauty by loggers.
23. Other members of Caswell's Midwestern School included the *Columbus Dispatch*'s Billy Ireland, the *Chicago Tribune*'s John T. McCutcheon, and the *Des Moines Register*'s Ding Darling. Caswell, "The Midwestern School of Editorial Cartooning," 198.
24. Block, *Herblock: A Cartoonist's Life,* 33–37.
25. Ibid., 33.
26. See, for example, Block, "Weighing in before the Big Fight," *Evanston News-Index,* October 3, 1928, which depicts Thomas Nast's Tammany Hall Tiger atop a scale that has been overbalanced by the weight of "Hoover['s] Worldwide Achievements," and Block, "After the Landslide," *Evanston News-Index,* November 8, 1928, which shows the Tammany Tiger in a trash can as voters fruitlessly search for "the fellow who said Hoover would be a weak candidate."
27. Block, "A Suggestion for Mr. Hoover," *Chicago Daily News,* January 6, 1930; Block, "Housing Plans," *Chicago Daily News,* November 25, 1931.
28. Block, "The Pleasure Is All Ours," *Chicago Daily News,* July 16, 1929.
29. Block, "Stock Market Fever Chart," *Chicago Daily News,* October 14, 1929.
30. Pacyga, *Chicago,* 249–53.
31. Block, "The Needier Case," *Chicago Daily News,* January 29, 1931; Block, "Profit and Loss," *Chicago Daily News,* September 25, 1930; Block, "Smoke Clouds and Silver Linings," *Chicago Daily News,* August 19, 1931.
32. Block, *Herblock: A Cartoonist's Life,* 43–51.
33. Brinkley, *The End of Reform,* 9.
34. Quoted in ibid., 10.
35. Block, *Herblock: A Cartoonist's Life,* 56.
36. Block, "Dealing with Both Hands," Syndicated Cartoon, March 14, 1933. The Herbert L. Block Collection at the Library of Congress houses fourteen thousand original ink and graphite Herblock cartoons, spanning Block's career from 1929 when he started at the *Chicago Daily News* to his death in 2001.

37. Block, "The Difference," Syndicated Cartoon, January 5, 1935.
38. Block, *Herblock: A Cartoonist's Life,* 61–62.
39. "Coughlin Rebuked by M'Nicholas; Papal Step Hinted," *New York Times* (hereafter *NYT*), September 26, 1936.
40. Block, "The Spoken Word," Syndicated Cartoon, October 7, 1936.
41. Block, "Louisiana—There She Stands," Syndicated Cartoon, August 4, 1934; Block, "The Long, Long Trail," Syndicated Cartoon, August 5, 1934; Block, "Feeding the Hungry," Syndicated Cartoon, November 16, 1934; Block, "The Crown Jewels," Syndicated Cartoon, April 18, 1935.
42. Block, "Attention, Committee on Un-American Activities," Syndicated Cartoon, August 29, 1938; Block, "Wait Till the Dies Committee Hears about This!" Syndicated Cartoon, December 3, 1938.
43. Block, "Some Day There'll Be an Uprising," *Chicago Daily News,* April 25, 1929.
44. Block, "Cheer Up! The Worst Is Still to Come," *Chicago Daily News,* April 27, 1929.
45. Block, "Fairy Tale," *Chicago Daily News,* October 4, 1930.
46. Block, "Then and Now," *Chicago Daily News,* August 29, 1930.
47. Titled "A Word to the Wise," the cartoon depicts in its top frame a politician (labeled simply "Politics") accepting money, and therefore influence, from a criminal while rhetorically stating, "If the long arm of the law doesn't function. . . ." The cartoon's bottom frame answers this statement by showing the politician, relabeled "Crooked Politics," being kicked out of office by a public vote, represented by the "Long Foot of the Public." Block, "A Word to the Wise," *Chicago Daily News,* August 29, 1930.
48. Block, *Herblock: A Cartoonist's Life,* 10–15. Indeed, Block's first mention of his mother in *A Cartoonist's Life* is in the context of her cooking. Ibid., 1.
49. Bederman, *Manliness and Civilization,* 13.
50. Block, "'Tis a Sad Story, Men!" *Chicago Daily News,* May 6, 1929.
51. Block, "It Can't Happen Here," Syndicated Cartoon, May 28, 1936.
52. Block, "Nobody Knows de Trouble I've Seen," Syndicated Cartoon, November 12, 1935.
53. See Block, "The Next Great Discovery," *Chicago Daily News,* July 5, 1929; Block, "The Universal Topic," *Chicago Daily News,* February 6, 1932; Block, "Explaining the Large Numbers," *Chicago Daily News,* March 28, 1932; Block, "If Things Keep On—," Syndicated Cartoon, March 1, 1933; Block, "Right with Him to the Very End," Syndicated Cartoon, April 21, 1936; and Block, "Africa," Syndicated Cartoon, April 4, 1939. The sole exception to this was drawn in June 1932, when Block sketched the Mills Brothers, a popular jazz quartet that he had seen in concert the previous day. Block drew the group in negative colors, however, resulting in them being

depicted with white faces. Block, "Four Mills Brothers," *Chicago Daily News,* June 11, 1932.

54. Block, "The Spirit of Democracy," *Chicago Daily News,* July 29, 1932.
55. Block, "One Reason for Gandhi's Costume," *Chicago Daily News,* September 17, 1930.
56. Block, "The Land of Opportunity," *Chicago Daily News,* November 20, 1930.
57. For a full description of how cartoonists developed and used these stereotypes, see Fischer, *Them Damned Pictures,* 70–120.
58. Katz, "Herblock's History," 13.
59. Block, "Evolution in Germany," *Chicago Daily News,* October 18, 1930; "Hail Hitler!" Syndicated Cartoon, January 1933; Block, "The World as It Looks Right Now," Syndicated Cartoon, March 12, 1934.
60. Block, "In World Affairs—," Syndicated Cartoon, August 3, 1936.
61. Block, "Hands across the Sea," Syndicated Cartoon, September 30, 1940.
62. Block, "Waiting," Syndicated Cartoon, August 24, 1940.
63. Block, "American Labor," Syndicated Cartoon, August 31, 1940.
64. Block, *Herblock: A Cartoonist's Life,* 65–68.
65. "Parsons Wins Pulitzer Prize for Herald Tribune Editorials," *New York Herald Tribune,* May 5, 1942.
66. Block, "British Plane," Syndicated Cartoon, March 7, 1941.
67. Block, *Herblock: A Cartoonist's Life,* 60–68.
68. As a member of the 45th Infantry Division, Bill Mauldin is the most celebrated American cartoonist from the World War II era. He famously created "Willie" and "Joe," who represented the average American soldier and their experiences of war in the European theater. For more on Mauldin, see DePastino, *Bill Mauldin,* and DePastino, *Drawing Fire.* His World War II cartoons are collected in Maudlin, *Willie and Joe.*
69. Gregor Duncan was killed by a German shell while riding in a jeep in Italy on May 29, 1944.
70. Block, *Herblock: A Cartoonist's Life,* 89–92.
71. For examples of Block's work for the army, see the digital resource "United States Army, 1943–1945," in Johnson and Katz, eds., *Herblock.*
72. Block, *Herblock: A Cartoonist's Life,* 95; Graham, *Personal History,* 169. The *Post*'s previous cartoonist, Gene Elderman, had proved unreliable and ultimately drank himself out of a job. Roberts, *The Washington Post,* 243.
73. Roberts, *The Washington Post,* 257.
74. Block, *Herblock: A Cartoonist's Life,* 95; Graham, *Personal History,* 169. See also Eugene Meyer to Herbert Block, October 11, 1945, Box 49, Folder 4, HBP.
75. Block, *Herblock: A Cartoonist's Life,* 95.
76. "Block, Editorial Cartoonist, to Join Post Staff January 2," *WP,* December 26, 1945. Block's first published cartoon at the *Post* depicts two men

standing together on a globe. The first is a scientist, reading a book about atomic energy, but the other, who is labeled "Narrow Nationalism" and holding a giant ax, is shown rolling up his sleeves as he declares, "Brother, I'll Show You How to Split Something Big!" Block, "Brother, I'll Show You How to Split Something Big!" *WP*, January 3, 1946.

77. Roberts, *The Washington Post*, 202–13.
78. On economic policy, see Block, "End of Another Lid-Lifting Experiment" *WP*, January 4, 1946, and Block, "Hey—A Guy Could Slip on That!" *WP*, January 12, 1946. On congressional obstructionism and corruption, see Block, "Horatius at the Bridge," *WP*, January 15, 1946; Block, "It's Terrible, People Refusin' to Work!" *WP*, January 16, 1946; and Block, "I Got No Control over Myself," *WP*, January 29, 1946. On atomic energy, see Block, "Job No. 1," *WP*, January 26, 1946, and Block, "This That Junk You Were Telling Me About?" *WP*, January 31, 1946. On interventionism, see Block, "The World's Last Chance," *WP*, January 10, 1946.
79. Annette Bulow, "Herbert Block," Letter to the Editor, *WP*, January 9, 1946.
80. Johnson and Katz, "Herblock *Knew*," 51.
81. Block, "Strange Idol," *WP*, March 5, 1946. The Office of Price Administration (OPA) was established by executive order in 1941 to control inflation and rents after the outbreak of World War II.

2. "THE FEAR-AND-SMEAR RACKETEERS"

1. Block, *Herblock Book*, 128.
2. Ibid., 128, 137, 138–39.
3. Block, *Herblock Looks at Communism*, 1.
4. Block, "Put Me In, Coach! Put Me In!" *WP*, March 9, 1947.
5. Harry S. Truman, "Special Message to the Congress on Greece and Turkey: The Truman Doctrine," March 12, 1947, in Truman, *Public Papers of the Presidents . . . 1947*, 176–80.
6. Block, "I'm Here to Stay, Too," *WP*, March 13, 1947; Block, "Remember, This Is for Him," *WP*, March 14, 1947.
7. George Kennan to James F. Byrnes, February 22, 1946, in U.S. Department of State, *Foreign Relations of the United States, 1946*, 696.
8. Weart, *The Rise of Nuclear Fear*, 75–78, 102–3; Cuordileone, "'Politics in an Age of Anxiety'"; Sontag, "The Imagination of Disaster."
9. Block, "What's Going on Here?" (unpublished manuscript), ca. 1947, Box 182, Folder 7, HBP.
10. Block, "Job No. 1," *WP*, January 26, 1947.
11. Block, "A Choice of Genii," *WP*, March 6, 1946.

12. Block, "I Ain't Got Any Traditions," *WP,* April 25, 1946.
13. Block, "Pardon Me, Mister—Do You Know What Time It Is?" *WP,* August 27, 1946.
14. Storrs, *The Second Red Scare and the Unmaking of the New Deal Left,* 107–47. See also Knight, *How the Cold War Began,* and Haynes and Klehr, *Early Cold War Spies.*
15. Delton, *Rethinking the 1950s,* 13–14.
16. Hogan, *A Cross of Iron,* 254–55; Delton, *Rethinking the 1950s,* 16–23; Gillon, *Politics and Vision,* 5–16.
17. Culver and Hyde, *American Dreamer,* 419–26.
18. Gillon, *Politics and Vision,* 29–31.
19. Block, "Listen! Listen to the People Cheering!" *WP,* December 31, 1947. This was the second Herblock cartoon to comment on Wallace's candidacy. The first was published on December 24 and showed a member of the PCA eagerly pushing a somewhat anxious Wallace toward a waiting guillotine. Block, "This Is a Far, Far Better Thing You Do—," *WP,* December 24, 1947.
20. Block, "Get All The Sunshine You Can, Harry," *WP,* March 2, 1948; Block, "I Don't Scare Easy," *WP,* April 17, 1948.
21. Block, "You Betting on the Horses or the Jockeys?" *WP,* May 27, 1948; Block, Untitled Cartoon, *WP,* July 8, 1948.
22. Block, "How Do You Feel about Liberal-Baiting?" *WP,* August 2, 1948; Block, "Your Friends Got Bum Stummicks or Somepn?" *WP,* September 27, 1948.
23. Block, "The Big Train," *WP,* November 5, 1948.
24. Gillon, *Politics and Vision,* 57–58.
25. For example, Arthur Krock, "In the Nation: The Superior Articulation of the Left: II," *NYT,* July 19, 1949.
26. For details of these trips, see Box 2, Folders 6–8, HBP.
27. Arthur M. Schlesinger Jr., "What Is Loyalty? A Difficult Question," *NYT,* November 2, 1947.
28. Block, *Herblock Book,* 135.
29. Block, "You're with the State Department, I Presume," *WP,* October 13, 1947; Block, "Okay, Honey—Put It On," May 31, 1948; Block, "You Read Books, Eh?" *WP,* April 24, 1949.
30. Dekom, "Behind the Riddle of the *Washington Post,*" 11, 12, 15. For more on *Plain Talk*'s relatively short history and its impact on anticommunist rhetoric, see de Rosa, "Plain Talk, 1946–1950."
31. Block, "American, All the Way Back," *WP,* February 17, 1946.
32. Block, "Everybody Ready for Hallowe'en?" Syndicated Cartoon, October 8, 1947.
33. Block, "Suspicious Character," *WP,* April 10, 1946; Block, "I Got a Secret Weapon Too," *WP,* March 9, 1948.

34. Block, "It's Okay—We're Hunting Communists," *WP*, October 30, 1947.
35. Block, "That's a Joke, Son—You Don't Seem to Get It," *WP*, April 8, 1946; Block, Untitled Cartoon, *WP*, November 16, 1946; Block, "You Belong to an International Organization?" *WP*, March 27, 1947; Block, "I Don't See Any Danger of Fascism," *WP*, June 1, 1947.
36. Block, "Fire!" *WP*, June 17, 1949.
37. Block, "That's the Line We Want to Get Across, Pal," *WP*, January 31, 1950.
38. Schlesinger, *The Vital Center*, 130.
39. "The Shape of Things," Editorial, *The Nation*, February 23, 1946, 209.
40. Graham, *Personal History*, 194.
41. "Doubting Thomas," Editorial, *WP*, December 17, 1947.
42. Quoted in "205 Reds on Job in State Dept, McCarthy Says," *Chicago Daily Tribune*, February 10, 1950.
43. Bayley, *Joe McCarthy and the Press*, 16–22.
44. U.S. Congress, *Congressional Record*, 81st Cong., 2nd sess., 2062.
45. "Security Risks Kept in Jobs, Senator Says: McCarthy Tells Truman State Department Fired Only 80 Out of 300; Senator Cites Security Risks," *WP*, February 12, 1950; "Sewer Politics," Editorial, *WP*, February 14, 1950.
46. Block, "Seem to You There's Something a Little Odd Here?" *WP*, February 22, 1950.
47. On March 13, for example, McCarthy was shown hiding behind the U.S. Capitol's columns rather than answer questions from a throng of journalists, while three days later he was depicted hiding in the building's coat closet. Block, "Step Outside and Say That," *WP*, March 13, 1950; Block, "Pst—Is She Gone Yet?" *WP*, March 16, 1950. See also Block, "Hey—You're Cramping My Style," *WP*, March 10, 1950, and Block, "Somebody Around Here Is Helping the Commies!" *WP*, March 21, 1950.
48. Block, "You Mean I'm Supposed to Stand on That?" *WP*, March 29, 1950.
49. For examples, see almost any publication or discussion about either Block's work or McCarthyism, including Block, *Herblock: A Cartoonist's Life*, 133; Johnson and Katz, eds., *Herblock*, 130; Graham, *Personal History*, 204; Roberts, *The Washington Post*, 280; Lamb, *Drawn to Extremes*, 107; Kercher, *Revel with a Cause*, 41; Rovere, *Senator Joe McCarthy*, 7; Johnson, *The Age of Anxiety*, 29; Richardson, *How the South Won the Civil War*, 154; and Tye, *Demagogue*, 159.
50. Block, *Herblock: A Cartoonist's Life*, 133; Block, *Herblock Book*, 152.
51. Henry L. Stimson, "Loyalty in Washington," Letter to the Editor, *NYT*, March 27, 1950.
52. "Choice for Republicans," Editorial, *Christian Science Monitor*, March 28, 1950, emphasis added. For a detailed study of the *Christian Science Monitor*'s coverage of McCarthyism, see Strout, *Covering McCarthyism*.

Remarkably, Strout misses the significance of the date that the *Monitor*'s first use of "McCarthyism" occurred, instead writing in his introduction that Block created the term. Ibid., xii–xiii.

53. Marquis Childs, "Colorado Senator: Millikin-Carroll Race on Principle," *WP*, May 18, 1950.
54. McCarthy, *McCarthyism*.
55. Stalin appeared in twenty-five cartoons in 1952 and Truman in seventeen. Additionally, three symbolic characters made more appearances than McCarthy: Congress (76), Uncle Sam (54), and John Q. Public (29).
56. Block, "Stop Ganging up on Me!" *WP*, April 22, 1950; Block, "How about If We Just Set the Bar on the Ground?" *WP*, May 3, 1950.
57. "Nauseated Voter," "Bankrupt GOP," Letter to the Editor, *WP*, April 4, 1950; "B. R. D," "More on McCarthy," Letter to the Editor, *WP*, April 10, 1950.
58. Block, "That Odor around Here Isn't Coming from West Point," *WP*, August 8, 1951; Block, "You'll Take the High Road, and I'll Take the Low Road; I'll Be in the White House afore You," *WP*, January 23, 1952.
59. Block, "Say, What Ever Happened to 'Freedom-from-Fear'?" *WP*, August 13, 1951.
60. Block, *Herblock: A Cartoonist's Life*, 135.
61. Tye, *Demagogue*, 159; Reeves, *Life and Times of Joe McCarthy*, 316.
62. Bell, *The Liberal State on Trial*, 250–59.
63. Block, "Looks as if Congress May Save Us Money, Anyhow," *WP*, March 2, 1953. Other examples of Block's concern over McCarthy's attacks on Voice of America include Block, "We Killed 'Em in Europe, Boss," *WP*, April 23, 1953, and Block, "Nobody Here but Just Us Economizers," *WP*, July 24, 1953.
64. Block, "This One Doesn't Burn So Easily," *WP*, June 18, 1953. Other examples include Block, "Sometimes I Wonder What's in Those Darn Things," *WP*, May 31, 1953, and Block, "I Don't Smell Anything," *WP*, June 16, 1953.
65. Fried, *Nightmare in Red*, 137–38; "Ex-Major Cited by McCarthy Calls His Charges 'Nonsense,'" *WP*, February 4, 1954; "Testimony Shows Senator Branded General 'Not Fit to Wear Uniform': McCarthy Puts Off His Showdown with Army Secretary to Thursday," *WP*, February 23, 1954.
66. "Army Rejects McCarthy's Peress Order," *WP*, February 20, 1954; "Secretary to Produce Officers for Testimony: Agreement Cancels 'Showdown' Hearing on Army 'Coddling of Reds' Set Today; Stevens Yields to McCarthy on Inquiry," *WP*, February 25, 1954.
67. Block, "Spotlight," *WP*, February 5, 1954; Block, "Okay, Bud. When I Want You Again I'll Send for You," *WP*, February 25, 1954; Block, "We've Got to Avoid a Split with Him," *WP*, February 28, 1954; Block, "Have a Care, Sir," *WP*, March 4, 1954; Block, "Relax—He Hasn't Got to You Yet," *WP*, March 7, 1954.

68. Reeves, *Life and Times of Joe McCarthy*, 315–16.
69. See Letters to the Editor from Henry L. Abbott and Emily Rigdon, *WP*, March 1, 1954, and from R. P. Hartle, Richard W. Hogue, and Elizabeth Phelps, *WP*, March 2, 1954.
70. Paul D. Rheingold, "Cartoonist's Comment," Letter to the Editor, *WP*, March 16, 1954.
71. Herman, *Joseph McCarthy*, 253.
72. "Army Probes GIs' Allegations of 'Brass' Coddling Schine," *WP*, January 30, 1954.
73. Schrecker, *Many Are the Crimes*, 261–65.
74. Bayley, *Joe McCarthy and the Press*, 202–10.
75. Quoted in Katz, "Herblock's History."
76. Block, "Here Goes," *WP*, April 22, 1954; Block, "Quick, Officer—They Went That Way," *WP*, April 27, 1954.
77. Keith Saunders, "Cartoon of McCarthy," Letter to the Editor, *WP*, May 7, 1954.
78. Guy Sauterne, "Powerful Cartooning," Letter to the Editor, *WP*, May 11, 1954.
79. Don Patton, Letter to the Editor, *WP*, May 11, 1954.
80. "Cohn Admits All but Secretary and Schine Were Cut Out but Says That Isn't Important," *WP*, April 28, 1954; "Dirty Linen," *WP*, April 28, 1954; "Question of Good Faith," Editorial, *WP*, May 1, 1954.
81. "McCarthy Won't Name Informant: Senator's Refusal Follows Testimony 'Letter' Is Actually Part of a Report," *WP*, May 6, 1954; "Doctored Letter," *WP*, May 6, 1954.
82. Block, "I Have Here in My Hand—," *WP*, May 7, 1954.
83. Tye, *Demagogue*, 436–39.
84. Block, "Well, Why Doesn't He See a Psychiatrist?" *WP*, June 10, 1954.
85. "Senate Passes Resolution of Censure Condemning McCarthy by 67–22 Vote; Colleagues Base Their Judgment on 2 Counts," *WP*, December 3, 1954.
86. Bayley, *Joe McCarthy and the Press*, 148–51.
87. Graham, *Personal History*, 204.
88. Bayley, *Joe McCarthy and the Press*, 151; "Circulation 381,417 Daily; 392,580 Sunday: Post Reports Circulation," *WP*, July 12, 1954.
89. Block, *Herblock's Here and Now*, 280.
90. Quoted in Bayley, *Joe McCarthy and the Press*, 55.
91. "Herblock Wins Broun Award: New Yorker Is a Co-Winner," *WP*, February 24, 1950; "New Deal Mouthpiece," Editorial, *Chicago Daily Tribune*, March 25, 1950; Block, "The Herblock Award," Letter to the Editor, *WP*, March 8, 1950. Block argued that he was merely making the campaign contribution to a personal friend who he had known for seventeen years and that he was not "anti-Taft or anti-anyone else." But, he continued

without a trace of irony, "as [an] editorial cartoonist of an independent newspaper I deal with personalities only as they are involved with issues and principles." Block, "The Herblock Award," Letter to the Editor, *WP*, March 8, 1950.

92. Jane Harris to Herbert Block, May 8, 1950, Box 2, Folder 6, HBP. Despite the ADA's assurances that they would not publicize this event, the *New York Times* announced that the exhibit would benefit the ADA in a short article published on May 22, 1950.
93. Block, *Herblock: A Cartoonist's Life*, 140–41; Kercher, *Revel with a Cause*, 47.
94. "Herblock's TV Program Starts in Fall," *WP*, August 20, 1955; "Fulton Lewis Continues Comment on Fund for the Republic," September 16, 1955, Box 26, Folder 2, HBP; Block, *Herblock: A Cartoonist's Life*, 127–28. For more, see "Mass Media: TV Projects—Herblock, 1954–1958," Box 110, Folder 7–8, Fund for the Republic Records, Princeton University Library.
95. Schlesinger, *The Vital Center;* Richard Hofstadter, "The Pseudo-Conservative Revolt, 1954," in Hofstadter, *Richard Hofstadter*, 535–55.
96. John B. Oakes, "Report on McCarthy and McCarthyism: A Visitor to Wisconsin Analyzes the Political Strength of a Man Whose Significance Extends beyond State Boundaries," *NYT*, November 2, 1952; Fried, *Nightmare in Red*, 138.
97. Buckley and Bozell, *McCarthy and His Enemies*.

3. "THE MAJOR MORAL ISSUE OF OUR TIME"

1. "Takes Governor at Word Troops Will Keep Peace: Court Tells Little Rock to Carry Out Integration," *WP*, September 4, 1957.
2. "Law and Order," Editorial, *WP*, September 4, 1957.
3. Block, "The Gov. Faubus 'Peace' Plan," *WP*, September 5, 1957; Block, *Herblock: A Cartoonist's Life*, 159; Block, *Herblock's Special for Today*, 67.
4. "Takes Governor at Word Troops Will Keep Peace: Court Tells Little Rock to Carry Out Integration," *WP*, September 4, 1957.
5. Orval Faubus, news conference, September 9, 1957. Quoted in Benjamin Fine, "U.S. to Seek Writ to Force Faubus and Guard to Permit Integration," *NYT*, September 10, 1957.
6. Block, "Tears," *WP*, September 10, 1957.
7. Block, *Straight Herblock*, 142.
8. Block, "Oh Boy—Lots of Headlines," *WP*, September 13, 1957; "The Wart on Our Face," Editorial, *WP*, September 12, 1957.
9. Block, "Back to School," *WP*, September 25, 1957; Block, "How Can You Doubt My Good Intentions?" *WP*, October 3, 1957.

10. Block, "This Is an Explosive Situation," *WP*, September 6, 1957.
11. Berger, *Seeing through Race*, 88 (fig. 40), 98, 106–7.
12. One of the earliest of numerous national awards given to him in recognition of his commitment to civil rights was made in April 1949, when he was one of three men honored at the liberal American Veteran Committee's third annual Bill of Rights banquet. The other recipients at this event were Charles E. Wilson, chair of Truman's Presidential Committee on Civil Rights, and Dr. Edwin B. Henderson, principal organizer of the first rural branch of the NAACP and a lifelong activist against segregation in housing and education. "Wilson Awarded for Outstanding Civil Rights Work," *Atlanta Daily World*, May 13, 1949.
13. Block, *Herblock: A Cartoonist's Life*, 158.
14. Herbert Block, "Elmer Davis Memorial Lecture," speech delivered at Columbia University, December 3, 1963, Box 185, Folder 7, HBP.
15. Horton, *Race and the Making of American Liberalism*, 121, 137.
16. Myrdal, *An American Dilemma*, 13.
17. Schlesinger, *The Vital Center*, 190, 235.
18. Block, "It's Terrible, People Refusin' to Work!" *WP*, January 16, 1946.
19. Block, "I Hear Our Demonstrations Hurt American Prestige," *WP*, January 24, 1946.
20. Block, "I Got No Control over Myself," *WP*, January 29, 1946.
21. Cash, *The Mind of the South;* Cobb, *Away Down South*, 3, 47.
22. Bilbo is quoted in "Prince of the Peckerwoods," *Time*, July 1946, 24. For more on Bilbo's 1946 campaign rhetoric, see Fleegler, "Theodore G. Bilbo and the Decline of Public Racism."
23. Block, "Torchlight Parade," *WP*, June 29, 1946.
24. "U.S. Airs Vote Intimidation in Mississippi," *WP*, June 25, 1946; "Bilbo Campaign," Editorial, *WP*, July 1, 1946.
25. Block, "The Bilbo Election Case," *WP*, July 6, 1946. Subsequent cartoons to feature the efforts to prevent Bilbo's seating included Block, "Ha, Ha—See? I'm Laughing," *WP*, September 30, 1946; Block, "The Bloodhounds," *WP*, November 23, 1946; Block, "Winter Heat," *WP*, December 16, 1946; "Well, Well—Another Miracle!" *WP*, December 19, 1946; and Block, "Bad Apple," *WP*, January 3, 1947.
26. Bullock, Gaddie, and Buchanan, *The Three Governors Controversy*, 9–13, 109.
27. Tuck, *Beyond Atlanta*, 17–18; "Victory of Talmadge Called Reversion to Old Traditions," *WP*, July 19, 1946.
28. Block, "Thanks, Mr. Arnall! Thanks for Everything!" *WP*, July 19, 1946.
29. Block, "What's Going on Here?"
30. "White Blight," Editorial, *WP*, July 29, 1946.

31. Block, "It's Okay—Ol' Gene Will Be Back in Soon," *WP*, July 29, 1946.
32. Block, "Attention, Subjects!" *WP*, January 16, 1947.
33. Block, "What's Going on Here?"
34. Block, "We Don't Want None of Your Outside Interference," *WP*, January 18, 1947; Block, "You Too, Nosey," *WP*, January 22, 1947.
35. Block, "Not Guilty," *WP*, May 23, 1947; "Lynch Verdict," Editorial, *WP*, May 23, 1947.
36. Harry S. Truman, "Special Message to the Congress on Civil Rights," in Truman, *Public Papers of the Presidents . . . 1948*.
37. Block, "Bell-Ringer," *WP*, February 4, 1948.
38. Gillon, *Politics and Vision*, 47–50; Martin, *Civil Rights and the Crisis of Liberalism*, 81–88.
39. Block, "And in This Corner—," *WP*, July 9, 1948.
40. Block, "School Bell," *WP*, May 19, 1954. Block depicted the Liberty Bell in only one other cartoon drawn between 1946 and 1976, which again was focused on issues of civil rights. Block, "Hear Ye! Hear Ye!" *WP*, March 27, 1962.
41. Martin, *Civil Rights and the Crisis of Liberalism*, 123–26.
42. Roberts and Klibanoff, *The Race Beat*, 89–101. In total, the *Post* published only six stories on the Till murder in September 1955.
43. Eisenhower's heart attack on September 24 may have preempted an anticipated cartoon on the verdict itself, but this does not explain the lack of interest Block demonstrated in either the murder or the trial throughout the month of September.
44. Block, "Naive, Isn't He," *WP*, January 12, 1947; Block, "Hm—You Don't Say!" *WP*, December 11, 1949.
45. Roberts, *The Washington Post*, 292, 462.
46. Harris, *Little White Houses*, 69–70.
47. Roberts, *The Washington Post*, 294.
48. Roberts and Klibanoff, *The Race Beat*, 119–28.
49. "Exemplary Race Relations," Editorial, *WP*, February 24, 1956.
50. Block, "Somebody from Outside Must Have Influenced Them," *WP*, February 28, 1956.
51. Block, "Tote Dat Barge! Lift Dat Boycott! Ride Dat Bus!" *WP*, March 25, 1956.
52. Block, "Nah, You Ain't Got Enough Edjiccashun to Vote," *WP*, December 10, 1958. One reader, who saw the cartoon in the *Raleigh (NC) News and Observer*, declared it "marvelous" and wrote to Block praising the paper's owners for running it and "wondering how many other Southern papers" did likewise. Carson Ryan to Herbert Block, December 12, 1958, Box 70, Folder 4, HBP.
53. Berger, *Seeing through Race*, 8.

54. Block, "Poplarville, Mississippi, U.S.A., 1959," *WP*, April 28, 1959; Block, "Pray Keep Moving, Brother," *WP*, August 14, 1960; Block, "It Must Be Fine to Have a College Education," *WP*, January 11, 1961.

55. Block, "You Don't Understand, Boy—You're Supposed to Just Shuffle Along," *WP*, May 15, 1963. Other examples include Block, "We Don't Want You to Fall Down and Hurt Yourself," *WP*, February 20, 1957; Block, "Now Do You Want to Try for Nothing?" *WP*, July 29, 1957; and Block, "That Was for Paving the Road, Not Blocking It," *WP*, May 28, 1963.

56. Block, "Nah, You Ain't Got Enough Edjiccashun to Vote," *WP*, December 10, 1958; Block, "Oh Boy—Wait Till They Discover 'Black Beauty,'" *WP*, June 3, 1959; Block, *Straight Herblock*, 191.

57. Block, "You Know What I'd Like to Do? I'd Like to Push This Right Down over That Guy's Ears," *WP*, December 15, 1960.

58. Block, "And, Over Here, the Enemy—People," *WP*, February 28, 1964; Block, "I Got One of 'Em Just as She Almost Made It Back to the Church," *WP*, March 9, 1965.

59. Clyde T. Hall to Herbert Block, May 1, 1959, Box 34, Folder 7, HBP.

60. Block, Untitled Cartoon, *WP*, February 26, 1960; Gordon Peavy to Herbert Block, n.d., Box 64, Folder 10, HBP.

61. Block, "It's Getting So You Can Hardly Stone People in Peace Any More," *WP*, October 1, 1957; Block, "We Don't Want ANY Outside Interference," *WP*, September 2, 1962. Other examples include Block, "Somebody from Outside Must Have Influenced Them," *WP*, February 28, 1956, and Block, "Other Foreign News," *WP*, October 26, 1962.

62. Block, "We Don't Want No Troublemakers from the United States," *WP*, May 23, 1961.

63. Anonymous (name withheld) to J. Edgar Hoover, May 29, 1961, contained within the Herbert L. Block File, Federal Bureau of Investigation, Box 203, Folder 2, HBP.

64. The claim that King was "Hoover Enemy No. 1" is a reference to the FBI's wiretapping of King during the 1960s. King was referenced, but not depicted, in four other cartoons drawn between 1946 and 1976. Three of these were also published in the immediate aftermath of his assassination in April 1968, while the fourth was published on June 8, 1969, and referenced the FBI's wiretapping of prominent African Americans, including King, Cassius Clay, and Elijah Muhammad.

65. Ruby Bridges was depicted in Block, "Help!" *WP*, November 16, 1960. Charlayne Hunter and Hamilton Holmes were shown on a television screen in Block, "It Must Be Fine to Have a College Education," *WP*, January 11, 1961. James Meredith appeared in Block, "Other Foreign News," *WP*, October 26, 1962. Notably, none were explicitly identified by name,

and their identities are only evident because of the context of each cartoon.

66. For cartoons featuring William T. Coleman, see Block, "Your Keeping It Out Would Be a Serious Blow to Our Relations—With Our Allies, of Course," *WP*, December 17, 1975, and Block, "Passive Restraint," *WP*, December 8, 1976. For cartoons featuring Adam Clayton Powell, see Block, "Oh, Anti-Negro, Eh?" *WP*, February 22, 1963; Block, "He's Certainly Done a Lot for the Negro—It's Just That the Negro Happens to Be Him," *WP*, July 20, 1966; Block, "The Short Crusade," *WP*, January 11, 1967; Block, "What's Your Next Match?" *WP*, February 26, 1967; Block, "Brer Rabbit Ain't Going' ter Do Nothin' No More! Dis Is de End! Brer Rabbit Is Dead!" *WP*, March 2, 1967; and Block, "New Seat," *WP*, April 13, 1967. Although Coleman served in various executive roles within the NAACP and Powell was the first person of African American descent elected to Congress from New York, neither man was ever drawn in connection to civil rights–related activities.
67. Morgan, *What Really Happened to the 1960s*, 73.
68. Block, *Herblock: A Cartoonist's Life*, 158.
69. Block, "Tsk Tsk—Somebody Should Do Something about That," *WP*, April 3, 1956; Block, "And All This Time I Was Hoping You'd Speak Up," *WP*, August 28, 1958. Block extended this criticism of Eisenhower as an ineffective and aloof procrastinator to all aspects of his presidency, most famously in Block's March 27, 1957, cartoon "The Helicopter Era," which depicts a disinterested Eisenhower flying over a mob rioting over such issues as "Aid to Education," "Foreign Aid," "Immigration," "Civil Rights," "Trade," and the "Budget." Block, "The Helicopter Era," *WP*, March 27, 1957.
70. Block, "Medical Aid," *WP*, August 16, 1960.
71. Quoted in Dallek, *An Unfinished Life*, 604. In 1961 and 1962, Block instead depicted a representative from the Department of Justice as a proxy for the administration.
72. Block, "Washington, D.C., June, 1963," *WP*, June 13, 1963; Block, "Cold War at Home," *WP*, November 6, 1963.
73. Block, *Herblock: A Cartoonist's Life*, 194.
74. Block, "Come in, Friend—I Welcome Suggestions," *WP*, November 28, 1956; Block, "What Happened to That Plan for a House of Brick?" *WP*, June 26, 1957.
75. Kotz, *Judgment Days*, 27–28.
76. Block, *The Herblock Gallery*, 9; Block, *Herblock: A Cartoonist's Life*, 194.
77. Johnson's public statements are, however, referenced in three of Block's cartoons from this period. November 28, 1963's untitled cartoon and December 6, 1963's "Did He Say 'Let Us Continue' or 'Let Us Work Continuously'?" both reference, in the context of civil rights, Johnson's

November 27 appeal to the nation to continue his predecessor's agenda. March 17, 1965's "Literacy Test," meanwhile, includes a lengthy quote from the president's March 15 Voting Rights Address. Block, Untitled Cartoon, *WP*, November 28, 1963; Block, "Did He Say 'Let Us Continue' or 'Let Us Work Continuously'?" *WP*, December 6, 1963; Block, "Literacy Test," *WP*, March 17, 1965.

78. This is not to say that Block ignored other civil rights–related developments during this period. The white-on-Black violence that accompanied the civil rights movement's march from Selma to Montgomery in support of voting rights during March 1965, for example, was an event that outraged the nation and became the focus of nine Herblock cartoons during that month. Nevertheless, congressional (in)action on civil rights legislation accounted for over 53 percent (32 of 60) of the civil rights cartoons Block drew between November 23, 1963, and August 6, 1965.
79. June 26, 1963's "A Time for Greatness," for example, depicts Senators Strom Thurmond, Richard B. Russell, and John L. McClellan as inch-high figures standing in front of the doors to the Senate and holding a sign that reads, "The Old-Time Racist Politics Is Good Enough for Us." Block, "A Time for Greatness," *WP*, June 26, 1963. Other examples include Block, "It's Not Only the Committee Room—The Whole Country Is Being Packed with Those Damned American Civil-Righters," *WP*, July 14, 1963; Block, "Traitor!" *WP*, November 13, 1963; and Block, "We Mustn't Interfere with Customary Procedures—Doctor, Coroner, Inquest—," *WP*, December 8, 1963.

4. "NOTHING MORE THAN INFLAMMATORY PROPAGANDA"

1. Block, Untitled Cartoon, *WP*, November 23, 1963.
2. Block, "New Chapter," *WP*, November 26, 1963.
3. Block, Untitled Cartoon, *WP*, November 27, 1963.
4. Theodore L. Taylor to Herbert Block, December 1, 1963, Box 96, Folder 4, HBP.
5. James N. Greene to Herbert Block, December 3, 1963, Box 96, Folder 4, HBP.
6. Hartman, *A War for the Soul of America.*
7. Arthur M. Schlesinger Jr., "The New Mood in Politics," *Esquire,* January 1960, 58–60.
8. Schlesinger, "The Future of Liberalism."
9. Schlesinger, *Kennedy or Nixon*, 40, 42.
10. Block, *Herblock: A Cartoonist's Life,* 179–81.

11. For examples, see Block, "Nobody's Shoving, Chum," *WP*, May 25, 1959; Block, "Now It's Just a Question of Whose Kind of Peace," *WP*, January 18, 1960; and Block, "What's So Funny?" *WP*, May 10, 1960.
12. Block, "Chief, I Just Don't Think He's Ready for the Idea," *WP*, January 21, 1961.
13. Block, "Test," *WP*, March 26, 1961.
14. Block, "New Frontier," *WP*, August 7, 1960.
15. Block, "Gateway to the New Frontier," *WP*, November 17, 1960; Block, "It Looks Like the Same Old Tribe at the Pass," *WP*, January 29, 1961; Block, "Saddle Up. We Can Still Head 'Em Off at the Gulch," *WP*, March 28, 1961.
16. Dan Wakefield, "William F. Buckley, Jr.: Portrait of a Complainer," *Esquire*, January 1961, 49–52.
17. For cartoons advocating voting rights in Washington, DC, from this period, see, for example, Block, "Aloha," *WP*, March 13, 1959; Block, "It's Interesting to See What They're Doing in the United States," *WP*, November 8, 1960; Block, "Ho Hum—It's Sure Dull around Here" *WP*, August 8, 1962; and Block, "Have Another Pen," *WP*, August 6, 1965. On migrant worker voting rights, see Block, "The Still-Forgotten Man," *WP*, August 18, 1961.
18. Examples from the early 1960s include Block, "Grandpa, I'd Like to Do My Own Hunting," *WP*, August 26, 1960; Block, "There's Some Dangerous Radical Talk about Democracy Going Around Again," *WP*, December 27, 1960; and Block, "I'd Hate to Have Him Aiming at a Small One," *WP*, December 10, 1964.
19. William F. Buckley Jr., "The Magazine's Credenda," *National Review*, November 19, 1955, 6.
20. Richard Hofstadter, "The American Right Wing and the Paranoid Style" (1959), in Hofstadter, *Richard Hofstadter*, 960.
21. Block, "Go Back! Wrong Boat!" *WP*, May 25, 1947; Block, "Yoo Hoo! Boys! Are You Displaying the Flag Properly?" *WP*, April 18, 1952; Block, "And Some of Those Countries Aren't American at All," *WP*, April 24, 1953.
22. Evelyn N. Sherrill, "Letter to the Editor: Herblock's 'Daughters'" *WP*, April 26, 1956.
23. Block, "You See—Propaganda Everywhere," *WP*, April 19, 1957; Joseph F. Brisebois and M. H. Raitt, "A Prickly Harvest on the DAR Congress," *WP*, April 26, 1957.
24. Block, *Herblock Book*, 41–46.
25. Quoted in Mulloy, *The World of the John Birch Society*, 16.
26. Alan Barth, "Report on the 'Rampageous Right,'" *NYT*, November 26, 1961.
27. Hofstadter, *Paranoid Style*, 44
28. Block, "They're ALL Communists Except Thee and Me—," *WP*, April 5, 1961.

29. Block, "He Does Seem to Be out of Uniform—or Something," *WP*, July 26, 1961; Block, "Oh, the Army Isn't Sponsoring—It's Just Assisting," *WP*, September 29, 1961; Block, "We Off-Limit Boys Have to Stick Together," *WP*, August 2, 1963; Block, "Always Glad to See Somebody in There Pitching," *WP*, December 21, 1961; Block, "Exactly! Why Shouldn't He Break Away?" *WP*, December 30, 1962.
30. Phillips-Fein, *Invisible Hands*, xi–xii. Welch himself had been a successful businessman before founding the Birch Society, even serving on the board of directors of the National Association of Manufacturers (NAM), and many of the earliest members of the society had similar backgrounds. Among its founding members were two former presidents of NAM and the presidents of several major corporations, including Fred C. Koch, president of Kansas's Rock Island Oil and Refining.
31. Schoenwald, "We Are an Action Group," 22, 28.
32. Welch, *The Blue Book of the John Birch Society*, 101.
33. Robert Welch, "Republics and Democracies," September 17, 1961, in Welch, *The New Americanism*, 103, 111.
34. Block, "Elmer Davis Memorial Lecture."
35. Block, "If You Don't Like This Situation, You Can Cast Your Twentieth of a Vote against It," *WP*, October 13, 1961.
36. "Principles of the John Birch Society," *Congressional Record*, 87th Cong., 2nd sess., A4292.
37. Giglio, *Presidency of John F. Kennedy*, 101–2; Erwin Knoll, "Catholic Heads Open Fight to Put Church-School Aid in U.S. Plan: At Odds with Kennedy," *WP*, March 3, 1961; Fred M. Hechinger, "Education: Church and State. Catholic Hierarchy Hardens Stand on Aid to Parochial Schools," *NYT*, March 12, 1961.
38. Block, Untitled Cartoon, *WP*, April 30, 1947. Block's support for schools and teachers preceded his employment by the *Washington Post*. In July 1936, for example, he imagined a demure teacher being accused of not being patriotic by a flag-waving congressman. A series of shadowy figures—representing politics, schoolboards, contractors interested only in making a profit, and textbook scandals—loom large over the scene, representing the various groups who all sought to impose their priorities on America's schools. Block, "Are You Patriotic?" Syndicated Cartoon, July 13, 1936.
39. There are too many examples to cite here, but the first cartoon to explicitly address the overcrowding of schools was January 8, 1946's "This Year's Big Game." The first cartoon to depict children crammed into a small classroom or school was September 6, 1949's "The Bent Twigs." Block, January 8, 1946's "This Year's Big Game," *WP*, January 8, 1946; Block, "The Bent Twigs," *WP*, September 6, 1949.

40. Block, "This Little Kid's Got a Big Guy with Him," *WP*, February 21, 1961.
41. Block, *Herblock: A Cartoonist's Life*, 7.
42. Block, "Onward, 'Christian' Soldiers," *WP*, October 23, 1960.
43. Block, "Here Little Boy. Pull the Nice Horsie in with You," *WP*, March 8, 1961.
44. R. J. Grogan to Herbert Block, March 1961, Box 32, Folder 6; Thomas J. Dougherty to Block, May 20, 1961, Box 20, Folder 15, HBP.
45. Dierenfield, *The Battle over School Prayer;* Laats, "Our Schools, Our Country."
46. Block, "Leaving Religion to Private Initiative Is Un-American," *WP*, June 28, 1962.
47. Jacqueline Duffy to Herbert Block, July 12, 1962, Box 22, Folder 3, HBP.
48. Block, "What Do They Expect Us to Do—Listen to the Kids Pray at *Home?*" *WP*, June 18, 1963.
49. Block, "Elmer Davis Memorial Lecture."
50. Block, *Straight Herblock*, 153–54.
51. Wakefield, "William F. Buckley, Jr.," 51.
52. Goldwater, *Conscience of a Conservative*, 3. As Rick Perlstein wrote in his account of the 1964 presidential election, Goldwater's manuscript was actually ghostwritten by William Buckley's brother-in-law and Goldwater had minimal interest in its content until after publication. Perlstein, *Before the Storm*, 51–53, 61–63.
53. Goldwater, *Conscience of a Conservative*, 31, 40–43, 61–62, 68–75, 109.
54. Block, "Sometimes I Feel Like Running Away, Too, but I Don't Know Where to Go," *WP*, July 28, 1960.
55. Alan Barth, "Report on the 'Rampageous Right,'" *NYT*, November 26, 1961.
56. Arthur Schlesinger Jr., "The 'Threat' of the Radical Right," *NYT*, June 17, 1962.
57. Quoted in Rovere, *The Goldwater Caper*, 15.
58. Block, "On to the Old OLD Frontier," *WP*, December 11, 1960.
59. Block, "I Don't Want My Tax Money Spent on Your Kind," *WP*, July 25, 1961.
60. W. H. Bradfield to *Chicago Sun-Times* Editor, July 29, 1961; H. W. Dickson to Herbert Block, July 29, 1961, Box 96, Folder 4, HBP.
61. Block, "If You Had Any Initiative, You'd Go Out and Inherit a Department Store," *WP*, December 6, 1961.
62. William O. Sparks to Herbert Block, December 15, 1961, Box 96, Folder 5; Dan Trolio to Block, December 1961, Box 96, Folder 5; Agnes Adams to Block, n.d., Box 96, Folder 4; Chuck Fisher to Block, December 7, 1961, Box 26, Folder 12, HBP.
63. "Low Block," *Time*, December 15, 1961, 42; Block, *Straight Herblock*, 176.
64. John D. Hall, "Criticizes Cartoon," *Sacramento Bee*, December 14, 1961.

65. Paul W. Franz, "Objects to Cartoon," *Sacramento Bee,* December 17, 1961.
66. Geraldine L. Sherwood, "Disgusted with Herblock," *Sacramento Bee,* December 14, 1961.
67. M. H. Woodland, "Applauds Herblock," *Sacramento Bee,* December 19, 1961.
68. Barry Schiller, "It Strikes Home," *Sacramento Bee,* December 21, 1961.
69. Philip Cecchettini, "Socialism Ahead?" *Sacramento Bee,* January 1, 1962.
70. W. L. Earls, "Blasts Cartoon," *Sacramento Bee,* December 19, 1961.
71. Russell Kirk, "Conservatives and Fantastics," *America,* February 17, 1962, 644.
72. William F. Buckley Jr., "The Question of Robert Welch," *National Review,* February 13, 1962, 83–88.
73. Senator Barry Goldwater, Letter to the Editor, *National Review,* February 27, 1962, 140. For the *Washington Post*'s reporting on Goldwater's shifting views on the Birch Society, see, for example, Associated Press, "Goldwater Impressed by Birch Membership," *WP,* March 30, 1961; United Press International, "Goldwater Sees No Danger in Birch Society," *WP,* November 20, 1961; and Associated Press, "Goldwater Scoffs at Blanket Censure of Birch Society," *WP,* March 3, 1962.
74. "Transcript of Goldwater's News Conference on His Entry into Presidential Race," *NYT,* January 4, 1964.
75. Block, "Mind You, I Don't Put It Exactly That Way," *WP,* November 21, 1961; Block, "Why, Sure Enough—It's Fearless Barry Himself," *WP,* December 22, 1961; Block, "Sorry, Old Boy, but Your Wife and I Feel You're Becoming an Embarrassment," *WP,* March 6, 1962.
76. "Goldwater Scoffs at Blanket Censure of Birch Society," *WP,* March 3, 1962.
77. Block, "Tusk to Tusk," *WP,* June 25, 1963; Block, "You Guys Think You Have Trouble?" *WP,* May 6, 1964.
78. Block, "Birchhead," *WP,* February 20, 1963.
79. Schlafly, *A Choice Not an Echo,* 86.
80. McGirr, *Suburban Warriors,* 135–38.
81. Richard Hofstadter, "Eisenhower's Views Asked," Letter to the Editor, *NYT,* June 16, 1964.
82. Hofstadter, "Some Comments on Senator Goldwater, 1964," in Hofstadter, *Richard Hofstadter,* 879.
83. Daniel Bell, "Some Comments on Senator Goldwater," *Partisan Review,* Fall 1964, 586; Hans Morgenthau, "Some Comments on Senator Goldwater," *Partisan Review,* Fall 1964, 596.
84. Block, "An American Tragedy," *WP,* June 5, 1964.
85. Block, "Shake Hands—This Is a Time for Unity," *WP,* June 9, 1964.
86. Quoted in Perlstein, *Before the Storm,* 391.
87. Block, "Stand Upon Our Historic Principles—," *WP,* July 14, 1964.

88. Block, "We Want a Choice—*a Choice*—Not an Echo—*an Echo*—," *WP*, July 15, 1964.
89. Block, *Straight Herblock*, 64–66.
90. Block, "Elmer Davis Memorial Lecture."
91. Donald Janson, "Rightists Buoyed by the Election; Open New Drives: They See 26 Million Votes for Goldwater as Proof of Their Rising Power," *NYT*, November 23, 1964. The initial vote tallies after election day gave Goldwater 26,171,832 nationwide votes. It was not until mid-December that his final total of 27,175,754 was confirmed.
92. Ronald Reagan, "Proud Loser," *National Review*, December 1, 1964, 1055.

5. "I'M AFRAID TO LOOK"

1. Joseph Kraft, "Short-Term Swings of Opinion Blind LBJ to Basic U.S. Mood," *WP*, February 15, 1968; Thomas O'Toole, "Troop Call Seen Helping McCarthy," *WP*, March 11, 1968; Carroll Kirkpatrick, "Johnson to Speak Tonight: Hints at Major Decisions on Vietnam War," *WP*, March 31, 1968.
2. Lyndon Johnson, "The President's Address to the Nation Announcing Steps to Limit the War in Vietnam and Reporting His Decision Not to Seek Reelection," March 31, 1968, in Johnson, *Public Papers of the Presidents . . . 1968–1969*, 469–76.
3. Block, "Gave Proof through the Night . . . ," *WP*, April 2, 1968.
4. Block, *The Herblock Gallery*, 9.
5. Lyndon Johnson, "Remarks on the Signing of the Voting Rights Act," August 6, 1965, in Johnson, *Public Papers of the Presidents . . . 1965*, 840–43.
6. U.S. Riot Commission Report, *Report of the National Advisory Commission on Civil Disorders*, 38
7. Quoted in Dallek, *Flawed Giant*, 223.
8. Lyndon Johnson, "Statement by the President Following the Restoration of Order in Los Angeles," August 15, 1965, in Johnson, *Public Papers of the Presidents . . . 1965*, 882.
9. Gillon, *Politics and Vision*, 174–75.
10. Patterson, *Grand Expectations*, 662–63; U.S. Riot Commission Report, *Report of the National Advisory Commission on Civil Disorders*, 113; Feagin and Hahn, *Ghetto Revolts*, 105.
11. U.S. Riot Commission Report, *Report of the National Advisory Commission on Civil Disorders*, 2.
12. Block, *The Herblock Gallery*, 73–75.
13. "Emergency Alarm" depicts a group of schoolchildren bursting out of the windows of a school building, while "It's Too Small to Play House. Let's Play

School" shows three children evaluating a wooden crate as a prop in their imagined games. Block, "Emergency Alarm," *WP*, January 31, 1955; Block, "It's Too Small to Play House. Let's Play School," *WP*, January 8, 1961.

14. Prior to 1965, African American schoolchildren appeared in only seven Herblock cartoons, all of which were focused on school desegregation. The only one of these cartoons to depict both Black and white children was September 11, 1963's "Dropout," which was drawn in the aftermath of a federal court ruling that forced elementary schools in Huntsville, Alabama, to desegregate. The cartoon depicts four students—one of whom is Black—walking past a cigarette-smoking George Wallace, the cartoon's titular dropout, as they head to their newly integrated school. Block, "Dropout," *WP*, September 11, 1963.
15. Averbeck, *Liberalism Is Not Enough*, 2.
16. The cartoon depicts an African American man sitting in a house that has only two walls and no roof. He is speaking on the telephone, presumably to an administration bureaucrat, while his family sits around him, bundled up for protection from the cold caused by a snowstorm. On the wall is written "Administration Part-Way Housing Order," while the words "Housing Discrimination" appear in the sky. Block, "It's Fine—When Do You Think We'll Get the Other Walls and the Roof?" *WP*, December 20, 1962. Kennedy did issue an executive order to prohibit such discrimination, but it only applied to military housing.
17. Block, "Faster! . . . Here It Takes All the Running *You* Can Do, to Keep in the Same Place," *WP*, May 30, 1963. Carroll's original words, spoken by the Queen of Hearts rather than the Queen of Clubs, were "Now, HERE, you see, it takes all the running YOU can do, to keep in the same place. If you want to get somewhere else, you must run at least twice as fast as that!"
18. Sugrue, *The Origins of the Urban Crisis*, 101.
19. Block, "What's the Matter? We Don't Say 'Niggers' Up Here," *WP*, March 12, 1963. See also Block, "You Think That Equality Stuff Is Likely to Spread Up North Here?" *WP*, March 20, 1960; Block, "We'll See How Tough the New Cop Is," *WP*, March 14, 1961; and Block, "Picketing! Demonstrations! Government Meddling! I Don't Know What This Country Is Coming To," *WP*, June 6, 1963.
20. Block, "Those Alabama Stories Are Sickening. Why Can't They Be Like Us and Find Some Nice, Refined Way to Keep the Negroes Out?" *WP*, May 19, 1963.
21. Block, "You Ugly Devil!" *WP*, August 17, 1965; Block, "How Could Anyone Think We Might Have Any Responsibility for What Goes on Here?" *WP*, August 22, 1965.
22. "17 Dead in Coast Rioting; 'No End' of Trouble Seen: More Than 1000 Arrests Made as Los Angeles Considers More Troops," *WP*, August 15, 1965; "Los Angeles—The Rage and the Aftermath," *WP*, August 15, 1965.

23. Block, "The Built-In Bomb," *WP*, July 17, 1966.
24. Block, "Open Housing," *WP*, September 20, 1966.
25. These cartoons generally depicted Senate investigators as visiting the inner city to determine the causes of rioting but being blinded by their own agendas to the everyday hardships faced by residents. See, for example, Block, "These Weren't Damaged in the Riots—They Went to Pieces Years Before," *WP*, July 18, 1967; Block, "I Don't Understand It—Why Can't They Behave as If They Had Good Educations, Good Housing and Good Jobs?" *WP*, August 23, 1967; and Block, "One Side, Lady—We're Looking for a Conspiracy," *WP*, November 1, 1967.
26. Banford, *The Unheavenly City Revisited*, 220.
27. Patterson, *Grand Expectations*, 667; "Leaders in Congress Deplore Riots on Coast as Intolerable," *WP*, August 17, 1965; Upton, "The Politics of Urban Violence," 250; O'Reilly, "The FBI and the Politics of the Riots."
28. Erskine, "The Polls," 664.
29. Block, "Keep a Sharp Lookout for Outside Agitators," *WP*, July 13, 1967; Block, "Fiddler," *WP*, July 25, 1967.
30. "Civil Rights Revolution Stalled by Extremists, White and Black," *Boston Globe*, August 29, 1965; "The Negro after Watts," *Time*, August 27, 1965, 16–17.
31. Lyndon B. Johnson, "Remarks at the White House Conference on Equal Employment Opportunities," August 20, 1965, in Johnson, *Public Papers of the Presidents . . . 1965*, 898.
32. Quoted in Dallek, *Flawed Giant*, 223.
33. Block, *Straight Herblock*, 191.
34. "The New Racism," *Time*, July 1, 1966, 11–13.
35. "A Fiery Humphrey Denounces Society for Lag on Civil Rights," *NYT*, June 2, 1966; "Humphrey Asks a Halt in Civil Rights Protests," *NYT*, August 13, 1966.
36. Block, "Open Housing," *WP*, September 20, 1966; Block, "That's Showing Those Damned White Civil-Righters," *WP*, September 30, 1966.
37. Block, "Enemies of the Dream," *WP*, April 7, 1968; Block, "A Time of Testing," *WP*, April 9, 1968.
38. Block, "Dangerous Genie," *WP*, July 7, 1966.
39. Block, "Race," *WP*, May 28, 1968.
40. Joseph, "Black Liberation without Apology," 2.
41. Friedan, *The Feminine Mystique*, 16.
42. "The National Organization for Women's 1966 Statement of Purpose," National Organization for Women, https://now.org/about/history/statement-of-purpose/.
43. Block, "Irresistible Force and Immovable Object," *WP*, July 31, 1968; Block, "Patience—In Time They Accepted My Pill," *WP*, September 8, 1968. Notably, only the second of these two cartoons actually depicts a woman.

44. Block, "Would You Care to Join the Movement, Brother?" *WP*, January 17, 1967.
45. Block, "I've Been Deceived and I'm a Lonesome Little Girl," *WP*, June 24, 1956.
46. Block, "Tell Us about the Voices That Speak to You," *WP*, December 10, 1972.
47. Block, "Going! Going!—," *WP*, March 23, 1948.
48. Press, *The Political Cartoon*, 213–16.
49. Block, "What Happened to the One We Used to Have?" *WP*, October 9, 1946.
50. Block, ". . . Not Much Change in Temperature . . . ," *WP*, February 4, 1949; Block, "Hung Jury," *WP*, May 11, 1965; Block, "I Don't See Any Danger of Fascism," *WP*, June 1, 1947.
51. See, for example, Block, "Who's the Fairest One of All?" *WP*, June 27, 1975.
52. Block, "Sometimes We Almost Feel Like Giving the Kids a Break," *WP*, July 4, 1954; Block, "Shoo!" *WP*, April 21, 1955.
53. At the *Post*, the women's section was edited for over thirty years by Marie Sauer, who tried to subvert female stereotypes by including stories and profiles about women engaged in what were traditionally portrayed as "men-only" activities. Harp, *Desperately Seeking Women Readers*, 26.
54. In fact, the first two letters to be published by the *Post* in praise of Block's cartoons were both written by women. Annette Bulow, "Herbert Block," Letter to the Editor. *WP*, January 9, 1946; Elinor Ulman, "Herblock's Cartoons," Letter to the Editor. *WP*, March 19, 1946.
55. Meyerowitz, "Women and Gender in Postwar America," 1–2.
56. Block, "They're Claiming It Would Make Us Subject to Combat Duty," *WP*, November 18, 1977; Block, "It's All Right Because They're Sincere," *WP*, December 6, 1978; Block, "Not Negroes! Not Women! Not Gays!" *WP*, January 28, 1993. Any potential cartoon marking passage of the Supreme Court's ruling in *Roe v. Wade* to protect the right of a pregnant woman to an abortion may have been derailed by the death that same day of former president Lyndon Johnson, which Block did commemorate in the first cartoon published after both events. Block, "Landmark," *WP*, January 24, 1973.
57. Block, "Westward Ho, and Ho Ho Ho," *WP*, August 10, 1959.
58. Block, "Remember, It Would Be Unfriendly to Strike Back," *WP*, October 15, 1961.
59. See, for example, Block, "Oh, He's a Great Anti-Communist—It's Just That He Finds the Buddhists Are Easier to Get At," *WP*, July 10, 1963, and Block, "Those Crazy Buddhists—Setting Fire to Themselves," *WP*, August 30, 1963.

60. Block, "What a Dirty Trick, Sneaking Up on Us from Behind Like That!" *WP*, October 22, 1963. Block greeted news of the coup by showing Diệm fleeing from the flames he himself had started. Block, Untitled Cartoon, *WP*, November 4, 1963.
61. Block, "We Seem to Have That Paper Tiger in Our Tank," *WP*, February 10, 1965; Block, "What's the Matter with You—Can't You Read Signs?" *WP*, February 12, 1965; Block, *The Herblock Gallery*, 39; R. E. Joerese, "Negotiate," Letter to the Editor, *WP*, February 17, 1965.
62. Block, "The Falling-Domino Example," *WP*, February 23, 1965.
63. Gillon, *Politics and Vision*, 180.
64. "Professors Hold Vietnam Protest: 3 Bomb Threats Disrupt 'Teach-In' at Michigan U," *NYT*, March 25, 1965.
65. "The Big Viet-Nam Debate," *WP*, May 15, 1965; Block, "Go to the Foot of the Class," *WP*, May 18, 1965.
66. Block, "The Sidewalk Traffic Problem in Washington," *WP*, April 21, 1965. Along with a call to "Get out of Viet-Nam," the cartoon contains signs reading "Expel Alabama," "Get into China," "More Easter Eggs Next Year," "Pickets Unfair to Spring Sight-Seers," "Ban the N.Y. Yankees," and "Beagles Unfair to Cats."
67. Carroll Kilpatrick, "Larger U.S. Viet Role Denied," *WP*, June 10, 1965.
68. Block, "The Other Ascent into the Unknown," *WP*, June 10, 1965; Block, "Our Position Hasn't Changed at All," *WP*, June 17, 1965.
69. "Commitment in Viet-Nam," Editorial, *WP*, June 10, 1965.
70. Zelizer, *The Fierce Urgency of Now*, 162–225.
71. Schlesinger, *The Bitter Heritage*, 50.
72. Block, "Joint Session," *WP*, January 11, 1966. Other examples from 1966 included Block, "Watch That Carpet, Fella," *WP*, March 31, 1966, and Block, "Backlash," *WP*, December 6, 1966.
73. Block, "There's Money Enough to Support Both of You—Now, Doesn't That Make You Feel Better?" *WP*, August 1, 1967.
74. Quoted in Goodwin, *Lyndon Johnson and the American Dream*, 263.
75. Block, "We'll Teach You Patriotism and Respect for the Law," *WP*, May 7, 1967.
76. "McNamara Shouted Down at Harvard," *WP*, November 8, 1966; Block, "Harvard, Unfair Harvard," *WP*, November 9, 1966.
77. Block, *The Herblock Gallery*, 40.
78. Block, Untitled Cartoon, *WP*, May 5, 1968.
79. Block, "How Many Schools Have You Bugs Closed?" *WP*, December 17, 1968; Block, "Higher Education," *WP*, January 10, 1969. Other examples included Block, "And If You Don't Get Admitted There, What Other College Would You Like to Shut Down?" *WP*, April 22, 1969, and Block, "Groves of Academe," *WP*, May 9, 1969.

80. See, for example, "A Gallup Poll Finds 59% of Americans Would Continue War," *NYT*, November 11, 1967, and "Poll Reports 23% Voice Confidence in Johnson on War," *NYT*, November 14, 1967.
81. Don Robinson, "NSA Leader Plans Campus Drive to 'Dump LBJ' in '68," *WP*, August 24, 1967.
82. Schumacher, *The Contest*, 85–89; Andrew J. Glass, "Sen. McCarthy to Oppose LBJ in Four Presidential Primaries," *WP*, November 10, 1967. Block had been friends with Rauh, who was a noted civil rights attorney and one of the founding members of the ADA, since the early 1950s and later retained Rauh as his own personal attorney. See Block, *Herblock: A Cartoonist's Life*, 118, and Box 38, Folder 3, and Box 66, Folders 9–12, HBP.
83. Block, Untitled Cartoon, *WP*, January 2, 1968.
84. Block, "I'm Afraid to Look," *WP*, December 27, 1967.
85. Block, "Where Do You Think You're Going, Mac?" *WP*, December 3, 1967.
86. Gillon, *Politics and Vision*, 211–14.
87. Block, "Chief, Some Odd-ball Charging Like a Knight in Armor Thinks He Can—," *WP*, March 14, 1968.
88. Block, "Company Arrives," *WP*, March 17, 1968.
89. Block, "Friends, I Want to Remove Any Cause for Contention between You Two Fine Fellow Democrats," *WP*, April 26, 1968; Block, "Happiness Is a Basket of Warm Puppies," *WP*, May 30, 1968.
90. Cottrell and Browne, *1968: The Rise and Fall of the New American Revolution*, 175–76.
91. Block, "Politics of Happiness in Street without Joy," *WP*, August 25, 1968.
92. Schumacher, *The Contest*, 386–89.
93. Block, "War Casualty," *WP*, August 27, 1968; Block, "All Right, Ref—Start Counting Him Out," *WP*, August 28, 1968.
94. Block, "Prague, Eh? We Got It from the 'Security' Forces in Chicago," *WP*, August 29, 1968.
95. William Chapman, "McCarthy Refuses to Support HHH," *WP*, August 30, 1968.
96. Block, "The Overflowing Cup," *WP*, August 30, 1968; Block, "If You Can Fix Him Up, I'll Try Some Too," *WP*, September 1, 1968; Block, "All Right Now, Team—Heads Up—We Can Win This Old Ball Game," *WP*, September 5, 1968.
97. See, for example, Block, "Cannon to Right of Us, Cannon to Left of Us, and Oh, Brother—," *WP*, September 12, 1968.
98. Schumacher, *The Contest*, 426–27; Block, "I've Decided to Protest Too—I'm Gonna Vote for Humphrey and Free Speech!" *WP*, September 22, 1968.
99. Block, "Glue Sniffing," *WP*, October 10, 1968.
100. Block, "We've Invented a New Kind of Race This Year," *WP*, October 18, 1968.

101. Block, "You Sure There Won't Be a Re-Entry Problem?" *WP,* October 15, 1968; Block, "Then after Humphrey Gets Clobbered, We'll Pick up the Pieces," *WP,* October 22, 1968.
102. Block, "That's Odd—Somehow I Get the Feeling That We Didn't Win," *WP,* November 8, 1968.
103. Block, "He Really Shrinks on You, Doesn't He?" *WP,* November 12, 1968.
104. Alan F. Matthews to Herbert Block, November 13, 1968, Box 97, Folder 1, HBP.
105. Harold H. Lund to Herbert Block, November 14, 1968, Box 97, Folder 1, HBP.
106. Sheila M. Stewart to Herbert Block, Box 97, Folder 1, HBP.
107. Alan F. Matthews to Herbert Block, Box 97, Folder 1, HBP.
108. Block, "The Victims Were Often 'Persons Who Had Broken No Law, Disobeyed No Order, Made No Threat . . . ,'" *WP,* December 3, 1968.
109. Hubert Humphrey to Herbert Block, December 3, 1968, Box 34, Folder 3, HBP.

6. "THAT SON-OF-A-BITCH HERBLOCK"

1. The interview was conducted on December 20, 1972, and published in newspapers across the country on January 14, 1973, using different titles.
2. Saul Pett, "Nixon on Nixon: 'Great Decisions Require Calm,'" *WP,* January 14, 1973.
3. Ibid.
4. See, for example, Wills, *Nixon Agonistes,* 11–12.
5. Ralph Nader, quoted in Whitfield, "Richard Nixon as a Comic Figure," 116; Herbert S. Parmet, "Discussant: Herbert S. Parmet," in Friedman and Levantrosser, eds., *Watergate and Afterward,* 243; Parmet, *Richard Nixon and His America,* 539.
6. Hugh Sidey, "The Presidency," *Life,* February 7, 1969, 2.
7. Richard Nixon, "Remarks at the Swearing in of Walter J. Hickel as Secretary of the Interior," January 24, 1969, in Nixon, *Public Papers of the Presidents . . . 1969,* 13.
8. Christopher S. Wren, "Nixon's Haldeman: Power is Proximity," *Look,* August 24, 1971, 19, Box 200, Folder 4, HBP.
9. "The Private World of Richard Nixon," *Time,* January 3, 1972, 18.
10. Conversation between Richard Nixon and John Connally, 29, 1971, Nixon Tape Transcriptions, Tape 002–072, University of Virginia Miller Center Presidential Recordings Program, https://millercenter.org/the-presidency/secret-white-house-tapes/2-72.
11. Greenberg, *Nixon's Shadow,* xxvi.

12. For a full discussion of how Nixon was portrayed by the media during the first years of his political career, see ibid., 36–72.
13. Sam Stavisky, "People in the News: Nixon Considered Restraining Influence on Often-Spectacular House Committee," *WP*, December 5, 1948.
14. Block, "We Got to Burn the Evil Spirits out of Her," *WP*, May 16, 1948.
15. Greenberg, *Nixon's Shadow*, 44, 46–47.
16. The five-o'clock shadow returned in September 12, 1948's "How Did Atomic Energy Information Leak out to the Damn Scientists in the First Place?" but had again disappeared when Block next depicted Nixon in April 28, 1950's "Fellows, We've Got to Meet the Competition." Block, "How Did Atomic Energy Information Leak out to the Damn Scientists in the First Place?" *WP*, September 12, 1948; Block, "Fellows, We've Got to Meet the Competition," *WP*, April 28, 1950.
17. See, for example, Block, "Anybody Got a Good Idea for a Summer Show?" *WP*, June 27, 1948, and Block, "Fellow, We've Got to Meet the Competition," *WP*, April 28, 1950.
18. Block, *Herblock Book*.
19. John D. Morris, "A. D. A. Endorses Stevenson Ticket," *NYT*, August 18, 1952.
20. Block, "Middle of the Road," *WP*, August 25, 1952.
21. Many Republicans publicly urged Eisenhower to adopt what they called a "Middle of the Road" strategy, and by the end of the campaign the phrases "Middle of the Road" and "Eisenhower Republican" became synonymous. "Middle of Road Stand Urged for Ike Policy," *WP*, August 1, 1952; "Kuchel Calls Self Middle of Road Man: New Senator Wants to Reflect Views of California Citizens," *Los Angeles Times*, December 24, 1952.
22. Leo Katcher, "Secret Rich Men's Trust Fund Keeps Nixon in Style Far Beyond His Salary," *New York Post*, September 18, 1952.
23. "Nixon Should Withdraw," Editorial, *WP*, September 20, 1952.
24. Block, "Death of a Salesman," *WP*, September 20, 1952. Block's art was clearly based on the cover art of Viking Press's first edition of Arthur Miller's *Death of a Salesman*.
25. Block, Untitled Cartoon, *WP*, September 23, 1952. This cartoon complemented that day's main editorial in the *Post*, which ran under the title "Senator Nixon's Choice" and reiterated the paper's belief that Nixon owed it "to his party and to his country to take himself off the ticket." "Senator Nixon's Choice," Editorial, *WP*, September 23, 1952.
26. Block, "And Now for a Change in Tempo—," *WP*, September 25, 1952.
27. Patterson, *Grand Expectations*, 256–57; Nixon, *RN*, 101–4.
28. Greenberg, *Nixon's Shadow*, 65–66.
29. Block, "Sic 'Im, Checkers," *WP*, October 13, 1952; Block, "Here They Come Down the Stretch," Syndicated Cartoon, October 31, 1952.

30. Graham, *Personal History,* 203.
31. In contrast, Eisenhower is referenced in three cartoons and the Democratic ticket just once.
32. Patterson, *Grand Expectations,* 255.
33. Block, "Naughty Naughty," Syndicated Cartoon, October 29, 1952.
34. "Herblock's Pen," *Beaver (PA) Valley Times,* October 14, 1952, Box 199, Folder 5, HBP.
35. Graham, *Personal History,* 203.
36. "Herblock Isn't Mad, Just Resting Up, He Says," *Washington Daily News,* October 31, 1952, Box 199, Folder 5, HBP.
37. Reginald Valles to Herbert Block, October 31, 1952, Box 199, Folder 5, HBP.
38. Graham, *Personal History,* 203.
39. The controversy certainly didn't harm sales of Block's first book, *The Herblock Book,* which had been published earlier that month and soon reached a high of ten on the *New York Times*'s bestseller list. "Best Seller List," *New York Times Review of Books,* December 21, 1952, Box 199, Folder 5, HBP.
40. The July 2, 1954 cartoon "Ah, Yes—Isn't That Fellow McCarthy Terrible?" in which Eisenhower and the GOP elephant are innocently talking to a normal citizen, while Nixon rushes about in the background holding signs reading "Acheson Lost China" and "Democrats Didn't Care to Stop Communism," together with his old paint bucket, is a perfect example of this. Block, "Ah, Yes—Isn't That Fellow McCarthy Terrible?" *WP,* July 2, 1954.
41. Block, *Herblock Special Report,* 38–39; Roberts, *The Washington Post,* 326.
42. William Theis, "'Gutter Campaign' Charged to Republicans by Mitchell," *WP,* October 23, 1954.
43. Block, "Here He Comes Now," *WP,* October 29, 1954; Nixon, *RN,* 163.
44. Block, *Herblock Special Report,* 39.
45. Block, "Back Again! Together Again! Chotiner and Nixon," *WP,* September 25, 1962; Block, "Now, When You Get to This City You Turn Right and Come up at the Auditorium," *WP,* October 11, 1970.
46. Block, "Sweetest Little Feller—Everybody Knows—," *WP,* January 14, 1955.
47. Greenberg, *Nixon's Shadow,* 63–64.
48. Richard L. Strout, "President Takes High Line: Nixon Hailed," *Christian Science Monitor,* August 24, 1956.
49. "Adlai Derides 'New' Nixon, Attacks Ike on Civil Rights," *Newsday* (New York), September 12, 1956.
50. Schlesinger, *Kennedy or Nixon,* 2–18.
51. Block, "Let's See—What'll I Wear Today?" *WP,* February 15, 1956; Block, "Now You Kids Beat It," *WP,* October 26, 1956.
52. Some of the clearest examples of the "Nixon mask" can be seen in cartoons such as Block, "Will the Real Richard Nixon Please Stand Up?" *WP,*

June 9, 1960; Block, "Great Debate," *WP*, October 2, 1960; and Block, "Which Face and What Opinions Will Dick Put on Next? Tune in Again. . . ." *WP*, October 16, 1960.

53. Block, "Mirror, Mirror, on the Wall, Who's the Fairest One of All?" *WP*, January 2, 1960.
54. Block, *Herblock: A Cartoonist's Life*, 175.
55. "The Old Caricature," *Time*, January 18, 1960, 58.
56. Tris Coffink to Herbert Block, January 2, 1960, Box 14, Folder 14, HBP.
57. Robert S. Mendenhall, "Herblock's Horror," Letter to the Editor, *Chicago Sun-Times*, January 10, 1960, Box 84, Folder 3, HBP.
58. Quoted in Ambrose, *Nixon: Triumph of a Politician*, 11.
59. Small, *Presidency of Richard Nixon*, 22.
60. Ambrose, *Nixon: Triumph of a Politician*, 52–57.
61. Examples of both types of representation of Nixon from this time can be seen in, for example, Block, "Gee, That Was a Tough Break," *WP*, May 19, 1964, and Block, "California," *WP*, May 29, 1964.
62. Block, "Everything's Coming up Roses," *WP*, March 24, 1968. Nixon also appeared dressed as an undertaker in a cartoon published on September 13, 1968. It depicts a funeral procession in which the mourners are carrying signs reading "As a Mark of Respect for Czechoslovakia—We Propose Closing—The Prospects for World Survival." They are followed by Nixon who is holding a sign that reads, "Hold Back the International Nuclear Control Treaty." Block, Untitled Cartoon, *WP*, September 13, 1968.
63. Block, "Come Out, Come Out, Whoever You Are!" *WP*, September 18, 1968; Block, "The Apt Pupil," *WP*, September 11, 1968.
64. Quoted in Small, *Presidency of Richard Nixon*, 28.
65. Willie Howard to Herbert Block, October 11, 1968, Box 97, Folder 5, HBP.
66. Although anonymous, the postcard was postmarked northern Virginia. "A. Kruschev" to Herbert Block, November 17, 1968, Box 97, Folder 5, HBP.
67. Hazel Gruman to Herbert Block, October 1, 1968, Box 97, Folder 5, HBP.
68. Betty Candow to Herbert Block, November 6, 1968, Box 97, Folder 5, HBP.
69. Unknown to Herbert Block, n.d., Box 97, Folder 5, HBP.
70. Karl Johnson to Herbert Block, November 8, 1968, Box 97, Folder 5, HBP.
71. "Close Shave—Clean Shave," Editorial, *Meriden (CT) Morning Record*, November 11, 1968, Box 97, Folder 3, HBP.
72. Unknown to Herbert Block, November 8, 1968, Box 97, Folder 3, HBP.
73. Mrs. King C. Wang to Herbert Block, November 7, 1968, Box 97, Folder 5, HBP.
74. Block, *Herblock Special Report*, 83–84.
75. Graham, *Personal History*, 410.
76. "President-Elect Richard M. Nixon," Editorial, *WP*, November 7, 1968.

77. Block, Untitled Cartoon, *WP*, November 7, 1968.
78. Block, *Herblock: A Cartoonist's Life*, 225.
79. "Close Shave—Clean Shave."
80. William W. Gullett to Herbert Block, November 8, 1968, Box 97, Folder 3, HBP.
81. Carolyn Thomas, "The Herblock Barber Shop," Letter to the Editor, *WP*, November 10, 1968.
82. John D. Lofton Jr., "The Herblock Barber Shop," Letter to the Editor, *WP*, November 10, 1968.
83. Unknown to Herbert Block, November 7, 1968, Box 97, Folder 3, HBP.
84. Henry R. Schnitzer to Herbert Block, November 1968, Box 97, Folder 3, HBP.
85. "Down the Chimney Dick Nixolas Came with a Bound" depicts Nixon as Father Christmas, wearing a fake white beard, while "Transfer" imagines the president-elect as an astronaut whose helmet obscures his mouth and chin. Block, "Down the Chimney Dick Nixolas Came with a Bound," *WP*, December 10, 1968; Block, "Transfer," *WP*, January 19, 1969.
86. "The Unveiling," Editorial, *WP*, January 22, 1969.
87. Block, "Post-Inaugural Parade," *WP*, January 21, 1969.
88. Block, *Herblock: A Cartoonist's Life*, 225.
89. Perlstein, *Nixonland*, 549–50, 635–37.
90. Block, "Think of Yourself as Contributing to 'The New Prosperity,'" *WP*, November 25, 1971; Block, "Isn't There Some Simple Word for All That?" *WP*, April 13, 1972.
91. Donald Clancy to Herbert Block, October 10, 1969, Box 97, Folder 4; Alfred F. Dougherty Jr. to Herbert Block, April 11, 1970, Box 97, Folder 4, HBP.
92. Alfred E. Lewis, "5 Held in Plot to Bug Democrats' Office Here," *WP*, June 18, 1972. Although the *Post* gave greater prominence to the story than other national papers—the *New York Times*, for example, relegated the story to page 30 of their edition—its greater exposure in the *Post* is explained because of its local interest. "5 Charged with Burglary at Democratic Quarters," *NYT*, June 18, 1972; Roberts, *The Washington Post*, 432.
93. Alfred E. Lewis, "5 Held in Plot to Bug Democrats' Office Here," *WP*, June 18, 1972; Bray, *Pillars of the Post*, 124.
94. Nixon, *RN*, 626.
95. Ziegler, quoted in "White House Consultant Tied to Bugging Figure," *WP*, June 20, 1972; Bray, *Pillars of the Post*, 121; Greenberg, *Nixon's Shadow*, 103.
96. Ziegler, quoted in "White House Consultant Tied to Bugging Figure," *WP*, June 20, 1972.
97. Roberts, *The Washington Post*, 441–42.
98. In 1972, Block's cartoons were published five days a week—Tuesdays, Wednesdays, Thursdays, Fridays, and Sundays—meaning that he typically

worked only on weekdays, with the Sunday cartoon drawn the previous Friday.

99. Block, "Who Would Think of Doing Such a Thing?" *WP*, June 20, 1972.
100. Block, "Remember, We Don't Talk till We Get a Lawyer," *WP*, June 21, 1972.
101. Block, "Strange—They All Seem to Have Some Connection with This Place," *WP*, June 23, 1972. In his autobiography, Block recalled sharing this cartoon with Katharine Graham, the *Post*'s owner and publisher, who laughed but asked if he was really going to print it. When he replied that he was in fact on his way to the engraver's with it, she respected his editorial independence and said no more on the subject. Block, *Herblock: A Cartoonist's Life*, 235.
102. "White House Consultant Tied to Bugging Figure," *WP*, June 20, 1972.
103. For example, Block, "The New Security," *WP*, February 14, 1971; Block, "It's for Security—It Makes *Us* Feel More Secure," *WP*, March 14, 1971; Block, "Call Mrs. Beard's Doctor—There's Been a Terrible Accident," *WP*, March 22, 1972; and Block, "Tangled Web," *WP*, April 7, 1972.
104. Carl Bernstein, interviewed in *Herblock: The Black and the White*, dir. Michael Stevens, The Stevens Company, 2013.
105. Graham, *Personal History*, 463.
106. Block, "And When You Fellows Hold Your Convention Here in August, We Hope You'll Have a Good Time Too," *WP*, July 14, 1972.
107. Bob Woodward and Paul Valentine, "GOP Says 'Bug' Hearings Would Hurt Campaign," *WP*, July 11, 1972; Block, "Come Back after the Election—I'm Kind of Tied up Right Now," *WP*, July 19, 1972.
108. Block, "The Dark at the Top of the Stairs," *WP*, August 25, 1972; Block, "Keep the Lid on till after the Election!" *WP*, August 29, 1972.
109. Block, "Latest Item Pulled out of the Swamp," *WP*, October 1, 1972.
110. Perlstein, *Nixonland*, 651–53; Gillon, *Politics and Vision*, 231.
111. For example, the series of cartoons Block drew concerning Nixon's association with Mexican bank accounts. See Block, "It's—Uh—Sort of a Good Neighbor Policy," *WP*, August 31, 1972, and Block, "Stop the Music!" *WP*, September 3, 1972.
112. For example, Block, "And That's Just the Rug to Cover the Wall-to-Wall Money," *WP*, October 10, 1972, and Block, "The Newspaper Stories Are Despicable—And We Refuse to Answer Any Questions," *WP*, October 18, 1972.
113. For example, Block, "All Quiet along the Potomac," *WP*, October 4, 1972, and Block, "Time to Go Upstairs and Do the President-of-All-the-People Bit," *WP*, October 22, 1972.
114. Rose Abrahamson, "No Republican Protest?" Letter to the Editor, *WP*, September 24, 1972.

115. The *Post* did, however, print 201 stories written by its own staff, as well as a further 14 columns, on the subject of Watergate. Liebovich, *Richard Nixon, Watergate, and the Press,* 132.
116. Block, "Somebody Has to Think about Tomorrow," *WP,* April 27, 1973. Other examples include Block, "How Can Anything Touch Us after Our Landslide?" *WP,* March 25, 1973.
117. Lou Cannon and David S. Broder, "Bush Warns White House on Watergate Harm to GOP," *WP,* April 27, 1973.
118. Block, *Herblock: A Cartoonist's Life,* 237. In contrast, in their famous account of their reporting of the Watergate story, *All the President's Men,* Woodward and Bernstein only mention Block once—they reveal that it was Block, having heard the news on the radio, who informed Woodward about McCord's letter to Judge John J. Sirica on the morning of March 23, 1973. Bernstein and Woodward, *All the President's Men,* 275.
119. Block, "Shadowed," *WP,* February 27, 1973. See also Block, "Oops—Sorry—I Wouldn't Intrude on Highly Placed Gentlemen," *WP,* March 4, 1973, and Block, "'The FBI Needs a Leader'—L. Patrick Gray," *WP,* March 9, 1973.
120. Block, "Obstacle Course," *WP,* February 19, 1974; Block, "Streaking," *WP,* March 6, 1974.
121. Block, ". . . I Can Report Today That There Have Been Major Developments . . . ," *WP,* April 18, 1973; Block, Untitled Cartoon, *WP,* June 26, 1973; Block, Untitled Cartoon, *WP,* March 3, 1974; Block, "Tidal Wave," *WP,* July 28, 1974.
122. Block, Untitled Cartoon, *WP,* May 3, 1973.
123. Block, "National-Security Blanket," *WP,* May 27, 1973. Other noteworthy examples from this period include cartoons drawn on May 23 and June 28. Block, Untitled Cartoon, *WP,* May 23, 1973; Block, "Now We Issue Another Statement about How Your Trusted Counsel Was Trying to Cover Himself—Right?" *WP,* June 28, 1973.
124. David Bell, "Herblock Has 'Hate Hang Up,'" Letter to the Editor, *Middletown (NY) Times Herald Record,* February 24, 1973; Mack Goldman, "Herblock on Herblock," Letter to the Editor, *Middletown Times Herald Record,* March 24, 1973; George Noonan, "Chortles at Herblock," Letter to the Editor, *Middletown Times Herald Record,* March 24, 1973, Box 200, Folder 5, HBP.
125. Joseph Alsop to Herbert Block, April 19, 1974, Box 1, Folder 6, HBP.
126. Block, Untitled Cartoon, *WP,* November 1, 1972; Block, "In Retrospect, Looking Back, and with Hindsight—," *WP,* July 12, 1973; Block, "Tape Job," *WP,* August 28, 1973; Block, "Mugging," *WP,* October 23, 1973; Block, "How Can They Say He Hasn't Faithfully Executed the Laws?" *WP,* July 21, 1974.
127. Block, "I Am . . . Not . . . a Crook," *WP,* May 24, 1974.

128. Nixon, "Question-and-Answer Session at the Annual Convention of the Associated Press Managing Editors Association, Orlando, Florida," November 17, 1973, in Nixon, *Public Papers of the Presidents . . . 1973*, 956.
129. Block, "State of the Union," *WP*, January 30, 1974; Block, Untitled Cartoon, *WP*, April 4, 1974; Block, "If You Listen Very Closely, You Can Hear a Voice Saying, 'I Am Not a Crook, I Am Not a Crook, I Am . . . ,'" *WP*, January 20, 1974. Block also referenced the speech the day after Nixon gave his news conference but showed Nixon holding a paraphrased sign that read, "Frankly, I'm Innocent." Block, "Full Disclosure," *WP*, November 18, 1973.
130. Block, "There You Are, Boy—Nice Bone—," *WP*, September 17, 1972.
131. Block, *Herblock: A Cartoonist's Life*, 110.
132. Kutler, *The Wars of Watergate*, 530. For cartoons about San Clemente, see Block, "And If You Go to San Clemente, Don't Ask Him If the People Provided Him with That Property," *WP*, June 14, 1973, and Block, "Now, Is Everything Perfectly . . . ," *WP*, September 2, 1973. For commentary on Nixon's taxes, see April 4, 1974's Untitled Cartoon and Block, "A Little Backdating on a Deed—A Few Hundred Thousand Dollars Underpayment—We All Make Innocent Mistakes," *WP*, April 7, 1974.
133. Stephen D. Isaacs, "Post Probe, Broder Win Pulitzer Prizes," *WP*, May 8, 1973.
134. See, for example, Copeland, *The Media's Role in Defining the Nation*, 246–47; Marshall, *Watergate's Legacy and the Press*, 106–7; and Schudson, *Watergate in American Memory*, 103–4.
135. See, for example, Jim Fiebig, "Watergate Witch-Hunts," *Palm Beach (FL) Post*, April 13, 1974. Conservative writer Paul Johnson famously wrote that the "Watergate witch-hunt . . . was run by liberals in the media" and led to the results of the 1972 election being "overturned by what might be described as a media putsch." Johnson, *Modern Times*, 649, 653.
136. David B. Wilson, "If Anyone but Nixon Had Done It . . . ," *Boston Globe*, June 4, 1972.
137. See, for example, John Wood, "He Spotted Nixon Early," *Boston Globe*, December 15, 1974, and Richard J. Walton, "Wincing All the Way: Book World," *WP*, December 18, 1974.
138. Nixon, *RN*, 972.
139. Block, *Herblock: A Cartoonist's Life*, 234.
140. At the end of 1972, the *Post*'s daily circulation figure was reported by the *New York Times* at just over 527,000, rising to approximately 533,000 by the start of 1975. Anthony Ripley, "Washington Star Gaining Readers," *NYT*, October 8, 1972; Martin Arnold, "The Washington Star Struggles to Survive Circulation Battle," March 7, 1975. Block's syndication figure is quoted on the dust jacket of Block, *Herblock Special Report*.

141. Block, "We Got to Burn the Evil Spirits out of Her," *WP*, May 16, 1948.
142. Graham, *Personal History*, 463.
143. "President Nixon. Now More Than Ever," *WP*, August 9, 1974.
144. Schlesinger, *The Imperial Presidency*, 377.

EPILOGUE

1. Block, *Herblock Special Report*, 9, 235, 255.
2. Tom Engelhardt, "He Drew Nixon's Number," *St. Louis Post-Dispatch*, December 3, 1974, Box 200, Folder 6, HBP.
3. Herbert Block, "Progressive-Nation Dinner," speech presented in Washington, DC, December 16, 1975, Box 187, Folder 4, HBP.
4. Ben Bradlee, quoted in Hertsgaard, *On Bended Knee*, 3.
5. Block, "The War on Poverty, 1981," *WP*, March 10, 1981; Block, "Look at It This Way—Your Glass Is Half Full," *WP*, September 10, 1981.
6. Block, "Help the Poor? What Kind of Religion Is That?" *WP*, November 13, 1984; Block, "The Founders Would Have Loved It if They'd Thought of It," *WP*, January 24, 1985.
7. Block, "Damn Media! You Should Know Better Than to Report All the Dopey Things He Says," *WP*, January 28, 1983; Block, Untitled Cartoon, *WP*, January 22, 1984.
8. Block, "Leave the Facades—It'll Be Just Like Hollywood," *WP*, December 1, 1981.
9. Block, *Herblock Through the Looking Glass*, 15–17.
10. Block, *Herblock: A Cartoonist's Life*, 283–84.
11. Block, "Through the Looking Glass," *WP*, June 3, 1984.
12. Newspaper Association of America, "Newspaper Circulation Volume, 1940–2014," March 30, 2015, https://web.archive.org/web/20160219134047/http://www.naa.org:80/Trends-and-Numbers/Circulation-Volume/Newspaper-Circulation-Volume.aspx; Amy Watson, "Number of Daily Newspapers in the United States from 1970 to 2018," June 10, 2021, https://web.archive.org/web/20220415212815/https://www.statista.com/statistics/183408/number-of-us-daily-newspapers-since-1975/; Amy Watson, "Paid Circulation of Daily Newspapers in the United States from 1985 to 2018," July 1, 2021, https://web.archive.org/web/20220410124519/https://www.statista.com/statistics/183422/paid-circulation-of-us-daily-newspapers-since-1975/.
13. The Herb Block Foundation, "The Golden Age for Editorial Cartoonists at the Nation's Newspapers Is Over," December 2011, https://www.herbblockfoundation.org/sites/default/files/hbf2011whitepaper_f1.pdf.

14. Michael Cavna, "Another Cartoonist Loses His Job. This Does Not Bode Well for the Future of Newspaper Cartooning," *WP*, January 25, 2019; Michael Cavna, "The New York Times Cuts All Political Cartoons, and Cartoonists Are Not Happy," *WP*, June 11, 2019.
15. David Von Drehle, "The Man Who Made Presidents Cringe: HBO's Herblock," *Time*, January 27, 2014.
16. Jeet Heer, "Herblock Was a Fine Political Cartoonist. Liberals Don't Need to Deify Him," *New Republic*, January 26, 2014, https://newrepublic.com/article/116345/hbo-documentary-herblock-deifies-liberal-cartoonist; Andrew Ferguson, "Washington's Blockheads: The Perpetual Adulation of Herblock," *Weekly Standard*, February 10, 2014, 14–16.
17. Block, Remarks at the Opening of "The American Presidency in Political Cartoons: 1776–1976" Exhibit.

SELECTED BIBLIOGRAPHY

MANUSCRIPT ARCHIVES

Library of Congress, Washington, DC
    Herbert Block Papers (MSS 84974), Manuscript Division
    Herbert L. Block Collection, Prints and Photographs Division

Harry S. Truman Library, Independence, Missouri
    White House Central Files: President's Personal File

Princeton University Library, Princeton, New Jersey
    Fund for the Republic Records: Mass Media: TV Projects—Herblock, 1954–58

Richard M. Nixon Presidential Library, Yorba Linda, California
    White House Central Files: Alphabetical Name File

William J. Clinton Presidential Library, Little Rock, Arkansas
    Stephen Warnath Papers

Wisconsin Historical Society, Madison
    Americans for Democratic Action Records, 1932–2011

Yale University Library, New Haven, Connecticut
    Chester Bowles Papers (MS 628), Manuscripts and Archives

NEWSPAPERS AND PERIODICALS

America
Atlanta Constitution
Atlanta Daily World
Baltimore Sun
Boston Globe

Charleston (SC) News and Courier
Chicago Daily Tribune
Christian Science Monitor
Esquire
Life
Los Angeles Times
The Nation
National Review
New Republic
Newsday (New York)
Newsweek
New York Herald Tribune
New York Post
New York Times
Palm Beach (FL) Post
Partisan Review
Sacramento Bee
St. Louis Post-Dispatch
Time
Washington Post
Weekly Standard

ARTICLES AND BOOKS

Abel, Elizabeth. *Signs of the Times: The Visual Politics of Jim Crow*. Berkeley: University of California Press, 2010.

Adler, John. *Doomed by Cartoon: How Cartoonist Thomas Nast and the New York Times Brought Down Boss Tweed and His Ring of Thieves*. New York: Morgan James, 2008.

Aldous, Richard. *Schlesinger: The Imperial Historian*. New York: Norton, 2017.

Ambrose, Stephen E. *Nixon*, vol. 2, *The Triumph of a Politician, 1962–1972*. New York: Simon and Schuster, 1989.

Anderson, Benedict. *Imagined Communities: Reflections on the Origin and Spread of Nationalism*. London: Verso, 1991.

Averbeck, Robin Marie. *Liberalism Is Not Enough: Race and Poverty in Postwar Political Thought*. Chapel Hill: University of North Carolina Press, 2018.

Banford, Edward C. *The Unheavenly City Revisited: A Revision of the Unheavenly City*. Boston: Little, Brown, 1970.

Bayley, Edwin R. *Joe McCarthy and the Press*. Madison: University of Wisconsin Press, 1981.

Bederman, Gail. *Manliness and Civilization: A Cultural History of Gender and Race in the United States, 1880–1917.* Chicago: University of Chicago Press, 2008.

Bell, Jonathan. *The Liberal State on Trial: The Cold War and American Politics in the Truman Years.* New York: Columbia University Press, 2004.

Bell, Jonathan, and Timothy Stanley, eds. *Making Sense of American Liberalism.* Champaign: University of Illinois Press, 2012.

Berger, Martin A. *Seeing through Race: A Reinterpretation of Civil Rights Photography.* Berkeley: University of California Press, 2011.

Berger, Maurice. *For All the World to See: Visual Culture and the Struggle for Civil Rights.* New Haven, CT: Yale University Press, 2010.

Bernstein, Carl, and Bob Woodward. *All the President's Men.* New York: Simon and Schuster, 1974.

Block, Herbert. "The Cartoon." In *The Editorial Page,* edited by Laura Longley Babb, 151–60. Boston: Houghton Mifflin, 1977.

———. *Herblock: A Cartoonist's Life.* New York: Macmillan, 1993.

———. *The Herblock Book.* Boston: Beacon Press, 1952.

———. *The Herblock Gallery.* New York: Simon and Schuster, 1968.

———. *Herblock Looks at Communism.* Washington, DC: U.S. Department of State, 1950.

———. *Herblock's Here and Now.* New York: Simon and Schuster, 1955.

———. *Herblock Special Report.* New York: Norton, 1974.

———. *Herblock's Special for Today.* New York: Simon and Schuster, 1958.

———. *Herblock's State of the Union.* New York: Simon and Schuster, 1972.

———. *Herblock Through the Looking Glass: The Reagan Years in Words and Pictures.* New York: Norton, 1984.

———. *Straight Herblock.* New York: Simon and Schuster, 1964.

Boyle, Kevin. *The UAW and the Heyday of American Liberalism, 1945–1968.* Ithaca, NY: Cornell University Press, 1998.

Bradlee, Ben. *A Good Life: Newspapering and Other Adventures.* New York: Simon and Schuster, 1995.

Brands, H. W. *The Strange Death of American Liberalism.* New Haven, CT: Yale University Press, 2001.

Bray, Howard. *The Pillars of the Post: The Making of a News Empire in Washington.* New York: Norton, 1980.

Brinkley, Alan. *The End of Reform: New Deal Liberalism in Recession and War.* New York: Vintage Books, 1995.

———. *Liberalism and Its Discontents.* Cambridge, MA: Harvard University Press, 1998.

Brown, David S. *Richard Hofstadter: An Intellectual Biography.* Chicago: University of Chicago Press, 2006.

Buckley, William F., and L. Brent Bozell. *McCarthy and His Enemies: The Record and Its Meaning.* Chicago: Regnery, 1954.

Bullock, Charles S., Ronald Keith Gaddie, and Scott E. Buchanan. *The Three Governors Controversy: Skullduggery, Machinations, and the Decline of Georgia's Progressive Politics.* Athens: University of Georgia Press. 2015.

Bunker, Gary L. *From Rail-Splitter to Icon: Lincoln's Image in Illustrated Periodicals, 1860–1865.* Kent, OH: Kent State University Press, 2001.

Cash, W. J. *The Mind of the South.* New York: Vintage Books, 1991.

Caswell, Lucy. "The Midwestern School of Editorial Cartooning." In *Cartoon America: Comic Art in the Library of Congress,* edited by Harry Katz, 198–203. New York: Abrams, 2006.

Chafe, William H., ed. *The Achievement of American Liberalism: The New Deal and Its Legacies.* New York: Columbia University Press, 2002.

——. *The Unfinished Journey: America since World War II.* New York: Oxford University Press, 2007.

Cha-Jua, Sundiata Keita, and Clarence Lang. "'The Long Movement' as Vampire: Temporal and Spatial Fallacies in Recent Black Freedom Studies." *Journal of African American History* 92 (2007): 265–88.

Cobb, James C. *Away Down South: A History of Southern Identity.* New York: Oxford University Press, 2005.

Copeland, David. *The Media's Role in Defining the Nation: The Active Voice.* New York: Peter Lang, 2010.

Costello, Matthew J. *Secret Identity Crisis: Comic Books and the Unmasking of Cold War America.* New York: Continuum, 2009.

Cottrell, Robert C., and Blaine T. Browne. *1968: The Rise and Fall of the New American Revolution.* New York: Rowman and Littlefield, 2018.

Culver, John C., and John Hyde. *American Dreamer: A Life of Henry A. Wallace.* New York: Norton, 2001.

Cuordileone, K. A. *Manhood and American Political Culture in the Cold War.* New York: Routledge, 2005.

——. "'Politics in an Age of Anxiety': Cold War Political Culture and the Crisis in American Masculinity, 1949–1960." *Journal of American History* 87, no. 2 (2000): 515–45.

Dallek, Robert. *Flawed Giant: Lyndon Johnson and His Times, 1961–1973.* New York: Oxford University Press, 1998.

——. *An Unfinished Life: John F. Kennedy, 1917–1963.* Boston: Little, Brown, 2003.

Dekom, O. J. "Behind the Riddle of the Washington Post." *Plain Talk* 2 (March 1948): 11–18.

Delton, Jennifer A. *Rethinking the 1950s: How Anticommunism and the Cold War Made America Liberal.* New York: Cambridge University Press, 2013.

DePastino, Todd. *Bill Maudlin: A Life Up Front*. New York: Norton, 2008.

———. *Drawing Fire: The Editorial Cartoons of Bill Mauldin*. Chicago: Pritzker Military Museum and Library, 2020.

De Rosa, Peter L. "Plain Talk, 1946–1950." In *The Conservative Press in Twentieth-Century America*, edited by Ronald Lora and William Henry Longton, 461–69. Westport, CT: Greenwood Press, 1999.

DeSousa, Michael A., and Martin J. Medhurst. "Political Cartoons and American Culture: Significant Symbols of Campaign 1980." *Studies in Visual Communication* 8, no. 1 (1982): 84–97.

Dewey, Donald. *The Art of Ill Will: The Story of American Political Cartoons*. New York: New York University Press, 2007.

Dierenfield, Bruce J. *The Battle over School Prayer: How Engel v. Vitale Changed America*. Lawrence: University Press of Kansas, 2007.

Doherty, Thomas. *Cold War, Cool Medium: Television, McCarthyism, and American Culture*. New York: Columbia University Press, 2005.

Dowd Hall, Jacquelyn. "The Long Civil Rights Movement and the Political Uses of the Past." *Journal of American History* 91, no. 4 (2005): 1233–63.

Downie, Leonard, Jr. *All about the Story: News, Power, Politics, and the Washington Post*. New York: PublicAffairs, 2020.

Drucker, Johanna. "Not Sound." In *The Sound of Poetry / The Poetry of Sound*, edited by Marjorie Perloff and Craig Dworkin, 237–48. Chicago: University of Chicago Press, 2009.

Dudziak, Mary L. *Cold War Civil Rights: Race and the Image of American Democracy*. Princeton, NJ: Princeton University Press, 2011.

Edwards, Janis L. *Political Cartoons in the 1988 Presidential Campaign: Image, Metaphor, and Narrative*. New York: Garland, 1997.

Eisenmann, Linda. *Higher Education for Women in Postwar America, 1945–1965*. Baltimore: Johns Hopkins University Press, 2006.

Ericson, David F., and Louisa Bertch Green, eds. *The Liberal Tradition in American Politics: Reassessing the Legacy of American Liberalism*. London: Routledge, 1999.

Erskine, Hazel. "The Polls: Demonstrations and Race Riots." *Public Opinion Quarterly* 31, no. 4 (1967): 655–77.

Farber, David, and Jeff Roche, eds. *The Conservative Sixties*. New York: Peter Lang, 2003.

Feagin, Joe R., and Harlan Hahn. *Ghetto Revolts: The Politics of Violence in American Cities*. New York: Macmillan, 1973.

Feldstein, Mark. "Watergate Revisited." *American Journalism Review* 26, no. 4 (2004): 60–68.

Fischer, Roger A. *Them Damned Pictures: Explorations in American Political Cartoon Art*. North Haven, CT: Archon Books, 1995.

Fleegler, Robert L. "Theodore G. Bilbo and the Decline of Public Racism, 1938–1947." *Journal of Mississippi History* 66, no. 1 (2006): 1–27.

Fones-Wolf, Elizabeth. *Selling Free Enterprise: The Business Assault on Labor and Liberalism, 1945–1960*. Urbana: University of Illinois Press, 1994.

Forker, Martin. "The Use of the 'Cartoonist's Armoury' in Manipulating Public Opinion: Anti-Irish Imagery in 19th Century British and American Periodicals." *Journal of Irish Studies* 27 (2012): 58–71.

Fort Wayne, Indiana, City Directory (1874). Taylor, MI: R. L. Polk, 1874.

Fried, Richard M. *Nightmare in Red: The McCarthy Era in Perspective*. New York: Oxford University Press, 1990.

Friedan, Betty. *The Feminine Mystique*. New York: Norton, 1963.

Friedman, Leon, and William F. Levantrosser, eds. *Watergate and Afterward: The Legacy of Richard M. Nixon*. Westport, CT: Greenwood Press, 1992.

Gerstle, Gary. "Race and the Myth of the Liberal Consensus." *Journal of American History* 82, no. 2 (1995): 579–86.

Gerstle, Gary, and Steven Fraser, eds. *The Rise and Fall of the New Deal Order*. Princeton, NJ: Princeton University Press, 1989.

Giglio, James N. *The Presidency of John F. Kennedy*. Lawrence: University Press of Kansas, 2006.

Gillon, Steven M. *Politics and Vision: The ADA and American Liberalism, 1947–1985*. New York: Oxford University Press, 1987.

Gitlin, Todd. *The Whole World Is Watching: Mass Media in the Making and Unmaking of the New Left*. Berkeley: University of California Press, 2003.

Göçek, Fatma Müge. "From Empire to Nation: Images of Women and War in Ottoman Political Cartoons, 1908–1923." In *Borderlines: Genders and Identities in War and Peace, 1870–1930*, edited by Billie Melman, 47–72. New York: Routledge, 1998.

Goldwater, Barry. *The Conscience of a Conservative*. Shepherdsville, KY: Victor, 1960.

Gombrich, Ernst. "The Cartoonist's Armoury." In *Meditations on a Hobby Horse and Other Essays on the Theory of Art*, edited by Ernst Gombrich, 127–42. London: Phaidon Press, 1965.

Goodwin, Doris Kearns. *Lyndon Johnson and the American Dream*. New York: Harper and Row, 1976.

Graham, Katharine. *Personal History*. New York: Vintage, 1998.

Greenberg, David. *Nixon's Shadow: The History of an Image*. New York: Norton, 2003.

Guglielmo, Thomas A. *White on Arrival: Italians, Race, Color, and Power in Chicago, 1890–1945*. New York: Oxford University Press, 2003.

Halloran, Fiona Deans. *Thomas Nast: The Father of Modern Political Cartoons*. Chapel Hill: University of North Carolina Press, 2013.

Hamby, Alonzo. *Beyond the New Deal: Harry S. Truman and American Liberalism*. New York: Columbia University Press, 1973.

———. *Liberalism and Its Challengers: From F.D.R. to Bush*. New York: Oxford University Press, 1992.

Hariman, Robert, and John Louis Lucaites. *No Caption Needed: Iconic Photographs, Public Culture, and Liberal Democracy*. Chicago: University of Chicago Press, 2007.

Harp, Dustin. *Desperately Seeking Women Readers: U.S. Newspapers and the Construction of a Female Readership*. Lanham, MD: Lexington Books, 2007.

Harris, Dianne. *Little White Houses: How the Postwar Home Constructed Race in America*. Minneapolis: University of Minnesota Press, 2013.

Hartman, Andrew. *A War for the Soul of America: A History of the Culture Wars*. Chicago: University of Chicago Press, 2015.

Hartmann, Susan. *The Other Feminists: Activists in the Liberal Establishment*. New Haven, CT: Yale University Press, 1998.

Haynes, John Earl, and Harvey Klehr. *Early Cold War Spies: The Espionage Trials That Shaped American Politics*. New York: Cambridge University Press, 2006.

Herman, Arthur. *Joseph McCarthy: Reexamining the Life and Legacy of America's Most Hated Senator*. New York: Free Press, 2000.

Hertsgaard, Mark. *On Bended Knee: The Press and the Reagan Presidency*. New York: Farrar Straus and Giroux, 1988.

Hess, Stephen, and Sandy Northrop. *American Political Cartoons: The Evolution of a National Identity, 1754–2010*. Piscataway, NJ: Transaction, 2010.

———. *Drawn and Quartered: The History of American Political Cartoons*. Montgomery, AL: Elliot and Clark, 1996.

Higham, John. "The Cult of the 'American Consensus': Homogenizing Our Past." *Commentary* 27 (February 1959): 93–100.

Hirsch, Arnold R. *Making the Second Ghetto: Race and Housing in Chicago, 1940–1960*. Chicago: University of Chicago Press, 1998.

Hodgson, Godfrey. *America in Our Time: From World War II to Nixon—What Happened and Why*. New York: Vintage Books, 1976.

Hofstadter, Richard. *The Age of Reform: From Bryan to FDR*. New York: Knopf, 1955.

———. *The American Political Tradition and the Men Who Made It*. New York: Knopf, 1948.

———. *The Paranoid Style in American Politics and Other Essays*. New York: Knopf, 1966.

———. *Richard Hofstadter: Anti-Intellectualism in American Life, The Paranoid Style in American Politics, Uncollected Essays, 1956–1965*. Edited by Sean Wilentz. New York: Library of America, 2020.

Hogan, Michael J. *A Cross of Iron: Harry S. Truman and the Origins of the National Security State, 1945–1954.* New York: Cambridge University Press, 1998.

Horton, Carol A. *Race and the Making of American Liberalism.* Oxford: Oxford University Press, 2005.

Johnson, Haynes. *The Age of Anxiety: McCarthyism to Terrorism.* Orlando, FL: Harcourt, 2005.

Johnson, Haynes, and Harry L. Katz, eds. *Herblock: The Life and Work of the Great Political Cartoonist.* New York: Norton, 2009.

——. "Herblock *Knew:* Herb Block and American Editorial Cartooning." In *Herblock: The Life and Work of the Great Political Cartoonist,* edited by Haynes Johnson and Harry L. Katz, 37–58. New York: Norton, 2009.

Johnson, Lyndon B. *Public Papers of the Presidents of the United States, Lyndon B. Johnson. Containing the Public Messages, Speeches, and Statements of the President,* vol. 1, *1968–1969.* Washington, DC: U.S. Government Printing Office, 1970.

——. *Public Papers of the Presidents of the United States, Lyndon B. Johnson. Containing the Public Messages, Speeches, and Statements of the President,* vol. 2, *1965.* Washington, DC: U.S. Government Printing Office, 1966.

Johnson, Paul. *Modern Times: The World from the Twenties to the Nineties.* New York: Perennial Classics, 2001.

Joseph, Peniel E. "Black Liberation without Apology: Reconceptualizing the Black Power Movement." *Black Scholar* 31, nos. 3–4 (2001): 2–19.

——, ed. *The Black Power Movement: Rethinking the Civil Rights–Black Power Era.* New York: Routledge, 2006.

Kamen, Scott. "Rethinking Postwar Liberalism: The Americans for Democratic Action, Social Democracy, and the Struggle for Racial Equality." *The Sixties: A Journal of History, Politics and Culture* 11, no. 1 (2018): 69–92.

Katz, Harry, ed. *Cartoon America: Comic Art in the Library of Congress* New York: Abrams, 2006.

——. "Herblock's History: Political Cartoons from the Crash to the Millennium." *Library of Congress Information Bulletin* 59, no. 10 (2000): 1–64.

Keller, Morton. *The Art and Politics of Thomas Nast.* Oxford: Oxford University Press, 1975.

Kercher, Stephen E. *Revel with a Cause: Liberal Satire in Postwar America.* Chicago: University of Chicago Press, 2006.

Kimmage, Michael. *The Conservative Turn: Lionel Trilling, Whittaker Chambers, and the Lessons of Anti-Communism.* Cambridge, MA: Harvard University Press, 2009.

Knight, Amy. *How the Cold War Began: The Gouzenko Affair and the Hunt for Soviet Spies.* Toronto: McClelland and Stewart, 2005.

Kotz, Nick. *Judgment Days: Lyndon Baines Johnson, Martin Luther King Jr., and the Laws That Changed America.* New York: Houghton Mifflin, 2005.

Kruse, Kevin Michael. *White Flight: Atlanta and the Making of Modern Conservatism.* Princeton, NJ: Princeton University Press, 2005.

Kukkonen, Karin. *Studying Comics and Graphic Novels.* Malden, MA: Wiley-Blackwell, 2013.

Kutler, Stanley I., ed. *Abuse of Power: The New Nixon Tapes* New York: Touchstone, 1997.

——. *The Wars of Watergate: The Last Crisis of Richard Nixon.* New York: Norton, 1990.

Laats, Adam. "Our Schools, Our Country: American Evangelicals, Public Schools, and the Supreme Court Decisions of 1962 and 1963." *Journal of Religious History* 36, no. 3 (2012): 319–34.

Lamb, Chris. "Drawing Power." *Journalism Studies* 8, no. 5 (2007): 715–29.

——. *Drawn to Extremes: The Use and Abuse of Editorial Cartoons in the United States.* New York: Columbia University Press, 2004.

——. "Herblock Talks about Life as a Cartoonist; the Four-Time Pulitzer Prize Winner Discusses His 45 Years at the *Washington Post,* McCarthyism, Nixon, Bush, and More." *Editor and Publisher* 124, no. 26 (1991): 32–34.

Lang, Clarence. "Locating the Civil Rights Movement: An Essay on the Deep South, Midwest, and Border South in Black Freedom Studies." *Journal of Social History* 47, no. 2 (2013): 371–400.

Lang, Gladys Engel, and Kurt Lang. *The Battle for Public Opinion: The President, the Press, and the Polls during Watergate.* New York: Columbia University Press, 1983.

Lassiter, Matthew. *The Silent Majority: Suburban Politics in the Sunbelt South.* Princeton, NJ: Princeton University Press, 2007.

Latour, Bruno, and Peter Weibel, eds. *Iconoclash: Beyond the Image Wars in Science, Religion, and Art.* Cambridge, MA: MIT Press, 2002.

Lewin, J. G., and P. J. Huff. *Lines of Contention: Political Cartoons of the Civil War.* New York: Harper, 2007.

Lewis, Sinclair. *It Can't Happen Here.* New York: New American Library, 1935.

Liebovich, Louis W. *Richard Nixon, Watergate, and the Press.* Westport, CT: Praeger, 2003.

Long, Michael. "Cartoons without Humor: The Underwhelming Oeuvre of Herblock, America's Worst Political Cartoonist." *Weekly Standard,* November 13, 2000, 22–25.

Lordan, Edward J. *Politics, Ink: How America's Cartoonists Skewer Politicians, from King George III to George Dubya.* Lanham, MD: Rowman and Littlefield, 2006.

Lott, Eric. *Love and Theft: Blackface Minstrelsy and the American Working Class.* New York: Oxford University Press, 2013.

Lowndes, Joseph E. *From the New Deal to the New Right: Race and the Southern Origins of Modern Conservatism.* New Haven, CT: Yale University Press, 2008.

Marshall, Jon. *Watergate's Legacy and the Press: The Investigative Impulse.* Chicago: Northwestern University Press, 2011.

Martin, John Frederick. *Civil Rights and the Crisis of Liberalism: The Democratic Party, 1945–1976.* Boulder, CO: Westview Press, 1979.

Mattson, Kevin. *When America Was Great: The Fighting Faith of Postwar Liberalism.* New York: Routledge, 2004.

Matusow, Allen J. *The Unraveling of America: A History of Liberalism in the 1960s.* Athens: University of Georgia Press, 2009.

Maudlin, Bill. *Willie and Joe: The WWII Years.* Seattle: Fantagraphics Books, 2008.

May, Elaine Tyler. *Homeward Bound: American Families in the Cold War Era.* New York: Basic Books, 1998.

McAullife, Mary. *Crisis on the Left: Cold War Politics and American Liberals, 1947–1954.* Amherst: University of Massachusetts Press, 1978.

McCarthy, Joe. *McCarthyism: The Fight for America—Documented Answers to Questions Asked by Friend and Foe.* New York: Devin-Adair, 1952.

McClenahan, William M., Jr., and William H. Becker. *Eisenhower and the Cold War Economy.* Baltimore: Johns Hopkins University Press, 2011.

McGirr, Lisa. *Suburban Warriors: The Origins of the New American Right.* Princeton, NJ: Princeton University Press, 2001.

Meyerowitz, Joanne. "Beyond the Feminine Mystique: A Reassessment of Postwar Mass Culture, 1946–1958." *Journal of American History* 79, no. 4 (1993): 1455–82.

——, ed. *Not June Cleaver: Women and Gender in Postwar America, 1945–1960.* Philadelphia: Temple University Press, 1994.

——. "Women and Gender in Postwar America." In *Not June Cleaver: Women and Gender in Postwar America, 1945–1960,* edited by Joanne Meyerowitz, 1–18. Philadelphia: Temple University Press, 1994.

Michelmore, Christina W. "Old Picture in New Frames: Images of Islam and Muslims in Post World War II American Political Cartoons." *Journal of American and Comparative Culture* 23, no. 4 (2000): 37–50.

Mikailova, Yulia. "Intellectuals, Cartoons, and Nationalism during the Russo-Japanese War." In *Japanese Visual Culture: Explorations in the World of Manga and Anime,* edited by Mark Wheeler MacWilliams, 155–76. New York: East Gate Books, 2008.

Milkis, Sidney M., and Jerome M. Mileur, eds. *The New Deal and the Triumph of Liberalism* Amherst: University of Massachusetts Press, 2002.

Miller, Arthur. *Death of a Salesman.* New York: Viking Press, 1949.

Miller, Nathan. *New World Coming: The 1920s and the Making of Modern America.* New York: Scribner, 2003.

Mirzoeff, Nicholas. *An Introduction to Visual Culture*. London: Routledge, 2009.

——. *The Right to Look: A Counterhistory of Visuality*. Durham, NC: Duke University Press, 2011.

——, ed. *The Visual Culture Reader* London: Routledge, 2013.

——. "What Is Visual Culture?" In *The Visual Culture Reader*, edited by Nicholas Mirzoeff, 3–13. New York: Routledge, 1998.

Mitchell, W. J. T. *Picture Theory: Essays on Verbal and Visual Representation*. Chicago: University of Chicago Press, 1994.

Mittelstadt, Jennifer. *From Welfare to Workfare: The Unintended Consequences of Liberal Reform, 1945–1965*. Chapel Hill: University of North Carolina Press, 2005.

Morgan, Edward P. "The Good, the Bad, and the Forgotten: Media Culture and Public Memory of the Civil Rights Movement," In *The Civil Rights Movement in American Memory*, edited by Renee C. Romano and Leigh Raiford, 137–66. Athens: University of Georgia Press, 2006.

——. *What Really Happened to the 1960s: How Mass Media Culture Failed American Democracy*. Lawrence: University Press of Kansas, 2010.

Morgan, Ted. *Reds: McCarthyism in Twentieth-Century America*. New York: Random House, 2003.

Mulloy, D. J. *The World of the John Birch Society: Conspiracy, Conservatism, and the Cold War*. Nashville, TN: Vanderbilt University Press, 2014.

Myrdal, Gunnar. *An American Dilemma: The Negro Problem and Modern Democracy*. New York: Harper and Brothers, 1944.

Navasky, Victor S. *The Art of Controversy: Political Cartoons and Their Enduring Power*. New York: Knopf, 2013.

Nixon, Richard. *Public Papers of the Presidents of the United States, Richard Nixon. Containing the Public Messages, Speeches, and Statements of the President: 1969*. Washington, DC: U.S. Government Printing Office, 1971.

——. *Public Papers of the Presidents of the United States, Richard Nixon. Containing the Public Messages, Speeches, and Statements of the President: 1973*. Washington, DC: U.S. Government Printing Office, 1975.

——. *RN: The Memoirs of Richard Nixon*. New York: Simon and Schuster, 1990.

Offner, Arnold A. *Hubert Humphrey: The Conscience of the Country*. New Haven, CT: Yale University Press, 2018.

O'Reilly, Kenneth. "The FBI and the Politics of the Riots, 1964–1968." *Journal of American History* 75, no. 1 (1988): 91–114.

Pacyga, Dominc A. *Chicago: A Biography*. Chicago: University of Chicago Press, 2009.

Parmet, Herbert S. *Richard Nixon and His America*. Boston: Little, Brown, 1990.

Patterson, James T. *Grand Expectations: The United States, 1945–1974*. New York: Oxford University Press, 1996.

Pells, Richard. *The Liberal Mind in a Conservative Age: American Intellectuals in the 1940s and 1950s*. Middletown, CT: Wesleyan University Press, 1985.

Perlstein, Rick. *Before the Storm: Barry Goldwater and the Unmaking of the American Consensus*. New York: Nation Books, 2009.

———. *Nixonland: The Rise of a President and the Fracturing of America*. New York: Scribner, 2008.

Phillips-Fein, Kim. *Invisible Hands: The Making of the Conservative Movement from the New Deal to Reagan*. New York: Norton, 1999.

———. "If Business and the Country Will Be Run Right: The Business Challenge to the Liberal Consensus, 1945–1964." *International Labor and Working-Class History* 72 (2007): 192–215.

Press, Charles. *The Political Cartoon*. East Brunswick, NJ: Associated University Presses, 1981.

Reeves, Thomas C. *The Life and Times of Joe McCarthy: A Biography*. New York: Madison Books, 1982.

Richardson, Heather Cox. *How the South Won the Civil War: Oligarchy, Democracy, and the Continuing Fight for the Soul of America*. New York: Oxford University Press, 2020.

Roberts, Chalmers M. *The Washington Post: The First 100 Years*. Boston: Houghton Mifflin, 1977.

Roberts, Gene, and Hank Klibanoff. *The Race Beat: The Press, the Civil Rights Struggle, and the Awakening of a Nation*. New York: Knopf, 2006.

Rossinow, Doug. *Visions of Progress: The Left-Liberal Tradition in America*. Philadelphia: University of Pennsylvania Press, 2009.

Rovere, Richard H. *The Goldwater Caper*. New York: Harcourt, Brace and World, 1965.

———. *Senator Joe McCarthy*. Berkeley: University of California Press, 1959.

Sandbrook, Dominic. *Eugene McCarthy: The Rise and Fall of Postwar American Liberalism*. New York: Knopf, 2004.

Sayer, John. "Art and Politics, Dissent and Repression: The Masses Magazine versus the Government, 1917–1918." *American Journal of Legal History* 32, no. 1 (1988): 42–78.

Schlafly, Phyllis. *A Choice Not an Echo*. Alton, IL: Pere Marquette Press, 1964.

Schlesinger, Arthur M., Jr. *The Age of Roosevelt*. Boston: Houghton Mifflin, 1957.

———. *The Bitter Heritage: Vietnam and American Democracy, 1941–1966*. Boston: Houghton Mifflin, 1967.

———. "The Future of Liberalism: The Challenge of Abundance." *The Reporter*, May 3, 1956, 8–11.

———. *The Imperial Presidency*. Boston: Houghton Mifflin, 1973.

———. *Kennedy or Nixon: Does It Make Any Difference?* New York: Macmillan, 1960.

———. *The Vital Center: The Politics of Freedom*. Boston: Houghton Mifflin, 1949.

Schneider, Stefanie. "Stop Them Damned Pictures: Political Cartoons, the Study of Emotions, and the Construction of the Anglo-American Relationship." In *Emotions in American History: An International Assessment*, edited by Jessica C. Gienow-Hecht, 115–38. New York: Berghahn, 2010.

———. "Stop Them Damned Pictures! Political Cartoons, Visual Culture and the Construction of Anglo-American Relations." In *Visual Culture Revisited: German and American Perspectives on Visual Culture(s)*, edited by Ralf Adelmann et al., 81–99. Cologne, Germany: Herbert von Halem Verlag, 2007.

Schoenwald, Jonathan M. "We Are an Action Group: The John Birch Society and the Conservative Movement in the 1960s." In *The Conservative Sixties*, edited by David Farber and Jeff Roche, 21–36. New York: Peter Lang, 2003.

Schrecker, Ellen. *Many Are the Crimes: McCarthyism in America*. Boston: Little, Brown, 1998.

Schudson, Michael. *Watergate in American Memory: How We Remember, Forget, and Reconstruct the Past*. New York: Basic Books, 1993.

Schulman, Bruce, and Julian Zelizer, eds. *Rightward Bound: Making America Conservative in the 1970s* Cambridge, MA: Harvard University Press, 2008.

Schumacher, Michael. *The Contest: The 1968 Election and the War for America's Soul*. Minneapolis: University of Minnesota Press, 2018.

Shaw, Matthew J. "Drawing on the Collections." *Journalism Studies* 8, no. 5 (2007): 742–54.

Sheppard, Alice. *Cartooning for Suffrage*. Albuquerque: University of New Mexico Press, 1993.

Shikes, Ralph E. *The Indignant Eye: The Artist as Social Critic in Prints and Drawings from the Fifteenth Century to Picasso*. Boston: Beacon Press, 1969.

Small, Melvin. *The Presidency of Richard Nixon*. Lawrence: University Press of Kansas, 1999.

Smith, Kristen, ed. *The Lines Are Drawn: Political Comics of the War between the States*. Athens, GA: Hill Street Press, 1999.

Sontag, Susan. "The Imagination of Disaster." *Commentary* 40 (October 1965): 42–55.

Storrs, Landon R. Y. *The Second Red Scare and the Unmaking of the New Deal Left*. Princeton, NJ: Princeton University Press, 2013.

Strömberg, Fredrik. *Black Images in the Comics: A Visual History*. Seattle: Fantagraphics Books, 2003.

Strout, Lawrence N. *Covering McCarthyism: How the Christian Science Monitor Handled Joseph R. McCarthy, 1950–1954*. Westport, CT: Greenwood Press, 1999.

Sugrue, Thomas J. *The Origins of the Urban Crisis: Race and Inequality in Postwar Detroit*. Princeton, NJ: Princeton University Press, 2005.

Trilling, Lionel. *The Liberal Imagination: Essays on Literature and Society.* New York: New York Review of Books, 2008.

Trostle, J. P., ed. *Attack of the Political Cartoonists: Insights and Assaults from Today's Editorial Pages* Madison, WI: Dork Storm Press, 2004.

Truman, Harry S. *Public Papers of the Presidents of the United States, Harry S. Truman. January 1 to December 31, 1947.* Washington, DC: U.S. Government Printing Office, 1963.

——. *Public Papers of the Presidents of the United States, Harry S. Truman. January 1 to December 31, 1948.* Washington, DC: U.S. Government Printing Office, 1964.

Tuck, Stephen G. N. *Beyond Atlanta: The Struggle for Racial Equality in Georgia, 1940–1980.* Athens: University of Georgia Press, 2001.

Tuttle, William M., Jr. *Race Riot: Chicago in the Red Summer of 1919.* Urbana: University of Illinois Press, 1996.

Tye, Larry. *Demagogue: The Life and Long Shadow of Senator Joe McCarthy.* Boston: Houghton Mifflin Harcourt, 2020.

Upton, James N. "The Politics of Urban Violence: Critiques and Proposals." *Journal of Black Studies* 15 (1985): 243–58.

U.S. Congress. *Congressional Record.* 81st Congress, 2nd session. Washington, DC: U.S. Government Printing Office, 1950.

——. *Congressional Record.* 87th Congress, 2nd session. Washington, DC: U.S. Government Printing Office, 1962.

U.S. Congress. Senate. Committee on the Judiciary. *Control of Subversive Activities: Hearings before the Committee on the Judiciary, United States Senate. 80th Congress, 2nd Session. On H.R. 5852, an Act to Protect the United States against Un-American and Subversive Activities.* Washington, DC: U.S. Government Printing Office, 1948.

U.S. Department of State. *Foreign Relations of the United States, 1946,* vol. 6, *Eastern Europe; The Soviet Union.* Washington, DC: U.S. Government Printing Office, 1969.

U.S. Riot Commission Report. *Report of the National Advisory Commission on Civil Disorders.* New York: Bantam Books, 1968.

Wall, Wendy L. *Inventing the "American Way": The Politics of Consensus from the New Deal to the Civil Rights Movement.* Oxford: Oxford University Press, 2008.

Wallis, David, ed. *Killed Cartoons: Casualties from the War on Free Expression* New York: Norton, 2007.

Weart, Spencer R. *The Rise of Nuclear Fear.* Cambridge, MA: Harvard University Press, 2012.

Weisbrot, Robert, and G. Calvin Mackenzie. *The Liberal Hour: Washington and the Politics of Change in the 1960s.* New York: Penguin, 2008.

Welch, Robert. *The Blue Book of the John Birch Society*. Appleton, WI: Western Islands, 1959.

———. *The New Americanism and Other Speeches and Essays*. Boston: Western Islands, 1966.

Wheltle, Bruce. "Herblock: A Cartoonist's Life." *Nieman Reports* 48, no. 1 (1994): 95–96.

White, Theodore Harold. *The Making of the President, 1960*. New York: Atheneum, 1961.

Whitfield, Stephen J. "Richard Nixon as a Comic Figure." *American Quarterly* 37, no. 1 (1985): 114–32.

Williams, Carol, and Irwin Touster. *The Washington Post: Views from the Inside*. Englewood Cliffs, NJ: Prentice-Hall, 1976.

Williams, Kenny J., and Bernard Duffey, eds. *Chicago's Public Wits: A Chapter in the American Comic Spirit*. Baton Rouge: Louisiana State University Press, 1983.

Wills, Gary. *Nixon Agonistes: The Crisis of the Self-Made Man*. Boston: Houghton Mifflin, 1970.

Zelizer, Julian E. *The Fierce Urgency of Now: Lyndon Johnson, Congress, and the Battle for the Great Society*. New York: Penguin, 2015.

INDEX

Italicized page numbers refer to illustrations.